UNCONDITIONAL LOVE

Saskia Adams is a freelance writer and editor who worked at Penguin Books for ten years before deciding to devote more time to the cause of rescue pets. In 2011 she co-founded Forever Friends Animal Rescue, which now has several divisions around Victoria. She lives in the Yarra Valley with a large feathered and furry rescue menagerie, and when she gets a spare moment away from the tribe, she plays fiddle in her band, folkTrain.

Edited by Saskia Adams

UNCONDITIONAL LOVE

PetRescue's
Great Animal Stories

MICHAEL JOSEPH
an imprint of
PENGUIN BOOKS

MICHAEL JOSEPH

Published by the Penguin Group
Penguin Group (Australia)
707 Collins Street, Melbourne, Victoria 3008, Australia
(a division of Pearson Australia Group Pty Ltd)
Penguin Group (USA) Inc.
375 Hudson Street, New York, New York 10014, USA
Penguin Group (Canada)
90 Eglinton Avenue East, Suite 700, Toronto, Canada ON M4P 2Y3
(a division of Pearson Penguin Canada Inc.)
Penguin Books Ltd
80 Strand, London WC2R 0RL England
Penguin Ireland
25 St Stephen's Green, Dublin 2, Ireland
(a division of Penguin Books Ltd)
Penguin Books India Pvt Ltd
11 Community Centre, Panchsheel Park, New Delhi – 110 017, India
Penguin Group (NZ)
67 Apollo Drive, Rosedale, Auckland 0632, New Zealand
(a division of Pearson New Zealand Ltd)
Penguin Books (South Africa) (Pty) Ltd
Rosebank Office Park, Block D, 181 Jan Smuts Avenue, Parktown North, Johannesburg, 2196, South Africa
Penguin (Beijing) Ltd
7F, Tower B, Jiaming Center, 27 East Third Ring Road North, Chaoyang District, Beijing 100020, China

Penguin Books Ltd, Registered Offices: 80 Strand, London WC2R 0RL, England

First published by Penguin Group (Australia), 2013

Text copyright © this collection Penguin Group (Australia) 2013
Copyright © in individual stories and photographs remains with the authors, unless otherwise stated

The moral right of the author has been asserted

All rights reserved. Without limiting the rights under copyright reserved above, no part of this publication may be reproduced, stored in or introduced into a retrieval system, or transmitted, in any form or by any means (electronic, mechanical, photocopying, recording or otherwise), without the prior written permission of both the copyright owner and the above publisher of this book.

Cover design by Marley Berger © Penguin Group (Australia)
Text design by Samantha Jayaweera © Penguin Group (Australia)
Cover photograph by Alex Cearns / Houndstooth Studio
Typeset in ITC Stone Serif by Samantha Jayaweera, Penguin Group (Australia)
Printed and bound in Australia by Griffin Press

National Library of Australia
Cataloguing-in-Publication data:

Unconditional love: PetRescue's great animal stories / edited by Saskia Adams.
9781921901614 (paperback)
PetRescue (Organization)
Animal rescue–Anecdotes.
Pet adoption–Anecdotes.
Animal welfare–Anecdotes.
Other Authors/Contributors:
Adams, Saskia, editor.

636.0887

penguin.com.au

CONTENTS

Foreword by Dr Lisa Chimes vii

Introduction 1

Hero Pets 3

Against Impossible Odds 27

Dynamic Duos 67

The Cutest Critters 91

Perfectly Imperfect 115

We Are Family 139

Animals Healing Humans 161

Clever Creatures 183

Special Soulmates 205

Making a Difference 233

More Information About PetRescue 275

Contacts 279

Image credits 286

Acknowledgements 287

Foreword

Dr Lisa Chimes, from *Bondi Vet*

There are not many people who can say they truly love their job. I not only love what I do, I feel privileged to be a veterinarian. To be able to work with animals every day and understand how their bodies (and to some extent, their minds) function is something that I am so grateful for. Our pets provide us with unwavering companionship, unlimited smiles and unconditional love.

I call my dogs, Nelson and Lucas, my first- and second-born children. Both poodle-crosses, they accompany me everywhere and are rarely left alone. There is nothing like curling up on the couch with my 'boys' by my side at the end of a stressful day – they put things into perspective for me with their appreciation of the simple things in life. Their love and loyalty is palpable and, along with my husband and son, they really are my world.

Sadly, despite all that animals have to offer, they can fall victim to neglect and, in worse cases, abuse. As an emergency and critical care veterinarian, I see animals in distress every day. Some have fallen ill, others have been in accidents and misadventures and, unfortunately, there are a few that have been hurt or injured at the hands of humans. Like many in the medical profession, I've become accustomed to seeing the common problems, but no matter how many unwell animals

I treat, it is those that have been poorly cared for or intentionally harmed that often bring me to tears.

Euthanasia is without a doubt the hardest part of my job. I will never forget the first time I euthanised an animal – it was so hard to look into their innocent eyes and then watch as their family grieved. The only solace I take when 'putting animals to sleep' is in the fact that they are seriously unwell and I know that I'm doing the kindest thing for them.

On the other hand, the euthanasia of healthy animals is something that I cannot accept. Every year, around 40 per cent of dogs and 80 per cent of cats are euthanised in shelters and pounds because they are unable to find a home – this totals approximately 200 000 healthy animals.

I was always taught that vets are the advocates for animals. However, we aren't the only ones providing a voice for those that cannot speak. Organisations like PetRescue represent the unfortunate souls that end up in pounds as a result of poor breeding, puppy farms, impulse buying and mistreatment. PetRescue works tirelessly to give every rescue group, every foster carer and every single one of the community's homeless pets a voice. As stated by Animals Australia, it seems inconceivable that our society accepts the killing of thousands of healthy companion animals instead of demanding that the government finds ways to stop the unrestricted breeding and selling of pets and helps establish life-saving rehoming and desexing strategies.

Rescuing these animals from death row by adoption and foster caring is a true act of kindness. No matter what breed or species, these animals will enrich their new owners' lives with indescribable joy.

The best part of my job is witnessing the meows, barks and wagging tails of pets when they are reunited with their owners after treatment. I have no doubt that humans experience this same sense of excitement and warmth when they welcome a new pet from a shelter into their family.

Introduction

All animals, great and small, are blessed with a natural ability to bring joy to our lives in their own special way. Some inspire us with extraordinary acts of bravery and courage. Some amaze us with their incredible talents. But for the most part, they win and warm our hearts with their unconditional love. In PetRescue's book *Unconditional Love: PetRescue's Great Animal Stories*, we share tales from every corner of Australia in celebration of the all-round awesomeness of pets.

PetRescue is a growing national movement driven by animal lovers on a mission to empower communities to discover the joy of pet companionship and save the life of every healthy, treatable rescue pet.

Since the launch of our website in 2003, we've worked tirelessly to give homeless pets a voice and inspire all Australians to make the adoption option their first choice when looking for a pet. Today, with the amazing support of our growing community of pet lovers, PetRescue has become Australia's most visited charity website.

We firmly believe there is a home for every rescue pet and enough love to save every life.

We've come a long way, but still have far to go

It's hard to believe that around 40 per cent of dogs and 80 per cent of cats that enter Australian pounds and shelters are killed because homes aren't found for them. And while it can be easy to lay the blame solely on cruel and callous owners, the truth is that pets lose their homes for many reasons and usually through no fault of their own. An overwhelming majority of homeless pets have simply been lost and cannot be reunited with their families. In fact, less than 5 per cent of rescue pets have been surrendered or dumped. Rescue pets are just regular pets who need and deserve a second chance in life.

Ultimately, though, our great nation of pet lovers holds the power to put this right. Working together, with compassion and passion for pets, we can save every healthy, treatable pet.

Inspired by unconditional love

The unconditional love of pets is what drives everything we do here at PetRescue and all the hard work of the hundreds of rescue groups, pounds and shelters we proudly support. We also know it's what inspires more and more Australians to opt for adoption when choosing a pet.

Not all the pets starring in this book are rescue pets, but through these amazing tales of resilience, courage and true companionship, you'll find wonderment in the power of unconditional love to heal and bring happiness. We also hope you'll find the inspiration to adopt your next pet and support the vital work of your local rescue groups and shelters.

Our heartfelt thanks to all

We'd like to say a big thankyou to the hundreds of pet lovers who contributed their moving and often tear-jerking stories. Reading each and every one was a real labour of love – our only regret is not being able to publish them all. However, we're sure you'll agree, the biggest thanks should go out to the animals – a sentiment shared and beautifully expressed by Alison, who wrote in with a story about her dog, Malibu:

> *I am so proud of this scruffy little grey dog that nobody wanted. She does not judge, nor does she discriminate. Malibu sees not with her eyes, but with her heart.*

◇◇◇◇◇

HERO PETS

Some animals are really superheroes in disguise, going above and beyond the call of duty to transform their owners' lives. We think there should be a pint-sized medal of honour for these four-legged champions.

Emma Daisy, Lifesaver

When we adopted Emma Daisy in 2009 from Sydney Pet Rescue & Adoption, little did I know she would end up saving my daughter's life.

On her arrival, the twelve-month-old Australian bull Arab brought with her many unanswered questions. Had she been a stray? Had she been abused? Was she abandoned? We did not know, and would probably never know. What I did know was that I loved her. And in time she loved me too.

But first I had to study Emma's behaviour in order to understand her. She was nervous, anxious and unpredictable. She had aggression issues towards other dogs and humans. Overcoming her problems took time, patience, love and understanding.

People often make the mistake of assuming that a dog should show them loyalty and respect first. What they don't realise is the dog has almost never chosen them – they have chosen the dog! Respect and loyalty are only gained, I believe, once trust and confidence have been shown. So I decided the only way to gain Emma's trust and respect was by showing my loyalty to *her*. She needed to know she could count on me to be there for her – always. To guide her, teach her, nurture her, protect her and love her. Only then would she trust and accept all of us.

It worked. Emma healed. She confirmed my belief that in order to receive you must first give, and that man is not a dog's best friend – a dog is a man's best friend! Emma now has the courage to be herself – to display her true nature and personality. She has a beautiful, radiant soul that reflects in her eyes and smile. No longer aggressive towards dogs or humans, she is calm, affectionate and loving. She is obedient and protective of me and my children and is deeply bonded to my other female dog, Berry. They play, swim, eat and sleep together.

Emma's healing was our first little miracle. The night Emma saved my four-year-old daughter's life was the second. Madison has a sleep disorder called circadian rhythm disorder (CAD). It interrupts the body's internal 'clock', so Madison has difficulty falling asleep at the usual time and staying asleep. She can stay awake for up to three days straight.

On that fateful night, our four-legged Emma had only been with us about six months. Madison had been awake for eighteen hours that day and so when she had finally fallen asleep on our lounge, I gratefully scooped her up and took her to her bedroom and popped her into bed. I closed her door halfway so I could hear her if she stirred.

Madison's room is at the end of the hallway that adjoins our lounge room. Our lounge adjoins the kitchen, so I can also hear my children from the kitchen down the hallway.

Walking into the kitchen, I filled the kettle to make a cup of tea and put it on the boil. I had been standing there for just a minute when Emma suddenly came in and sat at my feet. She is always an inside dog, and she and Berry sleep at the foot of our bed at night.

Emma sat there, staring at me, and then made a very strange noise. I haven't heard her make this sound before or since. The only way I can describe it was that it was a cross between a growl, a yawn and a howl: 'Ahhhhrrrrrrrooooooool!' As Emma made this extraordinary noise she leaned forward and prodded me with her nose. Something was clearly wrong.

'What's up, Emma?'

She quickly hopped up to a standing position on her two back paws, and showed me the same kind of urgency and excitement as when I tell her it's time for walkies. All my senses were on alert now. Before I could do anything else, this dog latched her mouth gently around my wrist and proceeded to tug on me, pulling me out of the kitchen.

Heart thumping, I let her lead me into Madison's room. She nudged the door open with her nose and took me right up to my daughter's bed. Emma then let go of my wrist, lifted her head and emitted that same bizarre howl again. I looked at Madison's sleeping form; by this time she had only been in bed for two minutes and was now facing the wall. I gently rolled her back over to face me.

'Oh my God!' Madi's lips were a bright, dark blue colour. She wasn't breathing! Screaming, I lifted my daughter up and placed her on the floor, checking her mouth to see if she had swallowed something – maybe an object was blocking her airways?

Nothing.

Trying to think clearly, I turned her head slightly to the side and started performing mouth-to-mouth – it was all I could think of. Suddenly, she coughed and spluttered, then sat upright and looked at me bewildered, saying, 'Mumma, what are you doing?'

I laughed and cried out loud, all at once. Madison thought I was crazy, I'm sure, but I patted her on the back, scooped her up, popped her into the car and drove straight to my local doctor. He ordered tests to see what had caused her to stop breathing, and to check for any brain damage due to lack of oxygen, but Madi was fine. But if Emma had not alerted me to the tragedy about to unfold down the hallway, it would have been at least another ten minutes before I went in to check on my daughter. Ten minutes without Madison breathing would have been too long.

There is no doubt in my mind that my daughter Madison would not be alive today had we not adopted Emma, and had we not persisted with her during the early weeks and months when she was so confused, anxious and aggressive.

We are blessed to have Emma, and I hope she is as blessed to have us. Thankyou, Sydney Pet Rescue. You saved my best friend's life.

Holly, New South Wales

By My Side

This is the story of a beautiful labrador I intended to 'rescue' but who ended up rescuing me. After my previous dog had passed from old age, I spent a long time grieving and was not sure I could ever open up my heart to another dog. Then I became quite ill and everyday tasks such as grocery shopping, meeting friends and going to work caused great exhaustion. I struggled for years with depression, anxiety and agoraphobia. My doctors, knowing I'd always been an avid animal lover, suggested getting a canine exercise buddy. They obviously knew something I didn't: with canine support I would learn to manage my disability.

Finding the right dog was a long, arduous process. My doctors reckoned that I was too fragile to look after a puppy and that a more mature dog would be a better choice. And while I love puppies, I had to agree.

In my search for an older dog I contacted breeders, consulted rescue websites, joined online dog groups, went to the RSPCA almost every weekend, and checked the newspapers. Over the course of several months I met many different dogs great and small, but none of them was 'perfect' and I didn't feel like, 'That's the one!'

My main criterion was that I couldn't have a dog that might attack my cat, Maya. My cat is my source of comfort and has been by my side for many years, but is naturally not into long walks! And I really had to 'get moving' to increase my wellbeing. I had no idea what breed I wanted, but since I'm not a tall person and quite fragile it was best to avoid a huge dog that could take *me* for walks.

During one of my searches I stumbled across Labrador Rescue and thought I'd found the perfect dog. A lab–spaniel mix, she was much smaller than a lab, and described as sweet and social. More importantly, her foster home had other dogs and a cat, and the photo of her playing with a toy duck (which she seemed to take with her everywhere) was just gorgeous. Initially I hesitated, but decided to bite the bullet and contact the foster carer.

I called her and explained my interest in this lab. The carer, Linda, asked me a few questions, which I answered nervously, and then told me that she didn't think that particular dog would be the right fit for me. I felt so disappointed, but she then went on to explain that she did have another dog, Molly, who she believed would be perfect.

When I got to the front door of Linda's house, the sweetest littlest golden lab face greeted me through the screen door and I knew straight away we were meant to be.

While I spoke to Linda, Molly lay at my feet and rolled on her side, making herself completely comfortable. I saw her interact calmly with Linda's cat and respond to the 'leave it' command. She was a lot smaller than any lab I had ever seen and at three was already at her adult size.

Molly came home for a trial period, as the true test would be how she interacted with my cat, but the sweet girl did not make any attempt to chase Maya. Not only that, but she was also brilliant when introduced to my young nieces and nephews and a friend's toddler and baby. Molly was now my dog.

I had to walk Molly twice a day, which was a huge step for me since I hated leaving the comfort and safety of my home. I also decided to take her to dog obedience school to teach her to walk on a lead nicely, to socialise with other dogs and, in a way, to get me out of the house. The first class was a disaster due to nasty weather and a mix of badly behaved dogs. I did not cope well, and swore I wouldn't go back. But for Molly's sake, I pushed myself to keep on going. With the routine of consistent training she got better, even going on to win obedience awards! And with the help of my doctors I slowly became more confident about taking my girl out for walks and to obedience school.

I felt much calmer and much more relaxed with Molly around, but unfortunately she was not allowed in public places like malls, shops, cinemas and theatres, nor could she come to work with me. Getting out to shops and to work was still a huge struggle for me.

I then discovered an organisation called mindDog that was willing to help me train Molly as an accredited Assistance Dog. This would allow her to accompany me in public places and to my workplace!

Molly first had to take a public access test, where she would be observed with me in many new situations to see how she would cope. These included getting into a lift, walking into a restaurant and not misbehaving, walking in a grocery store with a shopping trolley, and so forth. Molly was a star and came out with a perfect score! I was so proud of her as this was not a test that many dogs pass. But she was a natural!

I still find it difficult to go to new places, or anywhere where there are crowds, but with Molly I know I can do it. Having her by my side has given me back my independence – even if it is just to get some groceries. I truly believe she knows she is working when she has her vest on. She has been great at ignoring people when she is 'on duty'.

The next step was getting Molly to come to work with me. This was huge, as I had never told people about my disability, and was afraid they would treat me differently. But since Molly was now an accredited Assistance Dog, she was legally allowed to accompany me everywhere – including work.

I approached my managers at work, spoke to Human Resources and showed them the legislation. I also worked with HR to provide factsheets educating staff about Assistance Dogs and the correct protocol for interacting with them. Once everything was finalised, Molly came to work with me.

Having Molly by my side during the day has made me so much more productive at work. It has made me realise just how wonderful my colleagues are. They have accepted me and my furry friend, and they look forward to seeing us both every day. They also understand that they are not supposed to touch Molly, talk to her or otherwise distract her without my explicit permission, and they are very accepting of the fact that I cannot place her 'off-duty' every ten minutes for someone to pat her. Just having her beautiful face around is enough.

Through Molly I have met truly wonderful people, some of whom have become close friends. I have also learnt that I am not alone. There are many people like me, and it is important we talk to each other.

I now volunteer with the wonderful Labrador Rescue group that introduced me to Molly. My life is so enriched having her, and I know how proud of us they are. I also support other people with disabilities in guiding them through the process of having their own dogs accredited as Assistance Dogs. Thankyou, Molly – for everything.

My gratitude to the inspirational Leko for helping me tell my story.

Chloe, New South Wales

◇◇◇◇◇

Cadbury Bear

In 2011, I made the decision to move to a sport-focused school, as sport was where I thought my future lay. Being the new kid wasn't easy, so it was lucky I had my much-loved pet rabbit, Sprite, for comfort.

In June I began to see posters around the school advertising 'free bunnies'. One of the teachers was a breeder with more than twenty rabbits, but had decided he didn't want them any more, and if they couldn't find homes within the next week he was going to dump them at the vet. Horrified, I went home and begged Mum to let me adopt one as a friend for Sprite, and she finally gave in.

The next day the teacher brought in three bunnies for students to meet. I noticed a little black female mini lop crouched in the back of the carrier. She was about five years old and absolutely petrified. None of the other students wanted her because she was so scared, but there was just something about her. I knew I had to have her.

The next day I brought in a carrier to take her home, and when I took her out she wet herself because she was so frightened. At home I put her in a pen just outside my bedroom, and if I tried to pat her she'd bite me and run into her hiding place. But I persisted – feeding her treats and paying her lots of attention. Sprite was in a pen on the other side of the room getting used to the presence of another bunny and the different smells. I decided to call her Cadbury Bear because when I first said it aloud she looked at me as if to say: *That's the one!*

Months went by and Cadbury turned into a totally different bunny. She loved pats and would lie on my bed or on the couch with me. She'd lick me and give me 'kisses', and she was confident and happy.

After she was desexed, Cadbury was finally introduced to Sprite. They fell madly in love! It only took a few introductions until they were completely confident with each other. Every time I'd look over at them together, they'd be grooming continuously for minutes. Bunny love is a different kind of love – one that brings out true happiness.

Watching Cadbury change from an anxious, frightened rabbit to a happy, frisky bunny made me realise I wasn't all that interested in sport – I just wanted to help animals. So I began volunteering with Rabbit Runaway Orphanage and the RSPCA. I ended up leaving the sports school and returning to normal school, with a new dream of working with animals.

Cadbury helped me on my journey: chewing my schoolbooks while I endeavoured to complete my homework, following me into the kitchen and sleeping on the end of my bed. She became my trusted companion and I adored her more than anything.

Then, in July 2012, Cadbury fell ill. Her previous life of constant breeding, bad diet and neglect had caught up with her. My baby girl suddenly stopped eating, so I rushed her to the vet and discovered she had spurred teeth and blocked tear ducts, and that her body had begun shutting down. For two weeks she was on pain medication and antibiotics. The vet couldn't operate on her teeth because she was too frail, so she had to be syringe-fed every two hours, which I gladly did for her, even through the night. Then, sadly, we learned that Cadbury had a brain tumour. When she took a turn for the worse, I made the most heartbreaking decision I'd ever made. She gave me a little goodbye lick just before she slipped away. I'll never forget the look in her eyes.

Cadbury changed my life. Because of her, I plan to become a veterinary nurse and later run my own animal shelter dedicated to her. She helped me find my true calling. Thankyou, Cadbury Bear.

Shannel, Victoria

◇◇◇◇◇

The Gift that Keeps on Giving

At the time I adopted Patch, I was running a small pet-sitting business and raising a Seeing Eye Dog puppy named Nancy. Little did I know how beautifully Patch would fit into my life.

Patch was a seven-year-old black-and-white border collie I found at the Animal Welfare League's Coombabah Rehoming Centre. When I extended my hand and she put her paw gently on my palm, I knew I had met my best friend.

Patch and Nancy became instant buddies. Patch had a wonderful calming influence on Nancy, the excitable pup. Within the first week, clever Patch caught on to the commands Nancy knew, and became her biggest mentor and supporter. Patch came with us to the Seeing Eye Dog meetings and they would use her as a 'distraction dog', to teach the puppies to ignore temptation, to walk and follow the owner's command. We were very proud when Nancy graduated in 2011, the first Seeing Eye Dog on the Gold Coast.

I work from home, so Patch sits next to me all day and walks with me each morning. She is my best friend, my work colleague and my baby girl. She has also been invaluable when it comes to assisting me with my part-time business, Proud Pet Sitters, and has helped look after many dogs needing extra companionship.

Lulu was a Dalmation we would care for three times a week. She was old and blind and had cancer. Patch was so gentle with her. She would sit by her, lie next to her and walk slowly with her. Often, Lulu would be lying still when we arrived, but she would smell Patch, get up and walk around looking for her. Patch increased Lulu's quality of life, so it was actually Patch who was hired, not me!

Lulu's owners then bought a Dalmation puppy, Georgia, to add to their family. Of course Georgia would often play-bite the older infirm Lulu and jump on her, as puppies do. But Patch nipped that in the bud, instantly showing the pup how to behave around her elders. It was wonderful to see Georgia respecting Patch and doing as she was told.

Hannah, an older German shepherd, was another dog we took care of. She had recovered from a spinal operation and would stay with us for a few months at a time while her mum worked interstate. Hannah's injury prevented her from having complete mobility, and I had to pick up her back legs if she fell. She loved watching Patch play and would walk behind her, bouncing with joy. When they went for walks together, Patch always travelled slowly to make sure Hannah could keep up.

Patch has helped bring understanding and friendship to so many dogs. We make a great team. She's with me every day, teaching me compassion, joy and to always live life to the fullest.

I get very close to the dogs I care for, so I thought it would be lovely to give their owners a memento of their time spent with us. I did this for Lulu and Hannah first, taking photos and writing poems to describe their personalities as I'd gotten to know them. I made a little book for each, and gave it their owners, who loved it.

Then the owner of The Dog Bakery in Hope Island, Katherine, asked me to create a book for their black poodle, Lily, the star of their café. Katherine liked it so much she suggested I start a small business selling them, and that she would display them in her store.

This got me thinking: if I did a book like this about shelter dogs, I could help raise money for the Animal Welfare League, from where I adopted Patch! When I approached the AWL with an example of a book, they thought it was a great idea. My creations, simply titled *Pet Poems*, are now sold at their Coombabah Adoption Centre. I now volunteer there also. Not a day goes by without me thinking how lucky I am to have my beautiful Patch, and this was my way of thanking them for rescuing her. She is truly a gift that keeps on giving!

Duonette, Queensland

Flexi the Wonder Cat

How my blind, bedridden gran had the accident we do not know, but she thinks she had a nightmare and fell out of bed one night.

It was around 4 a.m. on 7 June 2012, and I was sleeping in my room at my gran's house. She had been asleep in her bed, which has a half-bed rail along the wall side, and a very heavy bedside table on the other. During the night she had somehow fallen out of the bed and wedged herself between the two shelves of the bedside table. She'd tried to ring her bell, which is a doorbell attached to the table, but it had been broken in the fall.

Poor Gran called and called out to me for help but, being in a deep sleep, I didn't stir. Now here's the part where Flexi the Wonder Cat comes in. While I didn't hear Gran's cries for help, her seven-year-old moggy cat Flexi did.

We had adopted Flexi from a neighbour in our block a few years earlier when they were moving overseas. When he first arrived he was quiet and shy for weeks. After that he grew in confidence and now rules the roost. Being bedridden, Gran is home all day and Flexi loves to lie with her in bed. He is also very cheeky – he will not touch Gran's food but he will steal mine or anyone else's if you take your eyes off it for a second! But when he gets into trouble he runs straight to Gran, knowing she will stick up for him.

Anyway, the night Gran had her fall and couldn't get up, she realised Flexi was responding to her cries as she heard his bell on his collar come *ding, ding, ding* into the room, drawing closer to where she was stuck on the floor. Gran did the only thing she could think of: 'Flexi, please go and wake Leanne. I need help.' She heard him turn and leave the room at once. The first thing I knew about it all was that Flexi had jumped on me in bed and was whacking my face with his paw! Suddenly wide awake, I told him to bugger off, though he'd never done anything like that before.

But Flexi wouldn't be deterred. He kept slapping my face with his paw and meowing loudly. I was just about out of patience when I heard Gran call out. I rushed to her room and turned on the light. I was shocked when I saw her predicament. 'Oh my God! What happened?'

'I must have rolled out of bed,' she replied. 'I'm stuck!'

Knowing what a stalwart my gran was, I didn't quite believe that she wasn't hurt. I couldn't see any bleeding or bruising, and as she was conscious and speaking to me she seemed okay. So I took the legs off the bedside table to release the bottom shelf and lifted the table off her.

I then had to haul Gran up and get her back into bed.

What she said next surprised me. 'Can I have a cup of tea and a couple of chocolate biscuits? And can you give Flexi some treats too?'

I gave Flexi some treats for being the hero of the moment, but told Gran she couldn't have the tea and biscuits until she'd seen a doctor, 'just in case'. I rang the after-hours medical service, and the doctor came within half an hour. He checked Gran all over and said she was fine. However, he did say it was lucky that we found her quickly because it was a cold night. She might not have fared well if she'd spent several hours out of bed in such low temperatures.

'It wasn't luck,' I told the doctor, 'it was Flexi the Wonder Cat!'

Who would have thought our Flexi would turn out to be a hero? I would not have woken for many hours if Flexi hadn't roused me to help Gran. We love our chubby tuxedo-fronted terror!

Leanne, New South Wales

◇◇◇◇◇

My Four-legged Furry Inspiration

'Sharon, I have a dog for you!'

I was excited when Marie of the Schnauzer Club of Victoria contacted me with the news I had been waiting for. Being an advocate of Oscar's Law – a proposed reform to ban puppy farms – I had decided my next dog would be a rescue dog. So, when I was ready to adopt a companion for my miniature schnauzer, Blitzen (bought, of course, from a reputable breeder),

I put my name down with the Victorian and New South Wales Schnauzer rescue groups. I live in Adelaide, but hoped it still meant we could adopt when the right dog needed a home.

'Ava is a nine-month-old mini schnauzer,' Marie explained. 'She was surrendered to Melbourne's Schnauzer Club Rescue because her owner was moving into a rental property and could not have a dog there. I have a suspicion she may well have been a puppy farm dog, as the owner met the breeder in a park.'

This indeed set off alarm bells because I knew that disreputable puppy farmers often met prospective buyers in parks, car parks and others' private homes so that they could pretend the puppies were the result of a one-off or accidental mating, and not the product of neglected mother dogs imprisoned in a puppy farm.

Marie gave me the phone number of Janine and Michael, the lovely couple who were fostering Ava in Melbourne. They told me that Ava was in season when she reached them, which meant that her desexing had to be delayed for three weeks. My heart sank – I faced an agonising wait! However, during the weeks Ava spent with Janine and Michael we had many long conversations on the phone and on Facebook about my little girl. They said that although she was a Little Miss Bossy Britches, she had settled in nicely with their other dog, and that Ava and foster dad Michael had become the best of buddies!

At last, on 26 October 2011, Ava was on her way to Adelaide by plane. After a long, anxious morning, the flight arrived. But we still had to wait for the aeroplane to be unloaded. How would this little dog be feeling after such a bewildering experience? We need not have worried. When Ava popped out of her crate, the little one's tail was wagging madly with excitement. It had all been just one big adventure for her!

Soon she was in the car and on her way to her new home to meet Blitzen and my sixteen-year-old German shepherd, Xena. After a few tense moments during which Ava barked and growled to let the older dogs know she expected to be treated with respect, everything was fine. Ava settled in beautifully.

Soon, we took Ava to dog training with Blitzen. It immediately became obvious that Ava was very anxious around other dogs; even when walking, she became a little upset. So I booked a private lesson with my dog trainer, Amy Van Dyk, at Advance Behavioural Training. This was a great help. Amy thought that Ava had generalised anxiety with no definite known cause; anxiety can be caused by a genetic fault or by life experiences. However, Ava responded well to lots of hard work and intense therapy – and, with her brother Blitzen, even achieved her Canine Good Citizen Award. This award, designed by the Delta Professional Dog Trainers Association and the Delta Society, is a nationally recognised certificate that confirms the qualifying dog is a well-trained and sociable canine citizen. Next, Ava completed her Advanced Trick Training course, which involves learning how to take a bow, to ring a bell, put toys in a box, perform leg weaves and open draws, retrieve mail from a letterbox, and do 'high fives' and even 'high tens'.

Ava was sent to me for a reason. Not only has she taught me so much, she has inspired me to become a Delta Accredited Trainer myself, like Amy. I have also started part-time volunteer work for Advance Behavioural Training, and learning how to run classes.

My goal now is to help dogs with the more extreme behavioural problems – so often created by humans in the first place. I want to assist people in training their dogs – no matter where they have come from – so that they can be happy, well-adjusted members of their families. This way I can ensure they will not end up dumped or in shelters as unwanted dogs. I believe there is no such thing as a bad dog – just a badly trained one – and it is up to us to help them.

I thank Ava for taking me down this path and am glad she is with me every step of the way. Every day she gives me the strength to forge ahead, no matter how hard the road.

Sharon, South Australia

◇◇◇◇◇

Malibu's Heart

My home was quiet. My life was lonely. My two greatest friends had died – my father and my beloved dog Lucy, who I had rescued from the pound in 1997. She was killed by a brown snake two weeks after my father's passing, and I was shattered.

One day in February 2006, I found myself visiting Monika's Doggy Rescue in Sydney, and my life changed forever.

Once inside the shelter, all the dogs in the enclosure overwhelmed me, bouncing up and down and demanding my attention. One grey, dishevelled mutt, with eyes like those of a baby seal, stood at the back of the pack. She gazed at me steadily and seemed to be silently begging: *Pick me! Please pick me!* As I gathered her up in my arms she licked me repeatedly on my face as if to say: *About time you came! I've needed you . . .*

Our first walk together in a nearby park across the road from Monika's was the beginning of our life together. Within minutes it was sealed – this little one was coming home with me.

On arrival home – still unnamed – I introduced her to her new brother Nova, my father's rescue dog, and they hit it off brilliantly. I sat watching them and celebrating by way of a Malibu and pineapple drink. Looking down at my glass and then at my new friend, I suddenly said aloud, 'Would you like to be called Malibu?' The little one wagged her tail and leapt up for a kiss, and from that moment on, Malibu it was.

There was something profoundly different about Malibu from the start – this scruffy mutt with fur like silk. The first morning after Malibu came home with me, I was woken by the little ball of fluff lying on my chest, her wet tongue licking my face and her tail wagging like mad. She had a smile from ear to ear – dogs *do* smile! – and what she was saying was clear: *Thankyou for giving me a second chance at life!*

Before long, I knew that Malibu was my soulmate of the dog world. She seems to be in touch with what I am feeling. Mal is always there by my side. She follows me like my shadow and always radiates such happiness. She brings me contentment with just her mere presence.

A few years ago, I decided to share the love and joy Malibu has brought into my life by telling our story on Facebook. I hoped 'Malibu Thomson's' Facebook page would increase awareness of shelters, pounds and the wonderful work done by rescue groups. 'Adopt your next best friend for life!' is our Facebook catchcry.

My project took off immediately. So many people were keen to tell their own story of how they adopted their new best friend. Very soon, fundraising and charity work became an additional focus. Online 'Malibu and Friends' raised $200 for K9 Cancer. We also helped run the online auction of a beautiful quilt consisting of squares made by people from all over the world. The quilt, which raised $1200 for Pawsitive Teams (a therapy and dog training centre), was donated back by the auction winner and now hangs proudly in the training centre. Malibu features on one of the squares!

Not long after that, I started taking Mal into nursing homes to visit the sick and old. This was a new adventure for her; she had not been out in public much. But she was a natural! On that first day she walked in and greeted everyone with loving gentleness. She touched so many hearts and brought many smiles to residents and staff alike. She had found her calling in life.

Now, on each of her visits to several local nursing homes, she announces her arrival by way of a gentle bark as we enter. 'Malibu's here!' the residents call out, all competing for her attention and affection as she arrives to spend the day with them. She shares her time with all the elderly folk, even if they are bed-bound, lying beside them for a snooze together. She shares chairs – and tea and cake! – while residents pat her tummy as she rests her head on their laps. She sometimes even perches proudly in their walkers, being pushed around the halls, looking just like 'Miss Malibu' from *Driving Miss Daisy*! And even when she just sits and listens to the elderly people talk, Malibu seems to understand.

While Malibu loves everyone, there was a gentleman named Den who Malibu had a special friendship with. He had no visitors; his family lived in England. Malibu and Den took to each other like they had been friends for years. Den could no longer walk and had Alzheimer's. Malibu would lie on Den's table across his bed with her head resting on his arm while he stroked her for the longest time. They would look into each other's eyes with a gentleness that could only be described as angelic. Den would share his cake or biscuits with her and he would smile – and that smile would light the whole room.

One time Den was unwell and bed-bound. Malibu chose to spend the whole day with him. Den had his arms wrapped around her, holding onto her like a special treasure, and the nurses would come in and say, 'Den, who's that you have there?' And he would simply smile – the nurses were in awe of how much Den lit up because of his four-legged friend.

One day Den looked at Malibu and said, 'I love you, Bu Bu,' and kissed her on her head. I had tears running down my cheeks.

When I saw how life-changing Malibu's nursing home visits were, I created the Facebook page 'Malibu Thomson – Love Ambassador for the Elderly' to inspire others to visit aged-care facilities with their gentle and friendly doggies. Many have written to me saying they are following in Malibu's 'paw prints' with their own rescue dog, offering comfort and companionship to their local elderly. I could think of no greater reward than hearing this.

I am so proud of this scruffy little grey dog that nobody wanted. She does not judge, nor does she discriminate. Malibu sees not with her eyes, but with her heart.

Alison and Julie, New South Wales

Tails from Home

From a long-term resident at the Perth-based Dogs' Refuge Home to the heart and soul of our local aged-care facility, ten-year-old labrador cross Alby is living proof that it's not always a sad tale for pound hounds that have had a rough start in life.

As soon as I saw Alby advertised on a poster at a local café, I knew he would be the perfect four-legged resident for the aged-care facility at which I worked. At the time I was the managing director of the facility, and was always looking for ways to enrich the lives of the residents.

So, I delved a little further and approached the Dogs' Refuge Home in Shenton Park about Alby and discovered their long-term resident had been returned twice because of his severe separation anxiety.

This challenging trait would require some attention but could potentially work in our favour, and I truly thought we could help. We had a home full of willing and able carers, who were guaranteed to always be there, and the Dogs' Refuge Home had Alby – a seven-year-old labrador mix – it was a match made in heaven!

So, on 31 August 2010, we chose to adopt Alby from the shelter. It was not an easy transition due to his diagnosis of separation anxiety and depression, but the brilliant trainers from the Home worked with us, introducing him to his new environment progressively. Eventually, with their help, time and love, Alby was able to settle in well and soon became a permanent member of our blended family.

Three years on and Alby no longer requires his anti-depressant medication. He is the heart and soul of the facility and has really made his mark on the home and residents. So much so, he has his own column in the facility's monthly newsletter! Therapy staff also worked with residents to develop a 2013 calendar in his honour, where he is featured on every page. Open to January and see Alby dressed up for Australia Day; turn to February and see him in a Valentine's Day costume, and so on. Our hugely loved four-legged friend thoroughly enjoyed dressing up and smiling for the camera. He's a natural poser!

Much to his enjoyment, Alby continues to be a very busy boy and his attention is in high demand. He starts off his day with a morning kiss and cuddle for every one of the residents, travelling from room to room, ensuring they all get their Alby affection quota for the day! He then immerses himself in daily activities with the residents, including ball games, craft and exercise sessions and bus outings. He also loves spending time participating in resident therapy sessions, helping people living with dementia learn to interact again. And after a full day, Alby turns in for the night at the nursing station or sometimes has sleepovers at the homes of a few of the staff members, which provides him with another opportunity to get spoiled.

Without doubt, Alby is the most beautiful dog – he is adored by residents and staff alike. He fills his role as 'home dog' remarkably well, making every effort possible to comfort residents, keep them company, entertain them and make them feel loved and needed.

It's been an unforgettable experience to watch a once homeless and unwanted dog blossom the way Alby has. We will be forever grateful that the staff and volunteers of the Dogs' Refuge Home didn't give up on Alby when many others would have, using the excuse of his behavioural challenges. But you could say that Alby didn't really have any behavioural challenges – he was just waiting on the right home *for him*. One person's problem dog was our perfect dog.

This story proves that all rescue pets, no matter their size or age, can flourish in the right home – and deserve to. I'm so glad Alby found his forever home with us.

David, Western Australia

Raphey's in da House

It was a trap, of course. Those six little words that had ensnared many others before me. 'Would you like to hold him?' And honestly, I did try to resist.

'No, thanks,' I replied, 'I've already got a cat at home. I'm looking for a doggy friend for him.'

Shortly before, I had been in the Shenton Park Dogs' Refuge Home. Unfortunately, none of the canines were a good fit for the role of cat companion. Disappointed, I decided to pop next door, to Cat Haven, and take a peek at all the gorgeous kitties there. Just for fun. Now, staring at Raphey, a little fluff ball that kept bouncing around to get my attention, I relented. And once I held him, squirming in my arms, he was coming home with me, just like they knew he would!

At home, I introduced my cat Bruce to newcomer Raphey. Bruce immediately walked up to Raphey, sniffed him, gave him a massive lick, and assumed the role of a big brother. Relief!

It was very sweet to watch the two cats' relationship grow. Raphey would bounce off the walls and Bruce would patiently let him be silly. When Raphey fell into a kitten sleep in the middle of all his toys, Bruce would check on him, and nuzzle and groom him.

Raphey is definitely a cat's cat. He appreciates Bruce's affections, despite the daily biffo between them (which Bruce always wins!). He is tolerant of the two humans and the two dogs that have since joined us in our happy home, but he turns away from human cuddles. And if he's in a sulk, he looks for one of the dogs to take it out on! One of his favourite pastimes is sitting on the lounge armrest, swiping at the unsuspecting canines as they go past. He also regards certain spots as his turf, and guards them strongly. Try sitting in Raphey's chair at your peril!

Who would have thought this over-developed sense of possession would end up protecting us and our home from criminals? It was a hot night, and my wife was home alone. She had left the back windows ajar to allow some airflow through the house. While she was in the front lounge watching a movie, she heard Raphey making an odd sound – loud, sharp warning meows. Standing up, she looked down the hallway to see Raphey, staring, rigid, into the bedroom at the back of the house. When she next heard a scuffling noise, my wife realised our clever boy was alerting her to the presence of intruders! Without thinking, she ran down the hallway, yelling at the top of her voice and bravely wielding the television remote control. Surprised, two figures scooted through the house and out the back door. Thanks to Raphey, the would-be thieves fled without taking anything, and were subsequently caught by the police. Yay, Raphey!

Despite his incredibly cute, fluffy exterior, Raphey is a tough gangster on the inside; but so far I have resisted the temptation to buy him a large gold chain to lend street cred to his big fur coat!

Raphey, our hero.

JB, PetRescue, Western Australia

◇◇◇◇◇

AGAINST IMPOSSIBLE ODDS

◇◇◇◇◇◇◇◇◇

Rescue pets beat the odds! Despite sometimes being the victims of violence or neglect, with the love and loyalty of new families, these courageous and resilient animals can overcome heartbreaking adversity to enjoy the happy lives they so deserve.

The Miracle of Earl

Earl's list of injuries from the Nepean Animal Hospital read:
- Broken pelvis
- Shattered hips
- Broken rib
- Broken jaw
- Herniated intestines.

Not a nice way for a story to start, but that is the list of horrific damage inflicted by a hit-and-run driver on Earl, a four-year-old staffy. Left for dead, Earl was found by two young girls and rushed to the Nepean Animal Hospital.

I first became aware of Earl's plight when I saw a notification on a friend's Facebook page. The next twenty-four hours were critical for Earl, and my friend was desperately trying to locate his owners. I can't explain what prompted my next steps, but they were to change two lives forever – mine and Earl's.

I called the hospital to check on Earl's condition, and to offer to help in any way that I could: to put up posters, door-knock in the area, raise funds for his surgeries. It was imperative that treatment began immediately, and the compassionate vet, Dr Tony Karolis, generously offered to meet half of Earl's projected $3000 costs.

The first operation was performed that evening. Tony called to tell me that he had been stunned by Earl's internal state. How was this dog not dead? He'd worked for hours to correct the placement of Earl's intestines, but did not know if he'd make it through the night. I waited . . .

To my immense relief Earl *did* make it through the night – although he was not eating, and would need a lot more hospital care.

Earl's story made it to the local papers, donations flooded in and his owners came forward. Unbelievably, despite being told that all hospital bills would be met by Tony and No Kill Pet Rescue, Earl's owners requested that he be put down. We were all stunned. Thankfully Tony suggested to the owners that they surrender Earl to the care of No Kill Pet Rescue, which they did without even visiting him to say goodbye.

I went to see Earl as often as I could, and my heart sank to find him staring forlornly at me from his hospital cage. You could tell he was thinking, *Where are my mum and dad?*

After two weeks Tony deemed that a home environment would aid Earl's recovery, and there was no doubt whose home that would be. He was still a very poorly boy, and I had to carry him from the hospital in a sling. At home, I slept next to his crate for the first night, too afraid to leave him on his own. We soon settled into a daily routine of treatment and medication. Like a true staffy, Earl took it all stoically, never once complaining.

However, the need for hospital treatment was far from over. A stomach parasite resulted in severe dehydration for Earl, and another week back in hospital. On his return home, the routine resumed. Earl began to eat more, and started walking without the aid of a sling. But his hips were still a problem, and it was time for X-rays to determine whether treatment was possible. I had to do everything I could to give Earl the chance of a normal life.

The day the X-rays were taken, Earl spent the night on my bed – and early the next morning I was woken by howls of pain. There seemed to be no end to the poor boy's misfortunes, for his paws had started to swell and his gums had turned a creamy colour. Earl was once again rushed to hospital, where he was put on fluids and subjected to a battery of tests. Eventually it was determined that Earl had contracted IMHA (immune-mediated haemolytic anaemia – a disorder where the immune system destroys red blood cells faster than the rate at which new ones are produced). He began to slowly recover following a blood transfusion, but it was a few weeks before the full damage to his paws and tail became apparent. Half of Earl's tail dropped off, and he lost two toes from each front paw. Hard to believe one boy could suffer so much.

Now, nineteen months after his accident, I sit on my back verandah and watch Earl run towards me. He kisses me on the face, and runs off down the paddock again, zooming from left to right.

It has been a long rehabilitation for Earl. As a result of his misfortunes he is a little different from other canines, with his missing tail and toes, and his misshapen spine. He will always run a little slower than my other rescues – but he has more spirit and strength than any other dog I have ever known.

Was it worth it? Just ask Earl!

Neva, New South Wales

◇◇◇◇◇

A Magical Week with a Kookaburra Family

'Can you help with a baby kookaburra?' the man's anxious voice asked. 'I just found him on the road!'

As a volunteer with the Native Animal Trust Fund in Port Stephens, we receive calls twenty-four hours a day through our Rescue Hotline. Many caring members of the public contact us when they find an injured or orphaned native animal, and on this afternoon in November 2012, a baby kookaburra entered my life. I have cared for a number of injured adult kookaburras and a juvenile once before, but I'd never experienced anything like what was to occur.

On arriving at the caller's home, he told me, 'He was just in the middle of the road, being attacked by Indian myna birds.' Looking down into the dark box in front of me, I saw a baby male kooka who was too young to be out of his hollow. While its unknown exactly how the little one ended up on the road, it is possible that he was attacked in the nest and dragged out by the Indian mynas and was frantically trying to escape them. He was also in poor condition – thin and covered in a dark, sticky substance. I took him home and washed and fed him. He was calm, but no doubt quite bewildered, and very cute – especially after his bath, towel-dried and fluffed up! I left him overnight in a basket on my enclosed verandah.

The following morning I was woken to an almighty kookaburra chorus. What on earth was going on? I stumbled out onto the back verandah. The local kookaburra family had found my baby!

I couldn't believe my eyes. Two adult kookaburras had flown up to the house and were getting as close as they could to the little one in his basket. One sat on the guttering and peered down at him, and one perched in the tree nearest to the verandah. My kooka baby was vocal, too, making a low, throaty chuckling noise back. They were all clearly talking to each other and others further away, because two other adult kookaburras suddenly flew up, as though summoned by the others. But what were they saying to the little one? I wondered. *Who are you and where do you come from?* perhaps! Did the kooka family see my baby as an unwelcome trespasser in their territory and want to harm him, or did they recognise an orphan in need of care? He was certainly no relation to my own kookas. Naturally, I was familiar with the local family, especially their very early-morning chorus, but I don't believe in feeding wildlife, so I'd never seen them so close to the house like this.

Being optimistic, I hoped they had arrived because they heard the cries of one of their own, who was clearly an orphan in need. There was no doubt they could do a much better job of raising him than me, so I decided to take a chance and put the little one outside in a cockatoo cage. While I did this, the adults anxiously called to one another, flying back and forth. Next, I retreated and waited to see what would happen.

What I witnessed was unforgettable.

One by one, I watched the four adults fly down to the cage and line up with food in their beaks to feed the grateful orphan. It took a little while, but they soon worked out how to push the generous offerings through the wire. It was food they could have eaten themselves or fed to their own young . . . but instead, they recognised one of their own in need. I was amazed. It was a beautiful thing to witness.

Then, while I watched this wonderful event play out from the stairs, one adult flew up to the rail right next to me, staring me in the eye. Was he warning me off, saying, *You can go now, we've got this covered!* or was he also trying to feed me the delicious-looking winged creature in his beak? I took it as a warning to go, given that his feathers were standing up on his head, a common sign for, *Look how big and scary I am!* So I retreated and let the wonderful family event continue outside.

A little while later, on a table under the verandah, I set up the cocky cage with branches poking out from the inside for the adults to perch on while feeding the baby, and a chair nearby for them to land on. I was hoping what I witnessed that morning wasn't a one-off, and that over the next few days they would continue to visit to feed the little orphan. And they did.

Young kookaburras make an unusual and distinct noise when calling to their family, and for food. After hearing my baby make this noise, I realised the same call was coming from a number of nearby treed locations. The adult kookas had other babies they were also supporting! Then I saw them – two other juveniles slightly older than my baby, who were flying small distances from branch to branch.

This family of four adults was now caring for three juveniles, and it was clearly hard work, continually finding food for themselves and their hungry, demanding young. And, as my baby was underweight, he was very hungry and demanding! But still they stayed, and still they kept returning to look after the little orphan.

Since I'd added to their family I felt I should help them, so each day I put some meat out for them and fed the baby occasionally. I once found one of the adults on a sloped rail of the stairs, asleep to the point of its beak resting on the rail! I was slightly worried, so I approached and asked her if she was okay. She looked up calmly as if to say, *Yes, I'm just resting*. I left her alone and after a while she flew off in search of more food. And while I was helping, I could not provide the vital lessons or natural diet necessary for a healthy, socialised baby kookaburra.

As many people have experienced, kookaburras are calm birds that don't frighten easily and appear to be very intelligent. The 'locals' soon realised that my tending to the baby, such as moving him to where the adults could access him, was not a threat, and they would come in close to feed him regardless of my presence. I spoke to them and a few times they spoke back – a low, throaty, guttural noise. I really believe they realised I was also helping the little one.

After a few days I moved the baby to my aviary to enable him to practise flying, and again set up chairs and perches for the adults, cutting holes in the wire to enable beaks and food to get through. Able to watch from a nearby spot, I observed the amazing array of food kookaburras find and eat – they fed the baby spiders, grasshoppers, crickets, worms, a baby snake (or legless lizard) and once, to my horror, a baby bird about 10 centimetres long! I thought, *He will never get that down!* But, to my astonishment, he thrashed it as kookas do and then swallowed it whole.

After watching my little one in the aviary over a couple of days, flying across the width and up from the ground to the perches, I knew it was time for him to truly join his loving adoptive family. Things didn't go well, though – picking him up, I launched him up towards a tree but he landed awkwardly on a tall tree fern; then it started to rain and he was drenched, but too high to retrieve! I anxiously watched for the adults, hoping they would find him, and when they did, they were too heavy to land alongside him on the fern leaves. However, I then delightedly watched my baby fly confidently up several metres to a higher branch.

Over the following weeks, the little family with its new addition stayed nearby in our bush reserve while all their young grew stronger. He came and visited my backyard a couple of weeks later – older, wiser, but I could tell it was him. I watched him searching for his own food, now free and part of a family group. Next year he too will help feed his family's new offspring.

My honorary membership of a kookaburra family for a week was a joyous and unforgettable experience. Some people think of nature as 'cruel', or of it being a 'survival of the fittest'. However, the story of the caring birds in my backyard who selflessly adopted an orphan kookaburra tells a very different tale.

Caitlin, New South Wales

◇◇◇◇

Ben of the Big Heart

Everyone in my rescue group thought it was hysterically funny that I wanted to adopt a golden retriever.

I'd lived with cats all my life (I had many foster felines and cats living with me at the time) and had never actually owned a dog, so they thought I was away with the fairies!

Ben had been in the pound for about three weeks when I heard his story. After receiving reports from concerned residents, the rangers had picked up this emaciated dog that was wandering the streets. When further investigation revealed a history of neglect, the rangers decided Ben deserved a second chance.

First Ben had to be taken to the vet for desexing, but the vet said he was so old and malnourished that he would not survive the operation. The ranger then contacted rescue groups to see if anyone could take him, but they were all full to bursting. So Ben stayed in the pound where he actually started to put on weight.

When a friend who volunteered with another rescue group told me about Ben, I couldn't stop thinking about him. I knew that golden retrievers were supposed to be lovely dogs and Ben was an old boy. I couldn't bear the thought of him surviving such dreadful neglect only to be put to sleep because no one had room for him. He deserved to spend his last years living a happy life!

I rang my friend back and asked, 'Do you know what Ben is like with cats?' She replied he was fine, so I volunteered to foster him.

When I collected Ben from the pound he looked miserable, but still managed to wag his tail a little. He was so weak that he had to be lifted into the car. Even though he had put on weight, his ribs were visible, his pelvis prominent, and I could see every single vertebra. His lovely golden coat was matted and dull and he looked like an animal that had lost all hope.

I brought him home and hand-fed him raw meat. He was unbelievably polite and took the meat very gently, without snapping at it. That first night I probably gave him four small meals. He took each one with the same politeness, and each time his tail wagged a little more.

I took Ben to the vet for a check-up and called the local dog groomer. Every couple of days I took him for a short walk down the main street of the small country town where I live. At first (before he started gaining weight), people were shocked at the sight of Ben's emaciated body and many regarded me with disgust until I explained his story.

Then, as he gained weight, people started greeting Ben and crossing the street to say hello. He always wagged his tail and welcomed every pat and caress. As Ben gained strength and became more confident he decided that my backyard was a cat-free zone. My cats have the run of the house, but any cat that entered his area was chased off! My foster cats have their own enclosed area, but one of them, Felix, was very dominant, and was finding it difficult being with the others so I put him in with Ben, under supervision. They bonded so well that they now sleep together and eat together, and when I walk Ben, Felix comes too! Ben shares with all the cats, but Felix is his best friend.

My initial intention had been to find Ben a wonderful forever home once he was well enough, but locals kept telling me how much they would miss seeing him and that he'd been through enough. It made me realise how much I loved him, and that he had to stay.

Ben prefers going for walks in the bush, but every few days we deliberately go down the main street of St Arnaud. People come up to me and ask, 'Is this Ben the dog I have heard so much about?' They then chat away to Ben and rarely ask me my name. Others will say, 'Hello, Ben! Hello, Kaye!' even though I don't know who they are. Best of all, many locals now ask me about rescue groups and how they can help dogs like Ben. Some have even gone on to adopt animals from my organisation or gone to the pound to find their perfect companion. Others have donated pet food and toys to us – sometimes even money! Ben has become an extraordinary ambassador for animal rescue. Every time he walks down the street he educates someone about the myths of rescue pets. Dogs like Ben aren't 'defective', 'second-hand' or 'broken' – they've simply been neglected by people who failed in their duty of care. But we can change that by telling the world how wonderful rescue pets truly are.

Ben has the biggest heart and the gentlest nature. He adores people, and everyone who meets him can't help but adore him too.

Kaye Hanlon, Save-A-Pet Inc., St Arnaud, Victoria

◇◇◇◇◇

Shelley's Lament

'Hi, Helen, nice to meet you. Thanks for coming all this way,' I said, waving her in.

Helen is one of the rare breed of rescue volunteers willing to give up her time so that homeless dogs can tear up the back seat of her truck, chew through her leads and spread pound pong on her towels while she ferries them around the state.

Today she had brought me Shelley, a grey-and-white husky mix, and the latest rescue dog to be sprung from Renbury Farm. As a foster carer for Siberian Husky Rescue, I had agreed to look after Shelley until she was on her feet again and could find a forever home.

Shelley, like most pound dogs, looked somewhat dishevelled, but her eyes were bright and when the truck door opened she was two feet out before Helen caught her and pushed her back in to unclip her collar.

On the way from the truck to the dog run, Shelley gave a few well-timed coughs and stopped to look up at me with big brown eyes. Damn. She had kennel cough. And wow, she sure had a talent for the sad-eyed face.

I took Shelley into the dog run, closed the gate and turned around to size her up more closely. Poor girl. She had part of her left ear missing, a good dose of fly strike on her right ear and an elegantly placed cut across her nose that was scabby and in need of cleaning. On the upside, she had wonderful teeth, so clean and shiny they gleamed. She obviously worked hard at keeping them that way, because when I left she started cleaning them again on the wooden gate, trying to buzz-saw her way out of the compound. In the end she must have decided that either she'd made sufficient sawdust for today or her teeth were clean enough. In any case, she stopped chewing and moved on to the more serious business of howling.

To be honest she was not a bad howler, nor was she a bad chewer. She was just feeling hard done by after enduring three days in the pound, two hours tethered to the back seat of a strange truck and now being condemned to solitary confinement in an unfamiliar dog run.

The howling stopped before long, mostly because I was bathing her and it's quite hard to howl through soap bubbles. She needed a bath; her coat was oily and dirty, her skin was flaky and she still had that awful Clorox disinfectant smell that takes weeks to disappear – I didn't want a dog that smelled like a hospital corridor. After her bath she decided to leave off the chewing and howling, go back to the sad eyes and just leave it at that.

Time passed and she nursed herself through kennel cough, helped along by a particularly distasteful course of antibiotics. When the worst symptoms passed and she was well enough, the vet admitted her for desexing. Of course her cough was still somewhat infectious, so desexing was by special arrangement to minimise the impact any contagion would have on the vet's regular business.

When I picked her up that afternoon she looked really good. She had that happy expression that only a horse-sized dose of painkillers can bring, with the glazed-over eyes and the tail that wags for no reason.

The next morning was Sunday, and although she'd had a peaceful night's sleep on a comfortable velour-covered foam bed, something was not quite right. She looked miserable.

Mid-morning the vomiting started, just a little at first and only bile. I called the vet, who advised me to keep her off food and water for twenty-four hours.

By late afternoon she was throwing up more often and I was running out of paper towels, not to mention clean covers to put on her bed. It wasn't her fault, and she looked so distressed each time it happened – as if she knew she was making a mess and wanted to apologise, the poor thing. I caught myself pacing around the room and realised I was more worried than I'd let myself admit.

Just after 9 p.m., she vomited dark bile. It was time to drive to the emergency vet clinic. After a thorough examination, the vet's diagnosis was inconclusive. Then, after another vomit, he said firmly, 'She's staying overnight; I want her on a drip.'

The next day Shelley was transported from the emergency clinic back to my regular vet. She had ultrasound tests to look for internal haemorrhaging, but the results were unclear. Yet, by the end of the day she was showing some signs of improvement and apparently had not thrown up for some hours, so I went to visit her. To witness the look of recognition on her face and the light in her eyes when she first saw me approaching was an unexpected but wonderful surprise. She turned into a happy, wiggly puppy and the pain dropped away from her face. Despite the improvement, however, the vet still recommended she stay overnight for observation, and to see if the vomiting had truly passed.

That second evening at home without her was distinctly lonely. It was sad to think of what Shelley had been though, but I knew she was in the right hands and the hope that she could come home tomorrow gave me something good to look forward to.

The next morning's call from the vet brought the bad news that Shelley had worsened overnight. He had taken another ultrasound and X-ray and was disturbed to see what appeared to be a blockage in her intestine. He reported that the shape and material were not readily recognisable, but that it looked flattish and round. 'It could be anything,' he said. 'We will need to go back in to find out, and if it's a foreign object, remove it quite simply with a small incision along the bowel.'

This was not the news I had been expecting, but there wasn't really a choice. Shelley had to get well and if another procedure was needed for her to keep moving forward, then so be it. 'Go ahead,' I said.

I struggled to concentrate on my work that day. I racked my brains, trying to work out what Shelley could have gulped down over the weekend. Did she eat something at home? What do I own that's flattish and round? I couldn't come up with anything, but I couldn't leave the question alone.

The vet called late that afternoon. 'It wasn't an obstruction; I checked her out from stomach to rear end four times and there is no blockage. Her lymph nodes are exceedingly swollen and her intestinal walls are thickened due to irritation. It looks like a viral infection that's causing her ileum to stop functioning, and without her intestines moving fluid through properly, she's having to vomit.'

It took four long, precarious weeks for Shelley to recover. The things she endured are almost unbelievable. Yet she made it through and now the vet and I both joke that Shelley is the benchmark against which all other cases are measured. ('Well, yes, your dog is unwell, but let me tell you about this case we had a few weeks ago . . .!')

In the end, I was calling her Patches: she had fur shaved from both front paws where the intravenous needles went in, a shaved patch on her neck where they took blood for her heartworm test, fur missing from the graze on her nose, bald patches on both ears from fly strike and of course a completely shaved belly from all the surgery.

But then I got the call to say that Shelley had found a forever home.

Now with her new family, Shelley lives like a queen with the run of the house, company throughout the day, loads of exercise and doting owners who love her enough to give her the training and discipline she needs as well as the treats and toys she loves. In return, Shelley will bring them joy, love and energy and, twice a year, more fur than they know what to do with.

Intelligent, loving, unpredictable and occasionally infuriating, Shelley's a handful but no more than any other husky. She is one of the most magnificent creatures I have invited into my life. I still have a photo of her on my desk.

Andrew, New South Wales

◇◇◇◇◇

Our Little Ray of Sunshine

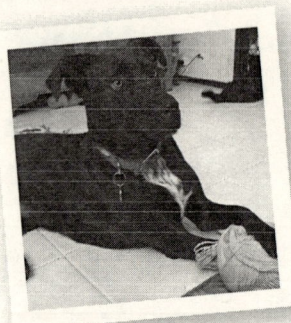

I first saw the sign on a community noticeboard in my local shopping centre in September 2011:

Missing dog: Holly
I rescued her from K9 Rescue 4 weeks ago
She is 9 months old and very scared

The photo of Holly, a beautiful black kelpie–labrador mix, brought tears to my eyes. The poor girl must have already had a difficult start to life if she'd been rescued as a puppy, and now she'd escaped from her new family, slipping her collar while on an outing with them. She was lost and frightened, with no food or comfort, roaming the huge bushland in Port Kennedy.

As a foster carer for cats through 9 Lives Cat Rescue, I was well connected to animal rescue social media. For months, I kept an eye on Facebook postings to see if anyone had spotted her, and every chance I had I drove by the area of bush where she'd escaped, hoping for a sign she was still alive. The summer of early 2012 was a scorcher, with heatwaves of 44°C, and I knew Holly was somewhere out there, still terrified and eluding capture.

Then, seven months later, in March, local retailers told me she'd been sighted again in the bush close to the road's edge, scavenging for food. So I knew she had survived the dreadful summer – somehow.

Months passed again and still no one had been able to capture this terrified soul. I'd begun to lose hope for Holly when, in July 2012, 'Pets of Perth – Lost and Found', a social media group, began receiving posts about daily sightings of a skinny, lost-looking dog on the edge of a fast and busy road in Port Kennedy. It had to be Holly! She was alive and extending her range from where she had previously been sighted, scavenging for road kill. I asked people to continue to report the date, location and time of their sightings so that I could try to find her paw prints and track her. In addition, a Facebook page was set up to help with the search.

Once we narrowed down Holly's territory, I started tracking her prints through the thick scrub and along the firebreaks, trying to read her movements in an effort to understand her patterns of behaviour. Next, I set up two food stations, one near the highway and one at the opposite end of the bush, on the quieter Bakewell Drive, and checked sand tracks near each to determine what animal was taking the food. Bingo! After a few days the prints showed me that Holly had found the Bakewell station, so I focused on that area. When I saw her for the first time, I didn't know whether to laugh or cry, so I did both. It was her, this elusive wanderer, still alive after an incredible ten months surviving alone in the bush. But she bolted off in panic as soon as she spotted me.

I dropped biscuits on the firebreaks and buried treats in the sand. The next morning they were all gone, with prints left to show that a fox, a crow and a dog had been in the vicinity, but that the dog had taken the food. This was how I introduced myself to Holly, leaving my scent around the food crate, with the treats, and with an item of my clothing.

For weeks, I would park my car some distance from the feeding station and strain to see Holly come for her meals. At first she'd only appear if she thought no one was around. But she was intelligent and soon worked out the association between me, the car and her food. Sometimes I would arrive and she'd be there, standing on the firebreak, waiting and watching for my car, running off into the scrub to hide as I set out her food. Other times when there was no sign of her, I'd walk along the firebreak, letting the breeze take my scent into the bush where she might be hiding, hoping that she would come out and I'd get a closer sighting of her. It became a daily game for me, trying to work out where she went during the day, where she slept at night, and what she experienced between my visits.

Attempts at capturing Holly in a large dog trap were trialled and failed. I spent weeks leaving her food near the trap, moving it closer each day, then placing the food inside. And when I thought she'd be able to get right into the back of the trap, I baited it with her favourite food – a lamb shank and sardines – and waited for it to work. But when Holly saw a rabbit enter the trap and set it off with a frighteningly loud metal clatter, she never went near it again.

Eventually, I was able to park close to the food station and leave my car door open so she could see me in the car, not presenting as a threat, and not making eye contact. She'd walk past on the firebreak, wary and watchful. As long as I made no sudden movements she'd tolerate my presence. After many more weeks, I was able to sit on the ground outside my car, and then on the firebreak where Holly walked each day. I'm a knitter, so for an hour or so each morning I sat with my pointy sticks and yarn, head down, seemingly uninterested in her and focused on my work, and Holly would inch a little closer.

Meanwhile, more and more people were now following Holly's story on Facebook, and a community of compassionate volunteers wanted to help. They donated lamb shanks and marrow bones, pigs' ears and chicken. She was wormed, watered and well fed. The community helped me help Holly, and every day I was thankful for their love and care.

But there was tension, too – we feared for Holly's safety. Trail bikes and four-wheel drives hooned through the bush regularly. There were no tall trees for shade and shelter, and on cold winter mornings I had to crack the ice on Holly's water bowl. Then when the weather warmed up that spring, the snakes came for her water. Bushfire was an ever-present risk. She was constantly on edge, always on full alert. And she'd bolt over the hill if she saw another human anywhere in the distance.

From the first day of my search for her paw prints, I knew that something had to be done to bring her out of the bush. And on that first day, I made a commitment to Holly that I would never give up on her. It didn't matter if I had to keep travelling to the bush to feed her every day for the rest of her life or mine; it only mattered that she should know there was someone there to help her. And if I could get her out safely, then I'd do everything possible to achieve that.

As a foster carer, I'd had some experience working with semi-feral cats and knew that if I had a boundary, progress could be made in taming a fearful animal. For months I'd wished there was some sort of boundary in the Port Kennedy bushland. I'd often thought a tennis court would have been handy – something with high fences and a gate that closes securely. But that was wishing for a miracle. So I continued visiting the feeding station each day, desensitising Holly to my presence, and trying to gain her trust.

After many months she was able to take food from in front of me while I sat cross-legged and peacefully still on the firebreak. But when I moved, she would run back to the edge of the bush, keeping a safe distance. I couldn't hand feed her, but I could interact with her in other ways. And it was during this time that I taught her to play.

I didn't care what anyone thought of seeing a little round granny on hands and knees on the firebreak, tossing a pig's ear or a toy around and doing play bows to a dog keeping its distance down the firebreak. I didn't care that I was developing a reputation for strange wanderings or for sitting on the track at dawn in a hostile environment and knitting! Every action was for Holly and every thought was focused on taming this wild dog and teaching her that interacting with this human was safe, predictable and joyful.

And then someone suggested hiring fence panels to build an enclosure. And so the actual possibilities of constructing a giant walk-in trap developed. I wanted the materials to mimic the industrial environment over the road from Holly's bush territory. She was familiar with chain-mesh fencing and star pickets. And an extraordinarily wonderful coming together of volunteers made it happen. Materials were donated, the expert services of a local fencing contractor were offered and volunteers came to clear the weeds and build the enclosure. It was triangular, because I wanted acute corners internally so that I could work with Holly once she was inside. Each side of the fence was about 10 metres long and 1.8 metres high, with the bottom of the wire buried into the ground. But it was built slowly, in stages, at non-feeding times, so that Holly would become accustomed to the changes in her environment. And every day I continued to sit and knit, to be a peaceful presence, and a safe and constant part of her world.

We all watched and waited to see Holly's reaction as each part of the enclosure was built. At first she panicked at the sight of a single star picket that had been driven into the ground. And she panicked when she scented that other humans had been there. She ran off without eating. But I continued to sit quietly nearby, knitting in hand, in case she was watching. I needed to show her there was nothing to be frightened of. And over the next few days and weeks, Holly grew used to each change made in her environment as we cleared more weeds and constructed the enclosure.

Four weeks after the first post went in, the day came when I knew the time was right: Holly was ready to trust me enough to be inside the enclosure with me. So sixteen months after she first escaped into the bush, and after six and a half months of a concerted rescue effort, Holly hesitantly stepped inside the fenced area with me. While her back was turned and she was at a far point within the enclosure, I quietly and calmly closed the gap in the fence behind her. She turned and saw her escape route had vanished and took a few steps towards me to try to get out. But I sat on the ground quietly and waited for her to understand that I wasn't going to harm her.

After twenty minutes, I approached her with a slip lead in hand. She paced backwards and forwards, and then I told her it was time. And she stopped. I slipped the lead over her head, and she jittered and then sat. We had our first touch when I put my hand gently but firmly on her shoulder. Her body shimmered with waves of muscle tremors, but, surprisingly, Holly leant into me. And we just stayed still together for a while, and let the world settle and waited for both our hearts to stop pounding. I eventually remembered to get my phone out and try to record the moment with some pictures, then posted on Holly's

Facebook page, 'I've got her!', and I knew it was all going to be okay.

Holly's adoptive family was thrilled to learn she was now safe in my care, but being sixteen long months later they had moved on, adopting another dog. They had agreed if Holly was ever found and caught, she would be relinquished back into the care of K9 Dog Rescue. So, with the family's blessing, I applied to the organisation to officially become Holly's new mum, and they happily said a very enthusiastic 'yes'.

Despite her earlier fears, Holly settled into domestic life without difficulty, sharing my home with Odie, my six-year-old chihuahua–Jack Russell mix, and numerous cats. I had been prepared for a challenge in bringing an almost wild dog into my home. Using a slow introduction technique, I showed Holly how to behave with little Odie and the cats. I made it clear from the start that they were with me and that I expected her to be gentle. She watched, understood and accepted them all with surprising tolerance.

Holly's rescue has brought tears of joy and happiness to me and the many people who followed her story – 'Holly's Army', as they're sometimes called! My dawn reports on her Facebook page were often accompanied by photos of the special girl with the early morning's rays highlighting her regal beauty. And so she became known as 'Our Little Ray of Sunshine' and, as such, has brightened up our whole world.

Jane, Western Australia

My First Penguin

I sat there staring at his little blue-and-white body and thought, *Oh my Lord, what have I gotten into now?*

It was early in 2010, and this was the first penguin I'd ever cared for as a volunteer for Wildlife Help on the Mornington Peninsula.

A member of the public had found the young chick and brought him in. He weighed only 600 grams – too small to be away from his mum.

I rang Denise Garratt at Help for Wildlife and she put me in touch with Marg Healy, a wonderful woman who would become my seabird mentor. Marg had run the Phillip Island Nature Park Wildlife Centre for over twenty-five years and many people turned to her for advice on anything that had feathers and eats fish.

Marg told me to start the little guy on fluids and gradually build up his fish intake. I was still petrified I was going to do something wrong, so she put me onto another great seabird carer, Mandy Hall, from the Altona Seabirds Shelter. Between the two of them, with me pestering them for advice every five minutes, that little penguin chick received some royal treatment.

A couple of months later, we released back into the wild at Flinders a chunky, cheeky and very fit penguin – weighing in at just over 1 kilogram. Phew! Penguins, unlike possums, don't look back once you release them. They are just happy to get away out there and do what penguins do.

My confidence now increased, I gradually moved on to helping other seabirds in need, and soon I was taking care of cormorants, fairy prions, storm-petrels and Australasian gannets.

Gannets are truly awe-inspiring, but are not one bit cuddly and best admired from a distance! I usually get five or six babies a year – youngsters that have fallen out from the breeding ground or haven't gotten the knack of fishing. They just float around, frightened and angry, until they are rescued on beaches by caring passers-by. Then it's gloves on, buckets of pilchards, and dodging very sharp beaks until the birds can figure it out for themselves. When we release them back into the wild we are quite grateful to see them go!

Seabirds face many challenges. There are fluctuations in fish populations due to overfishing and environmental degradation. Oil spills also take a horrendous toll not only on the birds but on their breeding grounds and food sources. And every year hundreds of petrel, albatross and gull chicks die from ingesting the plastic rubbish in our oceans. Others are injured from fishing lines or collisions with motor craft.

I love caring for seabirds, but this kind of wildlife rescue is not for everybody. The birds must have a deep saltwater pool to learn to swim in, and wide sandy pens to move about in. And you must quite like the smell of fish – we currently have three baby gannets in care and two penguins, and they are eating about a hundred pilchards a day!

Despite permanently smelling like fish, watching these birds return to the wild is unbelievably rewarding, and a fantastic way to help care for our coastal wildlife.

Klarissa, Victoria

◇◇◇◇

Poopie's Back!

When Nina Huynh first set eyes on Poopie, back in 2003, she fell in love – she couldn't resist the gorgeous little ball of Pomeranian fluff.

Poopie soon became a much-loved member of the family. Then, three years on in late 2006, the unthinkable happened – Poopie vanished. Nina and her family were distraught. They looked everywhere: rang around the pounds and rescue centres, and hit the streets – all with no success. What could have happened to her?

As time passed, Nina and her family gave up all hope of ever seeing Poopie again. They feared that – being so adorably cute – perhaps Poopie had been stolen. Then, out of the blue in July 2012, Nina received a phone call from the Sydney Dogs and Cats Home – her beloved Poopie had come into the shelter as a stray; would Nina like to collect her?

Nina didn't know what to do or say. 'I was in such shock, all I could say was, "Thankyou, can I call you back?!"' said Nina. 'We hadn't seen her in six years, and to hear that she was still alive and healthy – it was just so exciting and amazing!' After Nina regained her composure, she phoned the Home to arrange a time to collect Poopie. 'As soon as I got off the phone, I immediately notified every family member. I went to pick her up with my sister. My mother and grandmother kept calling to get updates on what was happening. The whole family was so happy to see her, it was an emotional reunion!'

Poopie has now settled in back at home. She sniffed around and toured the house as if she had never left, and the best part is that she now has a playmate! Nina got another dog about eighteen months ago, a Maltese–Pomeranian named Biscuit. Poopie and Biscuit have become the best of friends.

Now, if only Poopie could reveal to us what she has been up to for the past six years!

Amanda Stokes, Sydney Dogs and Cats Home, New South Wales

Gingermegs

The second I met Gingermegs the guinea pig, I knew my life would never be the same.

Our organisation, Australian Cavy Sanctuary, had been called out to help at a backyard breeder's home at Woodford, Queensland. There were over forty guinea pigs needing rescue that day. Living in filth, the piggies were in overcrowded random metal cages and bird aviaries on the property. The owner had been selling adults and babies at local markets where snake breeders would often buy the young ones as cheap live food for their reptiles. In addition, backyard breeders would also purchase the piggies for their own future money-making endeavours. In any event, to be sold at a market equals a very uncertain future for a guinea pig. There are no laws to protect them.

As I bent over all the little ones that day at Woodford, I saw many had fungal conditions, tumours and mange, and the owner's dogs were harassing them as well. We had to make two car trips to and from the property to ferry all the piggies to safety. I'll never forget coming back for the second trip and finding that a guinea pig I'd had in my arms only forty minutes earlier had been killed by one of the owner's dogs while I was gone.

It was on my second journey back to the property that we rescued a small female I was later to call Gingermegs.

Why was Gingermegs amazing? She was a teacher and guide in my eyes. I believe many animals are brought to earth to teach and share a message, and this was Gingermegs's purpose. She soon became a shining light of our Australian Cavy Sanctuary. Through my strong connection with her and the many outings I took her on, I shared this special girl and her love with thousands of people over the years. I watched her teach so many two-leggeds that guinea pigs are just as worthy of compassion, love, trust and unconditional loyalty as larger animals are. Guinea pigs are so very undervalued in our society, and yet Gingermegs helped change so many people's attitude towards them.

And while Gingermegs was such a wonderful public ambassador of our Australian Cavy Sanctuary, at home our bond only continued to grow. One very special yearly event we shared together was our Christmas lighting tradition. After dark, Gingermegs and I would get in the car and drive around Brisbane to the streets that were covered with the most bright and colourful decorations.

Last Christmas, I realised it was probably going to be the last Gingermegs and I would share together. During that, her seventh year since her rescue, she battled chronic kidney failure daily. We were back and forth to vets and appointments with natural therapists also. All this time, myself and other members of our team searched outside the box for new alternatives to chronic guinea pig diseases, and we all learnt a wealth of new knowledge in this field that we can now use to help other piggies.

But Gingermegs's time still drew to a close, despite her amazing strength and spirit. She passed away peacefully, and afterwards I was overwhelmed at the number of people who got in touch to express their sadness about our loss – people who had never even met Gingermegs! She was clearly so much more than your average piggy. That is what made her amazing – she taught people so much about guinea pigs by just being who she was.

Jessica, Australian Cavy Sanctuary, Queensland

Snowy Forever

For the first three years of his life, Snowy had everything his big fluffy heart could desire. A warm, safe bed, delectable treats, the best veterinary care, and constant love and affection. However, this life of privilege was not to last. When his owner was diagnosed with early-onset dementia at the age of fifty, she needed to move into care and couldn't take her cat with her. Melbourne Animal Rescue (MAR) came to her aid. When a volunteer arrived to collect Snowy, his mum said, 'Promise me you'll look after him.' 'Of course,' they replied.

Snowy is a gorgeous cat, but he found it very stressful settling into his foster home. He was not used to men, and was so fearful of the man of the house that he spent most of his time hiding behind couches. Eventually it was decided that Snowy should be moved to another foster carer.

In his new foster home, Snowy began to shine. He quickly won over his carers and resumed his princely role. But then, tragically, Snowy's world crumbled again. One hot summer's day, Snowy's carers left a heavy sash window open a crack, greatly underestimating the strength (and stubbornness) of their feline companion. Curious about the world outside, Snowy put his nose through and pushed the window up. He then fell four storeys down to the ground below.

Snowy was rushed to Lort Smith Animal Hospital, but the outlook was bleak. Miraculously, he had no internal or organ injuries; however, he suffered numerous compound fractures in both his rear ankles. Specialist surgery would be needed to repair the fractures, at an estimated cost of at least $6000. No rescue group has those sorts of funds.

MAR remembered their promise to Snowy's previous owner that he would be well looked after, so they gave the green light for his surgery. But a huge fundraising effort was going to be needed, and MAR's volunteers started this any way they knew how. A Facebook page for Snowy was set up, people phoned Lort Smith directly to donate, and with the amazing support of the public, the financial target was reached.

During the operation, Snowy's leg bones were pinned together with steel plates, and because he lacked sufficient bone to endure another operation, he was crated at Lort Smith for three weeks while his legs were healing to prevent further injury. He stood to lose both back legs if his rehabilitation failed. With a charming personality and good looks, Snowy was a popular patient at the hospital.

After three weeks he was allowed to go home to a new foster carer. She changed Snowy's bandages every four days, helped him go to the toilet, groomed him (which he hated), gave him his mountain of medication and comforted him while he cried during the night. After three months of much hard work, dedication and love,

Snowy was given a clean bill of health and was once again ready for adoption.

I'm Zoë, Snowy's forever mum. He first came into my life in a rather special way. Before he fell out of the window, I came across his profile on PetRescue. I was looking for another cat and a rescued one was all I wanted. Giving a home to an animal in need is an incredibly rewarding experience. Supporting no-kill organisations to continue their awesome work is also something really important to me.

So I narrowed down my search to two beautiful cats: Snowy, and an Abyssinian mix from Save-A-Pet. It was a difficult decision, but since I'd had Abyssinians growing up, we ended up adopting the gorgeous Atlas.

Yet I couldn't get Snowy's big, beautiful eyes out of my head. A couple of months after adopting Atlas, I checked to see if Snowy was still available for adoption. He was, but in the meantime he had had the terrible accident. I followed his story on the MAR Facebook page. Every time I saw him all bandaged up, I thought that if only I had adopted him, he wouldn't have fallen . . . but then I wouldn't have been enjoying life with beautiful Atty.

Another couple of months passed and Snowy healed. Still not being able to put him out of my mind, I enquired whether he needed a forever home. He did, and that was it – I *had* to meet him.

When I walked into the room, my first thought was how huge he was! Then I fell in love. Knowing him now, I realise what a big deal it was that he didn't run away from me; that he let me spend time with him and pat him. He obviously felt the same way I did.

I took him home for a trial run that night. After just a couple of hours, I knew he was never leaving.

Snowy now lives a happy life with his four feline siblings and three chihuahuas. He is very much the prince of the house, and spoilt rotten. He sits by me on the couch as I study, and is very vocal with his opinions. He is not as mobile as he once was. His ankle bones are fused and he cannot jump very high. He stays safely inside the house and likes to sleep on his back with his legs in the air!

There's no sneaking up on anyone for Snowy. The metal plates in his back legs means he makes a *thump, thump, thump* noise wherever he goes. It's one of my favourite sounds. I hear it as he runs up for hugs, or when he follows me around the house. He has become my best friend, and is a true inspiration for me. I love him dearly, and I am forever in debt to MAR, who worked so hard to give him the chance to find true love and happiness again.

Snowy's story inspired me to support the amazing work that animal rescue groups do. I now volunteer for MAR, and one of my jobs is to co-run the fundraising page that began with Snowy. We will keep raising money, rescuing and doing the work we do until they all have a home. Every animal deserves the happy ending Snowy has had.

Zoë, Victoria

Lilly the Filly

One of our hardworking Tasmanian RSPCA inspectors, Carrie, looked around the paddock, but could see only a small, white ball of fluff on the ground. She had been called out one night to investigate a report of a horse with broken legs. Thinking the ball of fluff ahead of her was a cat, she moved closer and was shocked at what she found. It was a tiny miniature pony, just days old, unable to get up. The little thing had clearly not been able to stand to get that first vital drink from her mum, or anything since. By now she was weak and dehydrated, and weighed just 9 kilograms.

Carrie wrapped the small being in a blanket, gently placed her on the front seat of her vehicle and drove to the local vet clinic, where X-rays showed the reason for the foal's predicament. It was revealed that she had congenital, bilaterally dislocating patellas – in other words, her kneecaps were sitting in the wrong position, preventing her from using her legs.

That first night, Carrie took the little filly home with her, and fed her from a tube every forty-five minutes during the night to hydrate her and prepare her for the operation she needed.

A day later, Carrie took the pony to the vet for knee surgery. It wasn't an easy operation, requiring two surgeons over several hours, after which the little one was in intensive care for four days. This was followed by several days of physiotherapy to help stretch out her spindly legs. But Lilly (as Carrie had now named her) was a strong-willed little girl, and was standing up and trying to walk within twenty-four hours.

Lilly needed a month to recuperate, and during that time she required a blood transfusion as well as frequent trips to the vet to have the fluid drained from her knees (mostly because she wanted to stand up instead of lying down and resting!). However, after five weeks of special care, Lilly's progress had exceeded everyone's expectations, and she was moving incredibly well. At that stage, she was still so tiny she was wearing a small dog coat as a horse rug!

Lilly's recuperation was at Carrie's house, so that the pony could receive the dedicated care she needed. Carrie's ten-year-old rescued racehorse, Chelsea, in the next paddock, showed great interest in the tiny foal, and the two started communicating with each other through the fence. When Carrie saw them tenderly reaching out to touch noses, she wondered if she dared allow them in the same paddock together, aware of the enormous size difference and the fragility of the little filly. But, as they seemed determined to make friends, she finally decided to open the gate and let them meet properly. It was the right decision. The big mare immediately took over the care of the tiny foal, teaching her important 'horse stuff', and keeping a close protective eye over her as she slept in a pile of hay. Lilly became equally attached to her surrogate mum – even stepping underneath the bigger horse's body when it was raining. It was beautiful to behold.

But the best was yet to come. Carrie decided to adopt Lilly, so the rescued pony and Chelsea can now live out their lives together in a safe and loving home.

Two years on, Lilly the Filly is a proud, strong little pony, with plenty of attitude. She is sharing Carrie's farm with a large family of other special animals, including two Alaskan malamute dogs, a cow, a goat, two lambs, four cats, chickens, ducks and birds.

I wonder if she knows what a lucky little girl she is!

Lorraine Hamilton, RSPCA Animal Care Centre, Launceston, Tasmania

Celine's Secret

Her pound picture showed a very pretty white-and-tortoiseshell kitten with a sweet face. Would we rescue her? How could we say no!

I'd been working with CatRescue NSW for about seven years when we collected Celine from a Sydney pound. We were told she had been sick but was recovering. She wasn't much more than a kitten, possibly around twelve months, and was noted as being a 'super smoocher'.

When she was dropped off at my place, I saw that she was very underweight and wouldn't eat, so I placed small amounts of food directly into her mouth. Very late that night she crashed severely and spent the next twenty-four hours 'hiccup breathing'. When cats do this it means it is so hard for them to breathe that they hiccup automatically to try to draw breath.

The next morning Celine and I were waiting at the vet before they opened. I was very worried about her. She was instantly given antibiotics and subcutaneous fluids. As Celine didn't improve during the day, we were back at the vet in the evening for a second dose of antibiotics and more fluids. Within a few hours the hiccupping stopped and Celine was now open-mouth breathing; an improvement at least. But the next day the dribbling and drooling started. The vet feared that Celine had feline calicivirus, but we couldn't find any mouth ulcers at that point – a common symptom. As she was still terribly ill, we added in a third antibiotic.

By day four of vet treatment, the drooling had stopped and I felt it was safe enough to start force-feeding our little one. I bought Celine minced meat, added water and some dietary supplement to the mix, and rolled it into little balls, putting them in her mouth one at a time. I managed to get her to accept about four balls before she got too upset, and I did this about five times a day. I was determined that Celine would live!

Days later, still on antibiotics and receiving daily fluid therapy at the vet, Celine remained extremely unwell. I went to bed at 11.30 p.m. on about day eight and felt Celine slipping away. I held her tightly for well over an hour, closed my eyes and willed her to live. At 1 a.m. I force-fed her more mincemeat balls and held her close again. Suddenly, I heard a noise she'd never made before. Celine was purring. Next, all of a sudden, her fur changed from hard and stiff to soft and silky. In a matter of seconds. Was it my imagination?

'Goodness,' my husband said, touching her. 'Celine's fur just went soft!' I knew then that we had Celine back.

Over the following days, Celine continued to improve. On the evening of day ten Celine started to sniff her food. She tried to eat but couldn't manage it. I put some of the balls into her mouth again and she purred. Over the next few hours she made a number of attempts to eat and finally she did. I cried – what an overwhelming moment. Celine was doing her best to go on!

In all, Celine was at the vet thirteen times during those ten frightening days. The vet didn't hold out much hope for her but wasn't going to give up, and I wasn't for a second either. We kept her on an unlimited amount of high-quality food normally given to babies and mums and, a week later, when she had put on some weight and was looking a lot better, she went to a lovely young foster carer called Tushka, who had just joined our team. She was instructed to keep Celine on the special food and to give her a few meals a day of raw meat. Our girl was still very skinny but looking better.

Three weeks later, I received a frantic phone call at eleven o'clock at night from Tushka. 'You won't believe this, Jenny,' she gasped, 'but I've just come home and found Celine with four babies!'

Both in shock, we talked for a while and I asked if the kittens were wet or dry. They were all dry and happily feeding from Celine. I explained that meant they had been born hours earlier and were all fine. This amazing girl had given birth and cleaned up her babies all on her own!

Tushka told me that Celine had been eating well and had put on some weight in the intervening three weeks, but hadn't looked pregnant. Doing some quick calculations, I realised that she must have been around four weeks' pregnant when she was so ill.

The next day we took Celine and her babies back to the same vet, who was utterly astounded. He said it was unheard of for a cat to maintain a pregnancy when it had been on death's doorstep and hadn't eaten for at least four days. These were miracle kittens!

Once Celine's babies reached ten weeks of age, they were adopted to loving owners. But the best news was yet to come: Celine finding her own forever home. She has now joined a family with children and a dog, who she adores. In fact, Celine and her new doggy friend take turns chasing each other around the house.

Jenny, New South Wales

A Healing Journey

Everything is dark. I can't open my eyes. My body hurts.
What happens from here is a blur.

We can only imagine the fear, pain, and how utterly frightened this cat is feeling, found nearly drowning in a well of oil. Words cannot even begin to capture the horrendous ordeal he has endured in his short life.

Rushed to Greencross Vets in Morwell, he appeared to be completely feral; he was so terrified his behaviours were erratic. But the vet staff knew this feline deserved a second chance at life and fought to give him that. They phoned us, Forever Friends Animal Rescue's Latrobe division (FFARL), asking if we would take on this disturbing case if the vet staff could save him. The answer, of course, was yes.

Thickly covered in oil, he was dubbed 'Hulk', as the cleaning agent the vets used was green in colour. In addition, he was a little angry, so reminded us all of the very green and grumpy TV character!

Unfortunately, after many baths, the oil wouldn't lift and rather than traumatise the scared boy any further, the only option the vet staff had was to shave his fur off completely. His road to recovery was going to be long and painful, and it was still unknown how well he would recuperate. But Hulk's angels never gave up on him.

Hulk went into foster care with Lyn and her family for three months. Lyn can still recall the horror at seeing him when she picked him up from the vet. Underweight and furless, Hulk appeared to have cigarette burns to his legs and had no whiskers. These were obvious signs of abuse and it left us all with no question as to how Hulk came to be in the well of oil. He also had a strong fear of men, which only confirmed our fears.

It was a cold winter's night when Hulk arrived at Lyn's, and after the ordeal he had been through, he couldn't control his shaking. She attempted to comfort the terrified cat and make him feel warm and safe by wrapping him tightly in a cosy blanket, but Hulk wanted to search the house for a safe place to hide. Lyn made his chosen spot as comfortable as she could with a cosy sheepskin and his food and water nearby so he wouldn't have to venture out far. For the next two weeks, Hulk would only leave his safe place at night, when the house was quiet, to use his litter tray. The poor thing was too frightened to move.

Lyn dedicated much time every day to try to gain Hulk's trust, sitting and talking to him. He eventually allowed Lyn to pat him, and one day she made a wonderful breakthrough when he pressed himself against her hand and gave a small purr. Eventually, he allowed Lyn to give him cuddles. After three weeks, she would bring him into the lounge room with her, but he would quickly head back to his safe spot. Over time, Hulk remained longer in the lounge room with Lyn, but was petrified if a male ever entered the room.

Soon, Hulk started to let his guard down and would venture out to check what Lyn and the rest of his new family were doing. He would sit and quietly watch them, but he could not be approached, and if anyone entered his area he would quickly retreat.

After two months, Hulk became comfortable enough with Lyn to come to her for a pat and a cuddle. He would often jump on the couch and place his paw on Lyn's shoulder to let her know he was there, and after a cuddle he would curl up on his blanket for a nap.

Hulk still did not fully trust anyone, but it was time for him to find a forever home of his own. It would take a special person, though – someone who would be patient and willing to give Hulk time to gain trust.

In August 2012, Wendy attended an adoption day and met a timid boy who would steal her heart. Hulk sat quietly in the corner of his carrier. He didn't want to come out and meet anyone; he wanted to remain safe and out of harm's way. But Hulk made an exception for Wendy.

Wendy gave Hulk a cuddle and she can still recall the feeling of his fur, which had only just started to grow back and was bristly under her chin. Hulk shook the entire time Wendy held him but purred continuously. Hulk moved in with Wendy and her family a week later.

Naturally, Hulk needed time to adjust to his new family and home. He remained in the bathroom, within the safety of his carrier, which was covered in blankets. He only ventured out briefly to eat and have a quick explore when things felt safe. Every day, Wendy would go and sit with Hulk, stroking him while she quietly spoke to him. And after two weeks, Hulk would come out of his carrier when Wendy entered the room. He soon discovered a ball that he enjoyed playing with. On one occasion, the ball entered the hallway, and he quickly chased after it. However, as soon as he realised he was out of his 'room', he quickly ran back.

One quiet night, when everyone had retired to bed and the lights were turned off, Wendy felt a cat jump on the bed between her and her husband Ray. It was Hulk. This became Hulk's place to sleep from then on.

Hulk has come a long way since the day he was rescued. He has a very healthy appetite and has blossomed into a handsome young man with gorgeous soft fur. He now enjoys cuddles and pats from the entire family. Hulk has a brother cat called Peppie, who he enjoys annoying, and loves playing with his sister cat, Bella. He is always on the go, and now playing with his toys like the kitten he missed out on being.

In January 2013, Hulk discovered the big wide world of the outdoors and loves spending time in the garden. Wendy has said how thankful she is to the volunteers at FFARL for rescuing her boy, nursing him back to physical and emotional health, and for allowing him to become a part of her family. Hulk had angels watching over him the day he was rescued, but many could argue the blessings belong to those of us who have accompanied him on his journey.

Mel Palmer, Forever Friends Animal Rescue Latrobe, Victoria

The Miraculous Ollie

After Ollie disappeared in 2007, I never dreamt we'd see her again.

Ollie was our much-loved family dog: a black-brindle staffy who adored people, but probably children a little more. Everybody knew her well, particularly the local school children. I'm a glazier, and she came to work with me most days, and kept me company.

Ollie spent some of her time in our fenced front yard, and she had a kennel in the corner of the garden for when she felt like a nap.

One evening, I went out the front to bring her in and she was sleeping so soundly, I didn't have the heart to wake her. The next morning I asked my fifteen-year-old daughter to bring Ollie in for breakfast. I will never forget the look on Samantha's face when she came back inside. Ollie had vanished.

Samantha went back outside and sat at Ollie's kennel and cried until I took a blanket out to her. Distraught, we put up fliers and contacted all the animal pounds and shelters without success. Ollie was microchipped, so we prayed someone would hand her in, but we started to realise she had probably been stolen.

Six sad years passed without Ollie. We didn't get another dog, as there could never be another Ollie, and because deep down I hoped she would one day return. Meanwhile, Samantha looked twice at every staffy she passed on the street in case it was our beloved girl.

I was at work in Brunswick recently when my mobile rang. It was a woman calling from the RSPCA in Epping. She said, 'We have your dog, Ollie, here.'

At first I thought it was a joke – I just couldn't believe it.

When I found my voice, I told the caller that Ollie had disappeared six years ago. She replied that Ollie had been found roaming the streets of Lalor, about 16 kilometres away. When she was brought in they had scanned her microchip and my number came up. Did I want her back?

'Yes!' I shouted. 'In a heartbeat.'

It was Valentine's Day when I drove to the RSPCA to collect our Miraculous Ollie. When they walked me to her pen to see her, I can honestly say she remembered me after all these years. And although she was four years old when she went missing, the now ten-year-old dog hasn't missed a beat since coming home. It's like she's never been away!

Needless to say, we never leave Ollie out the front now – she's either inside, in the backyard or in the ute with me. I'm now sure she was stolen from us that night in 2007, and it may have taken her six years to try to make her way home, but she did. We adore her – and you would too if you saw the look of love in her eyes!

Joe, Victoria

◇◇◇◇◇

Journey's Journey

The emaciated mother, near death, was a skeletal amstaff mix. And while she had had a large and demanding litter of twelve puppies, it was her owners who were ultimately responsible for her severe neglect. They had been forced to surrender her to the council to avoid prosecution.

What chance for adoption would such a dog and her dependent puppies have in a country pound? Fortunately the caring staff contacted us, SAFE Perth (Saving Animals from Euthanasia), asking for help. Dubbed 'Journey', the severely ill mum was collected by our volunteer soon after and taken straight to the Swan Vet. Journey's puppies had been collected earlier by another rescue group.

The wonderful Dr Huber, who examined Journey on arrival, found that she had a temperature of over 40 degrees, and she was suffering from an infected uterus, severe emaciation and mastitis. She was placed on a drip in intensive care for four days, and all we could do was watch and wait. Would she survive? The vet staff were doing all they could, but we were told not to get our hopes up.

When we shared Journey's horrific story on our SAFE Perth Facebook page, her plight touched the hearts of people all over the world, and donations poured in from all over Australia, Canada, the US and the UK. People were deeply disturbed by the sight of her near-death state in the first photograph, and at what this poor soul had been through. We kept supporters informed with daily updates on Journey's progress, and the well-wishers continued to grow.

During her week in intensive care, Journey was fed small meals of critical-care food to try to help her gain weight, and to regain enough strength to be operated on to remove her infected uterus. Finally she was ready, and it was a huge relief to us when she pulled through the surgery. There were cheers all around when, a week after being admitted to the vet, Journey was able to go into the home of one of our longest-serving foster carers, Corrina, who continued to nurse this survivor back to health.

After just six weeks no one would have recognised Journey from her first photograph. Not only has she put on weight, but her beautiful nature has also had a chance to blossom. She loves everybody she meets with equal enthusiasm: kids, adults, other dogs and puppies included. She's even been kind and accepting to cats!

But Journey's ability to love and forgive the world doesn't end there. While in foster care, she has even taken under her wing two litters of neglected puppies who came into care, looking after them like a true mother. She has shared her food with them, cleaned them and shown them all the 'doggy ropes'.

Journey particularly loves the human children in her foster family, spending time on the couch with them watching television – and is now even referred to as a lapdog! Journey wants nothing more than to be close to those who have nursed her back to the wonderful state of health she is in now. She awaits the next significant step in her new life – her adoption into a loving forever home.

The father of Journey's puppies, who we dubbed 'Daddy', was also taken into our care and has recently found a loving family to love him as he deserves.

If anything, Journey's journey reminds us why the work we do is so important. Any soul who has been so cruelly treated but is willing to forgive and trust us humans – and the world – again deserves sunshine on her path every day forward. Travel on, Journey.

Sue Campbell, SAFE Perth, Western Australia

DYNAMIC DUOS

◇◇◇◇◇◇◇◇

Pets don't just adore their humans: their unconditional love can be shared with any creature under the sun! Here you'll meet a heartwarming bunch of pet pals and odd couples who are testament to the astounding capacity of animals to love.

Mr Wigglesworth and Sophie Find Love

I would never have imagined that love would blossom between such an unlikely pair at Animal Welfare League's West Hoxton shelter earlier this year.

Mr Wigglesworth, a cute, hairy, brown pig and Sophie, a rather feisty little goat, fell head over hooves for each other as soon as they met. Both were orphans; incredibly, Mr Wigglesworth was found wandering alone in the suburbs as a tiny piglet.

Originally, Sophie and Mr Wigglesworth were in separate pens and could only see each other from a distance. The day it all started, Mr Wigglesworth was out of his pen, being cheeky and running around while I was trying to bring him back inside. All of a sudden, Sophie started 'baaing' at him, and our cheeky little pig went straight over to her.

He stood on the outside of her pen, just staring at her. It was like she called him over and he understood.

Watching this all unfold, I saw that instant spark between these two as they came face to face, tails wagging and feet shuffling. It was like a love scene from a Hollywood film!

Later that day, I thought I might see if Sophie and Mr Wigglesworth would like to have a play together. As soon as they came into contact, they got on like they had known each other for a lifetime. They started to playfully buck heads and jump around as if dancing together.

Over the coming days and weeks, this unlikely friendship only seemed to grow – while Mr Wigglesworth continued to grow too! And while his piggy self was soon bigger than his darling Sophie, she always remained the boss in the relationship.

Having this romance unfold around us produced so many smiles on the faces of our staff. The happiness of the goat and piggy friends was infectious – just watching their joy in spending time in each other's company was so touching. When they weren't snuggled up in the straw, they were playing tag in their pen, or feasting on a trough of strawberries and apples. These two love birds were inseparable.

After some time at the shelter, the word about our unusual pals started getting around. Soon the media came knocking, and Sophie and her main piggy man were even featured on Channel 7 news! Next, families started to get in touch to offer the couple a home. After much discussion, we decided that the successful adopters were to be a lovely rural family with children, who promised to always keep the forever friends together.

On the morning after Sophie and Mr W arrived at their new home, one of the children, Sophia, was so excited she woke up at 6 a.m. and ran out to be with her new friends. Sophia even asked if she could sleep with them one night!

Mr Wigglesworth and Sophie's new family even bought both of them special harnesses so they could take them for walks every morning. Originally they tried to just take Mr Wigglesworth out; however, Sophie wouldn't stop screaming for him, so they had to turn around and go back – she couldn't bear to be separated from her piggy soulmate.

Thanks to regular updates and fun photos from the family, we've seen that Mr Wigglesworth and Sophie are having a great time splashing around in their water trough and hanging out with the family's dog, George. George loves having them around too!

The shelter staff are missing Sophie and Mr W terribly, but are filled with happiness when they think of them being well cared for and in the company of their best friend for life.

Stories like this help all of us at our shelter to keep motivated and striving for our animals' happiness. Every animal is unique and special, but when we get to see relationships like this form for life, it is such a treat. It reminds me how lucky I am to have this job. When I'm surrounded by such fantastic furry characters as these, I'm just like a pig in mud!

Alan Norris, Animal Welfare League, New South Wales

When Two is Better than One

What is better than one rescue dog? Two, of course! A few years ago I made the decision to adopt a pug. While all dogs are special, pugs in particular require a higher standard of care, and as a result a lot of them often end up with horrific health issues due to owner ignorance or poor breeding practices.

I had looked at a few different breeds in my search, and had taken several months to make the decision, but finally I decided my heart was set on a pug. Not wanting to support pet shops, puppy factories or backyard breeders, adoption was the only option!

I first spotted Gizmo on PetRescue after a friend sent me the link. It was love at first sight. He just looked so cuddly and sad – all he wanted was his own forever home. The process to adopt Gizmo from Pug Rescue was not a quick one. Jo from Pug Rescue put me through my paces with a thorough application process that included phone interviews, house inspections and 'meet and greet' sessions with my chosen boy.

When I was finally told that I had been successful I was thrilled, and I got to take Gizmo home a few weeks before Christmas.

What I wasn't prepared for were the psychological injuries he'd incurred at the hands of his previous owners and what it would take to heal him. Gizmo was frightened of other dogs, of men and crowds in general, and would circle anxiously for hours on end. We knew that he'd spent most of his days out in a backyard with a very large dog for a companion. Without knowing the full story, his general fear of large dogs and the infected scratches he had on his back indicated his experience with the other dog was not a pleasant one. Over two years later, while his chronic circling and general fear of strangers had relaxed, he still suffered anxiety. If more than a few people came to my house he would cower and tremble, and mixing with other dogs was out of the question – even my parents' friendly kelpie couldn't get him onside.

Finally, after I returned from a stay overseas and discovered Gizmo had taken on destructive behaviours, I sought help from a vet. He put Gizmo on anti-anxiety tablets, but I was never happy about medicating him and eventually asked what we could explore as an alternative. To my surprise he suggested that a younger female pug with the right temperament could be the perfect antidote to Gizmo's woes. *What a great idea*, I thought! So the adoption process began once more.

I reached out to Jo again. How could we find a younger female pug who would bond with Gizmo – hater of all other dogs? As luck would have it, Jo had a younger female pug with a docile temperament in need of a new home, so I got to meet Marli. All she wanted to do was love and be loved. She had an adorable personality, liked to make mischief and was a master ninja when it came to sneaking onto the bed while you slept. She was perfect, but it was with trepidation that we introduced Gizmo to Marli. I was unsure how he would react.

As it happens, Gizmo hated her. For almost two weeks Gizmo solidly ignored Marli, even snapping at her if she got too close. Marli, bless her, would not give up. She would try and snuggle up to him, sneaking an inch at a time while he steadfastly ignored her (he is rather famous for his silent treatments). She would follow him around the house, stare at him lovingly and try to share his food bowl (although we've since discovered this is just because she is a guts). We persevered, however, feeding them together, making them share a crate at night-time, hoping he would warm to her eventually and let his guard down – giving up was never an option.

Then one day, after almost three weeks, I heard a growling noise from the lounge room and crept in to see what was going on. They were playing! Gizmo was chasing Marli, and when he caught her she would lie on her back and wrestle with him. I'd never seen Gizmo behave like this with another dog before. Was this our breakthrough?

From there it was onwards and upwards. Gizmo's life changed. He became more relaxed around strangers, more comfortable around other dogs, and when Marli would bark, he would bark too! Aside from the occasional yap, we'd never heard Gizmo bark before. But once Gizmo found his voice, the barking became so enthusiastic we ended up having to do some extra training to get that under control, a problem we felt blessed to have after more than two years of silence! Now, nearly six months later, we're so happy we chose to adopt again – Gizmo is a new man and Marli was just the medicine he needed. It's as though she's said to him, *Everything's okay now, Gizmo – there's no need to worry!* They love each other dearly and on the rare occasions they've had to be separated, it's been very clear how attached they've become to each other.

So now, three years down the track, not only have my fiancé and I had the opportunity to give a home to two wonderful pugs in need, but I can genuinely say that they have improved the quality of each other's lives, and ours too!

Krystal, Victoria

Queen of the Castle

Phoebe came into my life about fifteen years ago from the Cat Protection Society at the tender age of eight weeks – a little tortoiseshell bundle of purrs and claws. I had been a foster carer for rescue pets for many years and usually took in dogs, so Phoebe entered a mysterious canine-filled world. I'm sure it must have been a shock to her tiny kitten system, but she proved to be very adaptable to her new home.

Just six weeks later, I received a beautiful birthday present, a ten-week-old Rottweiler named Conor. Rather than there being the immediate dog-versus-cat rivalry, the Rottweiler and tiny kitten formed an instant friendship. It was a delight to see the two of them together, rolling about on the floor, or playing chasey around the backyard. Sometimes Conor chased Phoebe; sometimes Phoebe chased Conor.

Conor was too young to leave alone while I went to work, so he came with me, much to Phoebe's disappointment. At that time I owned a restaurant, so keeping a rotty at work posed a bit of a problem. I eventually came up with a solution – he could stay in the change room just off the dry store at the rear of my restaurant. He soon became the most petted Rottweiler in Melbourne, as our waiting staff loved to take a quick five-minute break with him when the stress of demanding customers got to them. This proved to be wonderful for Conor's socialisation, and set the pattern for his future as a gentle giant. Mind you, woe betide us if the health department had caught even the slightest whiff of these goings-on!

Still, despite all the attention he received at work, Conor was pleased to come home to his little mate Phoebe. She was equally delighted to see him and away they went, meowing and woofing through the house together. After a hard day and night at the restaurant, their antics were a joy to watch (though, at two o'clock in the morning, somewhat tiring!) The best thing of all was watching little Phoebe climb on top of her Rottweiler friend when she was ready to go to sleep – relishing his warmth.

About a year later, ten-week-old Anouk, my German shepherd girl, joined our family, and the happy twosome became a threesome. But Anouk's entry into our household had another unusual effect on the canine–feline relations. Phoebe, who had been sleeping on top of Conor, realised when winter approached that she now had a better offer. Come June, Phoebe moved to sleeping on top of Anouk, who had a longer coat and was warmer in winter! When summer returned, Phoebe went back to Conor. Fickle feline.

Conor and Anouk have both crossed the Rainbow Bridge now, but Phoebe has made other canine friends. Paddy O'Reilly (a Rottweiler–Great Dane mix) has joined the gang, along with Bridie O'Flaherty (an Irish staghound–bull Arab mix) who is the tallest dog I've ever seen; Mouse McCheese (a whippet–greyhound mix), so-named because she is addicted to blue cheese; and Snoopie the Cow Dog (a staffy mix), whose coat is the same pattern and colour as a Friesian cow.

My four fur-kids are all rescue dogs from country pounds all over Victoria, and despite how much I loved Conor and Anouk, I would never buy a dog from a breeder again. All my fur-kids seem to know they have been given a second chance because they are so loving and beautifully behaved. Or perhaps their good manners have more to do with Phoebe, who will put any mutt in their place when she feels they are too cheeky. No matter how many dogs there are in this madhouse, my tortoiseshell girl is still Queen of the Castle!

Eric, Victoria

◇◇◇◇◇

The Devotion of Zodie and Cricket

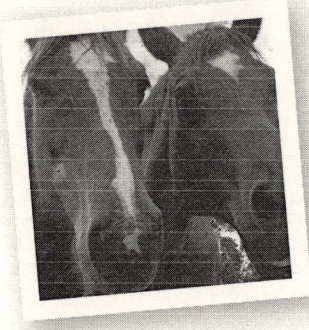

Zodie's fate changed dramatically the day Tegan found him. In May 2012, our friend Tegan had gone to a property in Victoria to purchase some horses, and noticed a lone horse in a dirt paddock with little feed. He was extremely emaciated, and Tegan was shocked to learn that he was still being ridden. She knew that if he were left over winter, he would likely starve to death, so she set about negotiating his purchase.

Happy to have rescued him, she transported him to her property. However, as she did not have the time to nurse him back to full health, she contacted me at Harmony Reins Animal Haven in Yarra Junction.

We were not in a position to collect Zodie immediately. We started talking to people in our network and then, amazingly, two strangers who we had never met before, Carly and her husband, stepped in, offering to collect and deliver Zodie at no cost. It was heart-warming to see so many people willing to help out.

With some breeds of horses it is standard practice to brand them. From Zodie's brands, we were able to discover that he was a purebred Arab and born in 1988.

On his arrival we were sickened by his poor physical condition. He had very little body fat and was completely covered in botfly eggs – the maggot stage of large flies. His belly was big and round, suggesting that it was full of worms. He was completely malnourished and neglected.

Our rehabilitation began with appropriate worming, a bath and some good food. We cut off his tangled, knotted mane and manually removed all the botfly eggs from his body. We found a toasty rug to keep him warm during the cold winter nights and hoped that the long-term neglect he had suffered would not have any lasting impact on his health.

Zodie fitted in very well with the routine at Harmony Reins. He slowly gained weight and proved to have the nicest temperament – everyone who met him became quite smitten. He is always happy to share his meals with any of our residents, and it's not unusual for Candy the donkey, Beavis and Popeye the goats, and Rory the dog to take full advantage of his generosity!

After six months in care, Zodie was looking amazing. With a healthy, shiny coat and a full belly, he was almost appearing fat. However, he never really bonded with any of the other horses, and we suspect this was because he had been paddocked alone for much of his life.

Then, in November 2012, Cricket arrived and everything changed. She had been purchased from the market to save her being sent to slaughter at a knackery. As soon as she arrived, Zodie showed interest in her. While she spent her time in quarantine, Zodie waited patiently and nickered at her to calm her. As soon as it was time to go into a shared paddock, Zodie was besotted with her. We'd never seen anything like it – they were inseparable. While they rested in the paddock they maintained constant contact, touching shoulders, bellies or noses. If they were people, they would have completed each other's sentences! When Cricket had her hooves done for the first time, Zodie gently rested his head over her shoulder to tell her it would all be all right. Watching them together was magical.

Sadly, in February 2013, Cricket unexpectedly took ill. We're not sure what happened but we think she may have been bitten by a snake. The vet came right away and there was nothing that could be done for her, so she was euthanised in the paddock with Zodie right by her side.

Cricket's passing affected all of us, but it affected Zodie more than anyone. She was such a gorgeous horse and was the centre of his world. He stayed by her side all night and did not leave her until it was time for her body to be removed the next day.

Since Cricket's passing, Zodie has found a friend in another Harmony Reins horsey resident, Jock, and he seems to be happier, bit by bit. We will give him time to grieve before we introduce him to any more of the ladies.

In such a short period our handsome Zodie has made his way firmly into our hearts. He is a kind soul who loves a cuddle and is always interested in the happenings on the farm. Some people find him hard to read as his ears are often pinned back against his head. This can be seen as a sign of aggression, but in the Arab breed it is quite common and is just his way of saying 'How're you doing?' He is lovely to handle in every way and we still wonder how such an amazing horse could end up so neglected. We are so blessed to have him with us and thank all those who helped to make a difference in his life.

Catherine Grayson, Harmony Reins Animal Haven, Victoria

Ellee Brave Heart

One weekend in 2007, my husband and I happened to be driving past the Lonsdale RSPCA when we both felt a strong urge to stop and have a look. This split-second decision would change our lives.

We had known for a long time that we wanted to get a whippet for our first pet. My husband had grown up with a rescue whippet named Dodger. The dog was a gentle and loving addition to his family, especially after the arrival of my husband's baby sister. Dodger would always watch over her and sleep next to her cot every night.

Whenever she started to cry, he would go and find her mum or dad and usher them towards the baby in distress. Meeting Dodger myself when he was much older and looking into the breed characteristics, I too fell in love with whippets, but hadn't done anything about it. Then that day in 2007, when we went into RSPCA Lonsdale, we met and fell in love with a beautiful three-year-old female whippet mix called Ellee.

Ellee was timid at first, and we knew we would have to work at gaining her confidence and trust. She slowly relaxed in our company, but would whine if we were out of sight, so we gradually left her for increasingly longer periods until she was fine to be alone for a couple of hours.

Things were hard with toilet training, too. We knew whippets were sensitive to voice tone, but Ellee took that to a whole new level. If she went to the toilet inside, we would just ignore her and clean it up. Meanwhile, every hour and a half we would take her outside and praise her if she did her business out there. This is simple enough in theory. But the problem was, when Ellee *did* go to the loo inside, she sensed she had done something wrong and would take herself outside and then refuse to come back in! In the end, my husband would pick her up gently and bring her back inside, but as soon as her feet touched the ground, she was off outside again. It was as though she felt she should be banished for her indiscretion. My husband would bring her in again, and one time I sat in front of the door so that when she tried to run outside again, I was there and ready to catch her. She was shaking as she tried to push past me, but I gently held her, stroked her and told her it was okay. I suddenly felt her lean into me with relief and slowly her shaking stopped. From then on, Ellee didn't need to punish herself any more.

Then, one day while we were watching *Bondi Vet*, a litter of newborn puppies began crying for their mum on the TV and little Ellee got up, looking worried, and searched all around the room trying to find them! She had never taken any notice of anything on the TV before, so this immediately got my attention. I had a talk with my partner and we decided perhaps Ellee needed a puppy in her life.

Soon after, we saw in the paper some female whippet puppies for sale near Murray Bridge. We arranged to meet the puppies, taking Ellee with us. We asked the owners to line up the puppies behind the fence so we could walk Ellee by and gauge her reaction. The first time we walked past, Ellee stopped at the fence to look in and one puppy came up to greet her. After a sniff, they both sat down opposite each other. It was amazing. We then put them together in a wide enclosed area. They interacted beautifully, Ellee watching the little one play and licking her if she came close by. There were no signs of aggression or fear in either of them. We bought 'Ellee's puppy' home and named her Phoebe.

Ellee took on the parenting role with little Phoebe with delight and, as we hoped, the surrogate mum blossomed into a loving, confident and playful girl. She now adored to run and jump. She would do laps with Phoebe, running from the bedroom, through the kitchen into the lounge room, leaping over the back of the armchair and, after pausing to stop, would jump back over the armchair and tear back to the bedroom. Young Phoebe couldn't jump like Ellee and would try to cut her off, but Ellee was too quick and could twist and turn with tight precision. It was a joy to watch.

Then, everything changed. In March 2012, I discovered I had a mutation in my DNA predisposing me to cancer at a young age. As a result, I had to undergo major surgery to prevent future risks, which meant an eleven-day stay in hospital. My brother had taken Ellee and Phoebe to his house for the interim as we were worried about the girls being on their own when my husband came to visit me.

Ellee and Phoebe had been to my brother's home a lot and they both enjoyed the company of his dog, Barney. It wasn't until I was given the okay to come home that my partner informed me that Ellee hadn't been coping all that well while I was in hospital. She had developed a lump on the left side of her neck, and had gone off her food. Considering I had been in hospital to try to prevent illness, it was very disturbing that our girl had become sick during this time herself.

A couple of days after I returned home, Ellee's lump was mysteriously gone and she was eating again, but there was clearly something still wrong. She just didn't seem her usual self.

Over the next few weeks, we found that the lump would come and go at random. It could appear and disappear in a matter of hours, or it could stay for days. Our vet tried the conservative approach at first – antibiotics and anti-inflammatories. These seemed to work, but they were really only boosting her appetite. The lump was still appearing and disappearing, but each time it seemed to grow bigger and then shrink to less.

The next step was a biopsy, but the vet only managed to get white blood cells. Exploratory surgery revealed two small lumps, one of which they removed, but they could get only a small sample of the other lump for testing. Once again, the lab test showed only inflamed white blood cells.

Ellee then needed to have an X-ray and MRI scan, but five days before the scans she had a seizure, so only the X-ray was taken. It showed multiple small growths in her lungs, on her heart and, going by the fact that she'd had the seizure, probably on her brain as well. The vet told us that the growth on her neck was most likely the primary tumour with the rest being secondaries.

My heart broke. We looked into chemotherapy for dogs but as Ellee had so many secondaries and in so many locations, it wasn't feasible or fair on her. All we could do was manage her pain. But within days Ellee lost her appetite. She would only eat cheese, and even then only if I told her it had her 'medicine' in it. From there, the cancer seemed to take her so quickly. The main tumour on her neck was changing every couple of hours.

When her time came, first we took Ellee out for a ride in the car. She couldn't run or play like she used to, but she still managed a smile. The vet staff were fantastic. They all came in to say goodbye, even the vet who had met her only once on the day of her seizure. We all cried at losing her. We brought Phoebe with us; you could tell that she knew what was happening too. Afterwards, Phoebe went up to Ellee and just laid her head down on her paw.

Ellee is the bravest and strongest girl I have known. We were blessed with her love for five years, and with how we got to watch her transform so much since that first day in 2007. Every day she healed a little more from whatever had happened in her past and grew more confident. She absolutely adored anyone that she got to meet. She went from shy and timid to strong and loving. Even though we have lost our Ellee, she still helps us get through the toughest moments in life. We have a saying now – 'Ellee would only drop her head for a scratch' – which reminds us of the essence of what Ellee had and what she went through, and that she didn't let it stop her from being *her*; it didn't stop her showing love, and no matter how bad things got, she always held her head up high. She was our little guardian angel who brought smiles, love and strength to us all.

Phoebe wasn't the same after we lost Ellee. She went off her food for the first few days. The only way I could get her to eat was to feed her by hand. She started to follow me around the house like a shadow and stopped playing. She looked so lost.

In January, I heard of a female whippet puppy up for adoption. After a phone enquiry, a photo of the puppy was sent to my phone. We fell in love with her face immediately. Over the long weekend we went for a road trip with Phoebe on board – just as we did with Ellee all those years ago. We brought Carlee home with us that day. She's another shy girl, but with Phoebe's and our love she is already coming out of her shell. Phoebe now follows little Carlee around the house. She has inducted her into how to play some of her and Ellee's favourite games. As happy as Phoebe is having a new friend, sometimes at night I wake up to hear her whimpering. At first I thought she had hurt herself, but I soon realised that she was just missing her Ellee, like the rest of us.

Jessica, South Australia

Man's Best Friends

An animal shelter is almost guaranteed to bring to mind some sombre and glum thoughts. Quite often the residents have been rejected by their families and thus far denied the happy life that should rightfully be theirs. However, in the summer of 2011, a story began that not only contradicts all that, but also warms the heart.

Bella, a ridgeback mix, came to Geelong Animal Welfare Society (GAWS) in a terrible condition. She was terrified and skinny, and afraid to the point that she would cower in the corner of her pen at the mere sight of people. At this point Bella was far from rehomeable, but our operations manager, Nadine, identified that despite Bella's fear and present condition, there was a beautiful-natured girl inside. She started spending extra time with Bella, and soon gained her trust. She slowly built Bella's confidence and nursed her back to health. Sure enough, it wasn't long before the dog's loving nature and personality began to shine through.

Bella soon spent her days with Nadine, greeting all the staff members in the morning, napping at the feet of the reception staff and joining everyone for a break in the tea room. She showed that she was friendly towards any other animal she met, including cats and even guinea pigs. Given her friendly nature and even temperament, Nadine, along with other staff members, started using Bella to temperament-test new dogs coming to the shelter.

Bella had built an extraordinary bond with Nadine, and all the staff had grown to adore her. She just seemed to fit in and it was soon apparent that no one at the shelter wanted to part with her. It was then determined that this would become her home and Bella had also decided that this was where she wanted to be.

Lucky the wolfhound mix came to the shelter as a surrendered dog – his family didn't want him any more. He suffered from a terrible skin condition that caused hair loss and sores, and was underweight. The staff ensured that Lucky got all the TLC he needed to recover. This was a long process and gave everyone the chance to get to know him. The team at the shelter quickly recognised that, just like Bella, he had a beautiful, goofy nature.

From their first encounter the bond between the endearing Lucky and the ever-sweet Bella was instant. Lucky's friendly, carefree nature brought out an unprecedented confidence in Bella. It fast became a partnership that would prove to be beautiful, not only for each other, but for their human counterparts too.

During his recovery, Lucky was spending more time in the house yard with Bella and often sneaking in to snooze at my feet in my office. It wasn't long before I realised Lucky brought a ray of sunshine and happiness to our long and sometimes stressful days. Surprisingly, no one had showed an interest in adopting Lucky, and as with Bella, he just seemed to fit into the daily routine of shelter life. As the two dogs were such good friends and the staff adored him, it seemed only right that he join Bella as a permanent shelter dog and that this become his home.

The two dogs spend their days with free range of the shelter grounds, having ample room to run and play. As well as being adored by the staff, they also enjoy attention, love and pats from the many visitors to GAWS. Both dogs are used for temperament-testing and helping other dogs to come out of their shells and gain confidence. Both these canines are friends with everyone they meet – humans, other dogs, the resident cat, Patsy, and any other animal that comes into the shelter. On occasions the staff visit nursing homes, and Lucky, with the infectious happiness that he seems to take with him, began to join them on their visits. He immediately put smiles on the faces of the elderly.

Through their tenacious will to survive and the love and care of the staff, these two amiable canines have a happy outcome. While unfortunate circumstances saw Bella and Lucky arrive at the shelter, it would appear it was happily destined to be. You could say that the loveable duo seemed to choose their life at the shelter as much as the staff chose to adopt them. Amid the long and sometimes sad days endured by staff, these two four-leggeds give much love and joy. Whenever things get tough, the staff only have to turn to Bella and Lucky to be reminded that dogs really are man's best friend.

Belinda Russo, Geelong Animal Welfare Society, Victoria

Roger Maximus Ram

Surprise, surprise, my son-in-law Juliano arrived home one night from his friend's farm carrying twins. Lambs, that is, or rams, to be exact. Orphans at birth. Oh, cripes!

We made them a comfortable, warm home in the corner of our family room. Lucky it had tiled flooring, as they did make a bit of a mess. They were real cuties, and we bottle-fed and nursed them constantly for the next few weeks until they were ready to move to the garden shed, where we continued to bottle-feed twice a day, until they grew larger and realised grass was for eating.

It soon became apparent that the brothers were Dorset sheep, a breed that doesn't need shearing or crutching, which was good news for us. As they grew, we would watch them running, jumping and happily playing together in the half-acre secure paddock behind our house. Being hand-fed they were extremely friendly and would come running whenever we went outside.

But, sadly, the time came to divide the house yard from the back paddock to create two pens, as the larger twin ram was becoming a little aggressive, while his brother Roger was a sweet and gentle fellow. Lucky for me, I knew a bit about rams. I had had a pet ram some years ago, and while I used to pat and rub his ears, one day he took three steps back, and as I wondered what he was doing, he flew forward into my knee caps and almost smashed them both. And I thought he was my friend! So I knew then what to expect from these two boys as they matured and never turned my back on either of them.

Then, one day, it happened. I had gone into the shed to clean it out. When done, I went to walk out but guess who was watching my every move? I knew that challenging look in his eyes and that determined pose. Yes, my sweet little bottle-fed lamb was now a big, tough boy ready to take on the world. I knew I would have to be hard on him because I couldn't run that fast any more, and it was a long dash back to the house. I grabbed a flat piece of board that I knew would make more noise than pain. The cantankerous ram stepped back and flew forward towards me, then *BANG!* His head hit the board, and although slightly shocked, he prepared himself for another go. I had to stand my ground and be sure this one hit home – but then came another and another. I was beginning to wonder if I would survive this attack! Eventually, my opponent accepted defeat and went back to playing with his brother. However, from then on I kept a board near the back door for when I had to go outside, as he came running as soon as he saw me.

I was interstate at the time when he tried to kill his brother, Roger. Juliano was home, fortunately, and able to fight him off. He sent him down to our neighbours who were fortunately after a ram for their ewes. So the remaining ram, Roger Maximus, was safe.

As time went on, the lone Roger became friendly with the rescue dogs I fostered, many as big as him. He would come to the fence and lie as close as he could beside them, with only the wire separating their bodies. My little Jack Russell, Buddy, started venturing into Roger's paddock to nibble his ears and nose softly. Roger loved it and would gently butt him, and Buddy would run in circles trying to get Roger to chase him, and sometimes he did. I believe Roger began to think of himself as a dog – with his brother gone, he obviously loved their company and felt safe while they were around.

The time eventually came for me to move, and Roger, of course, had to come too. He now resides with me on a picturesque farm in the Yarra Valley with his pals Gertie the Goat, Archie and Polly the rescue horses and many dogs. He is a cheeky fellow and gets grumpy if his food isn't ready when he wants it – he stamps his feet and bellows while kicking impatiently at the fence. *Hurry up!* I know that tilt of his head and that glint in his eye that means *I'm not real happy with you!* but he is really quite tame and still loves a rub on his ears, which seems to calm him instantly. Oh, and he's just developed a liking for carrots!

Lynda, Victoria

◇◇◇◇◇

Speckles and Tasha

Speckles always seemed to get left behind.

She came to us at Peninsula Cat Rescue in Mornington from a vet clinic at about twelve weeks old. A placid and gentle tortoiseshell, she mothered all the kittens who came into the foster kitten room. They always moved on to new homes, while Speckles stayed. Sadly, no one wanted to adopt her.

One day we took in a five-month-old tabby kitten that had been trapped at a caravan park. People at the park had felt sorry for her and fed her, but she was still quite wild and very timid. We called her Tasha.

Tasha never hissed or showed any signs of aggression towards us, which was a sign of her trust in us, but she didn't want to be touched. After her quarantine period, she was moved to the kitten room and it was interesting to watch how she changed under Speckles' guidance.

Tasha would often sit and observe all the other kittens at play and how they interacted with their human carers. The kittens would race up to their food bowl with Tasha timidly following. She began to accept being stroked and tickled under the chin – her first contact with humans. We began to feel optimistic about her chances of finding a home.

One day a lady called Lyn came to see the kittens and wanted two: one for her house as a pet and the other to be a mouser for the shed. She chose Speckles as the house pet and shy Tasha as the mouser, with the plan that Tasha would sleep in the shed at night and hopefully come into the house during the day.

It didn't quite work out that way, as this lovely collection of anecdotes from Lyn showed:

> Dear Joy and family,
>
> I thought I would send you a note and some pics of the two 'shed cats'. As you can see they seem very content in their new abode.
>
> At least a couple of times a day if not more, Tasha is now seeking out a big smooch with both of us, so it was certainly worth saving her because she has become a very affectionate puss indeed. Speckles is as loving as ever and likes to sit on your knee or the bed and have a cuddle.
>
> Tasha also doubles as an alarm clock, continuing to keep up the early-morning ritual of scratching at the carpet under the gap in the ensuite door. There's no chance of breakfast being missed in this family!
>
> They both love sitting on top of the piano. I even caught Speckles under the cover one day (I was wondering why there were strange noises coming from the piano knowing that the lid over the keys was down). Now I have to anchor down the

cover with a heavy pile of books at each end. Perhaps she is a thwarted composer!

Despite a selection of beds, sleeping together has become a nightly ritual even when it is hot, so they are indeed great mates! Tasha also loves lounging on the kitchen bench – so much so, I think she would be quite happy living in a pub where she could sit up and chat to all the bar flies! Her ability to jump on the bench results in her stealing cherries out of the fruit bowl and playing with them; something I discovered after stepping on one. She's fond of vine tomato stalks and is fascinated with bowls of water in the sink. One day I had left rocket draining in the sink and returned later to find it strewn all over the place . . . Tasha!

It is almost impossible to try and write anything on the kitchen bench as Tasha will come and walk all over the paper you are writing on and then proceed to chew the pen or rub against it so that the pen goes in all directions!

Speckles is so relaxed she has been known to fall off whatever she has been sleeping on. She loves snuggling up, particularly on lazy weekend mornings. If I doze off and she feels it's time for breakfast, she pats me on the face with her paw until I take notice and attend to her tummy. At other times, Speckles has these really mad moments that seem to come from nowhere – all of a sudden she will start careering round the place in a mad, ecstatic frenzy.

Tasha has become much more vocal – chatting when she would really like some cuddles or a play. On her last visit to the vet, Tasha was rather rudely described as a 'pudding' (I am sure it is because of all her fur) so we have started some daily yoga exercises. This involves her lying on her back and I tickle her haunches one at a time and this causes her to bend one way, then the other. Though I have to say after recently seeing a picture of a particularly obese cat (it looked like a roast chicken with pencils for legs) our gorgeous girls look positively svelte in comparison.

As far as relationships with household members goes, Speckles continues to boss little Major around (our Tibetan spaniel) as well as managing to get him out of his bed if that is in fact where Speckles would like to sit. He has been very long suffering and fortunately flexible enough to go and find somewhere else to sleep. One cosy winter's night I did catch Tasha and Roxy the red heeler having a lick of each other's faces – a rare occurrence for sure, but I think they have quite an understanding, those two.

One of Tasha's favourite spots is still my daughter Georgie's room – I think it is because none of the other animals go out there so she has claimed it for her own. She has been a great Year 12 study companion for her.

As you can see from these anecdotes the puddy tats continue to entertain, delight and fill our lives with so much companionship and love. Thank you for rescuing them. We love them to bits!

Love,

Lyn and Georgie

Joy Herring, Peninsula Cat Rescue, and Lyn Kirkham, Victoria

THE CUTEST CRITTERS

◇◇◇◇◇◇◇◇

There's nothing cuter than a fuzzy bunny, a fearless puppy or a curious kitten. Whether its their playful ingenuity, their hilarious antics or simply their cuddly fur and puppy-dog eyes, an adorable pet can be the quickest way to brighten your day.

Copernicus the Army Cat

At 1700 hours on 17 October 2005, an alarm sounded in the sergeants' mess at Warradale Barracks. Warrant Officer Stephen was first on the scene and switched it off. He immediately noted the sound of frenzied squeaking above the refrigerators and thought it was a bird trapped in the ceiling. Enlisting the help of Sergeant Alex, they climbed into the ceiling and investigated.

Nothing.

The squeaking continued, so off went the refrigerators. In the silence, they realised that the sound was more a squeal than a squeak and that it was coming from behind the fridge – specifically, from inside the plasterboard wall behind the fridge.

Fetching a large carving knife from the kitchen, Sergeant Alex carefully cut some of the plasterboard away. Reaching in, he gently pulled out fibreglass insulation and then a tiny, palm-sized, squealing black-and-white kitten. The little one was obviously not weaned and his mother had moved to another location. (Warradale Barracks had a feral cat problem at the time, and the mother cat had presumably gained access to the roof cavity and had her litter on the insulation. This little one had unfortunately fallen down the wall gap!)

At that point, WO2 Stephen offered to perform an action that would remove the kitten from the barracks (and existence). Sergeant Alex – now the kitten's Guardian Angel – calmly stated that if such a thing were to occur, the consequences would be immediate and severe!

Stephen's initial suggestion was hurriedly withdrawn. The kitten was gently placed in a gumboot – yes! – and began his journey to his new life, squealing all the way.

I received two voicemail messages that night from my father, Sergeant Alex: *'Meow!'* went the first one.

'You'd better get over here. He's got you a cat,' was the second one from my mum. And so little Copernicus came into my life.

I zoomed over to Mum and Dad's, collected my new little kitten and . . . was stuck. I was in the middle of moving house, and I didn't want the tiny being getting squished by boxes and furniture. Luckily my friends Kristyll and Carla came to the rescue, and took him in until the big move had happened. And then it was time for Copernicus to properly come home.

The following weeks of bottle-feeding the little mite every three hours weren't easy (it's every three hours throughout the night, too!) and although Copper was only two weeks old, he soon thrived. For the first few weeks he was confined to my bedroom, where he had his own special little heated pet dome and, inside it, a small ticking clock wrapped up in a towel. As he grew he explored more of the house – and met his new friend Merlin (my flatmate's kitty), who taught him how to be a real cat and use his litter tray and groom himself properly. Copper also developed the adorable habit of suckling his paw, to the point of bleaching it light brown, when purring on my lap.

Copernicus is now the seven-year-old boss of the house, demanding cheese and French fries, and telling the four other rescue cats who have since joined the family 'what for' if they get too uppity.

To me, Copper will always be my baby cat, even when he's nineteen and grumpy. I'm proud my dad was happy to show his soft, animal-loving ways that early morning at the barracks, and to step up to save my little sweetheart.

Debbie, South Australia

My Little Mexican

You know when you see children playing a game of chase-and-tag, and they're wildly running around screaming and having fun? Well that's kind of what my little rescue cat Charlie does with his bunny friends!

It all started when my beloved black-and-white cat, Jackson, moved on to the spiritual world. It was a heartbreaking time for my family. He made it to the incredible age of twenty-two, and Mum and Dad had him for eleven years before I was born.

Around four months later, my mum decided that it was time for a new family kitten. She took my brother and me to the RSPCA, but we didn't find what we were looking for. We drove home very disappointed. It just wasn't meant to be that day. But Charlie was . . .

The following afternoon, when my brother and I came home from school, there was the best surprise waiting for us – a gorgeous little ginger kitten! He had been saved from a country pound and was being fostered by our neighbour for Forever Friends Animal Rescue. Harry and I had no idea that we were going to get a kitten so soon. The day after we had looked at the kittens at the RSPCA, we came home and there he was, my little baby!

We have quite a barnyard outside at home – seven free-range eccentric chickens and two lazy bunnies. So for the first twelve weeks we had to take little Charlie outside on a lead – well, it wasn't really a lead, it was a headband as a collar attached to a handbag strap. We put Charlie near the bunnies to see how they got along. He inched up to them and they all sniffed each other, but I think the bunnies were a bit intimidated, so they chased Charlie away by charging at him. *Zoom!* Charlie ran away, all around the garden, but then he decided to be brave again, and came back up to the rabbits – and the same thing happened again and again! It was so funny to watch.

Charlie and the bunnies are still playing that game nine months later. My family calls it the 'Mexican Stand-off' – you know, when in a movie there are two men at either end of a small outback town? There's a close-up of one man's eyes as he squints, and then it shows the other man's eyes. Then the camera zooms out so that you can see both men, and a tumbleweed rolls across the road. Well, that's pretty much what it's like watching the rabbits and Charlie. Charlie pounces on the rabbits, the rabbits stand up on their hind legs, and Charlie speeds away.

I am such a lucky girl to have a cat like Charlie. He is so adorable and makes me so happy, even though Jackson is gone. I think everyone should adopt a rescue animal because they truly are friends forever.

Ruby, twelve years old, Victoria

◇◇◇◇◇

Mindy the Formula-One Shoebox Cat

Meet Mindy, our sweet, spoiled, furry ragdoll kitten.

Karla and I have both loved animals since we were children. I grew up in a family where we had all kinds of pets: fish, mice, rabbits, an Irish setter (Hogan) and two cats: Pebbles and Bam Bam. I should also mention that my mum used to look after sick birds from the local pet shop. When other birds picked the feathers off the weakest, my mum would take it home and look after it until all its feathers had grown back and the bird was strong again. At one point, we had more than ten cages in the living room, each with a different bird inside!

Karla is a vet and has a long history with dogs. At one stage she owned eight of them, after their mother gave birth and Karla couldn't bear to be separated from the puppies. Eventually her mum had to be very firm and the puppies found other homes.

We live in an apartment, so we decided to get a cat that wouldn't mind being indoors. I knew from my childhood cats that they like to sit or lie in anything that fits their body (a box, a bowl, a bag or even a pot plant). So not long after we got Mindy, I put a shoebox on the floor to see what happened. She jumped straight inside and played 'hide and seek' with me. But to keep the fun going, I pushed her around a bit.

'Look! She seems to like it,' I said to Karla. I'd push Mindy around and around the room, even the whole apartment. Sometimes we would stand on opposite sides of the room and push the box to each other. Mindy loves it! She even pulls in her ears as if she is trying to make herself more streamlined!

Every morning when we have breakfast Mindy doesn't stop complaining until we either push her around in her Formula-One shoebox or play with her some other way.

Her other favourite game is 'Fetch the Fake Brown Mouse'. And weirdly, it has to be a brown one – we've tried other colours (grey, white, black) but she ignores them.

When Mindy wants to play fetch, she pads over to us with the mouse in her mouth and drops it at our feet. Our job is to throw the mouse down the hall so she can speed after it, pounce on it, give it a bit of rough treatment and then return it to us so we can throw it again. This can go on for a quarter of an hour, as long as she isn't distracted by another toy, such as her feathered ball on a stick or her tunnel.

We've discovered that a mouse lasts for about a week before it's completely skinned to reveal its black plastic. Every month I buy her five brown mice toys.

Another favourite game is hide-and-seek, which we play every evening before we go to bed. I hide in the apartment somewhere and make a sound, which is the signal for her to try to find me. When she does, I jump out and chase her, give her a scratch and a cuddle, and then hide again.

We're not sure how much longer Mindy will be able to play Formula-One Moggy. She's actually grown so much that she no longer fits in her shoebox – her furry butt hangs over the edge while we push her around. It's good exercise for us to play with her, though. Although she's an indoor cat, she keeps us as busy as if we were walking a dog four times a day.

We love Mindy very much, and are just so happy to have her in our lives. But we need to find a bigger shoebox!

Daniel and Karla, Victoria

◇◇◇◇◇

Mr Hubbell

It's hard to believe Mr Hubbell was once a reject. Our Netherland dwarf rabbit was originally intended to be a show bunny, but he didn't make the cut, as he is apparently too small for his breed and is missing a couple of toes. It's the show world's loss and our gain, however, as the pleasure has been all ours – Hubbell has brought so much joy into our lives. He loves everyone he meets and will cover your entire face with kisses, just like a dog!

We adopted Hubbell through his previous owner when he was just twelve weeks of age. After debating all the traditional bunny names we finally settled on naming him after one of our favourite movie characters – 'Hubbell Gardner', from the classic film *The Way We Were*.

Hubbell currently lives happily alongside two dogs, two budgies and a cat. And they are all friends! He has a particular fondness for one of our birds, Alfie, and they love spending time together. Alfie will perch on the side of Hubbell's bowl as the two of them share food.

There is a huge sense of togetherness between our furry family members. We were very fortunate that our rescue dog, Hamilton, had previously been raised around rabbits, so Hubbell has nothing to fear – quite the opposite, in fact! Hamilton is very protective of the smaller members of the household and will go over to Hubbell or the birds, lie down next to them and make sure they are okay.

When Hubbell is outdoors, he has a hard time squeezing into his hutch, as the space is usually taken up by a dog or a cat – sometimes both! When Hamilton, our border collie–golden retriever mix, happens to be the one trying to squeeze inside the hutch with our cat, Calico, the three of them together make for a tight fit! Rabbits are known to be quite territorial, but Hubbell is more than happy for everyone to 'drop in' for a visit.

Did you know that rabbits are quite intelligent? Hubbell has learnt to respond to his name and will come when called, particularly when I say, 'Hurry, Hubbell, quickly!' Sure enough, in a flash, he charges over in the hope of getting a treat. His favourite snacks besides carrots are Jatz biscuits and any leftover millet that we feed to the birds. He will run like lightning into the kitchen the second he hears the biscuit jar opening, and will get himself into an absolute state when he thinks he could be getting some millet, hopping onto his back feet with front paws outstretched in sheer desperation. He will actually raise himself up on to his tiptoes, jiggle on the spot and flail his arms in excitement!

The other amazing thing about Hubbell is that his manners are impeccable. He toilet-trained himself, and has never chewed on one piece of furniture in the house. Hubbell lets you know when he is ready to come in or out by rising up on his back feet and scratching the door.

Hubbell also likes helping with the housework, or so he thinks . . . If you give him a folded-up towel he loves to rearrange where he thinks the creases should be by smoothing them out with his front paws until he is satisfied. My mum is a massage therapist and has a big Ikea bag filled with towels. This bag is one of Hubbell's absolute favourite places to be. He can rearrange the towels to his heart's content and when he is all tuckered out, he has a fabulous place to snooze. We don't even have to be in the same room to know what is happening, as he honks when he is happy (yes, rabbits *do* honk!) and sure enough we find him in the bag, legs stretched out, fast asleep.

I have grown up with pets my entire life and can honestly say I never thought adopting a rabbit could be so rewarding. Even our local vet and the nurses adore Hubbell; they love it when we bring him in to get his little nails trimmed. He is the only rabbit at the clinic who doesn't need to be brought in a carrier. He is quite happy to sit on my shoulder and wait for his name to be called. Hubbell really is the most amazing little guy – and how lucky are we to have him?

Tara, South Australia

Python the Guinea Pig

I often get asked, 'Why is your guinea pig called Python?!'

I adopted my little guy from Gold Coast Guinea Pig Rescue (GCGPR) in the middle of last year. Python earned his interesting name from his horrible past. He had been placed in a glass snake tank as live food when he was just a baby. Miraculously, however, he survived becoming dinner – as the snake was in the process of shedding its skin it was (thankfully!) uninterested in food. But for three horrific days Python sat in sheer terror next to the snake, without food or water. A family member finally felt sorry for the poor boy and brought him to Gold Coast Guinea Pig Rescue where he stayed for a long while. There he very slowly developed trust and confidence in humans, and they did a marvellous job rehabilitating him.

As a family that has only ever had female guinea pigs, adopting this handsome boy has been a new experience for us. We fell in love with him straight away when we saw him on PetRescue. I visited GCGPR's shelter to meet him, as we wanted to find a desexed male friend for my older girl, Cookie, who herself is shy and very skittish.

They were the perfect match, and I took Python home where he's been spoiled ever since. He has certainly turned into a little prince. He expects treats to be hand-delivered into his little 'pigloo' (his favourite igloo-shaped house) and loves 'table-time', where he gets to sit up on the benchtop to snack on some yummy celery leaves while getting brushed and cuddled.

He's cheeky, too – Python hates eating his vitamin C tablets and will use his little paws to push them away, and he also kicks up a fuss if he has to ride in the car, but all is forgotten once he gets scratched on his rump. When we do this, he makes a very contented purring sound and arches his back demanding more attention!

Python and Cookie are like an old married couple, and are the perfect match. They're constantly fighting over their favourite sides of the hutch as well as the last bit of vegetable left in their food bowls, and their piggy bickering can be heard from a mile away. Cookie was also a rescue pig, and both came to us with trust issues and to this day they are still very easy to startle. However, as soon as they hear or sense something strange, they will instantly run to find each other and cuddle up before realising everything's okay.

Python is mummy's little boy and while I love all of our pets at home, Python has a very special place in my heart. His spunk and recently discovered confidence is so heart-warming to see, and he deserves all the love and attention he can get. After his terrifying start to life, we are so lucky to have Python join our piggy family and we hope this gorgeous boy stays with us for a long time to come.

Katrina, Queensland

Wise Young Man

My husband Brett and I run Big Ears Animal Sanctuary, taking care of mistreated, unwanted or abandoned animals on our 10-hectare property in northern Tasmania. We have around 400 animals including cows, donkeys, sheep, goats, pigs, chickens, ducks, turkeys, cats, dogs and, of course, bunnies.

In 2012, we saw a rabbit farm for sale complete with bunnies, equipment and feed. Using our own personal savings (not Big Ears' donations) and generous financial support from other individuals and members of Freedom for Farmed Rabbits, we bought the farm and rescued 300 rabbits on that day. I noticed one of the many bunnies we had rescued looked very old and seemed to be sight- and hearing-impaired. We named him Wiseman (short for 'wise old man'), and though we had an outside pen, I brought him inside because I honestly didn't think he had very long left to live.

He just sat in his cage with his head down, showing no interest in his surroundings or even treats. When we picked him up and brought him into the lounge room for a cuddle, he didn't even move a muscle.

Then, as the days passed, it slowly became apparent that he could hear and see. He began making eye contact and showed an interest in trying out new foods. His once-droopy ears now stood up proudly, twitching and turning to hear what was going on around him. He would nudge at his cage, and stand up to receive pats when anyone walked past.

I let him out and he started running around the kitchen and doing 'binkies' – little leaps and jumps of joy.

After just a few weeks of being inside with us, a completely different bunny emerged – his personality could barely be contained within his little bunny body. Wiseman has shown us that he loves to play chasey, and will chase and chase you – a human, yes! – and then flop down for a rest. He is so confident now that he will even leap onto our laps and climb over us to find a spot to investigate or snuggle, often draped around our necks!

Wiseman now follows me about in the mornings – literally right behind me and under my feet. When I have my breakfast I also use this time to check emails. Wiseman soon realised that this was a perfect time for pats, and sits on my lap hoping for a nibble of toast.

Witnessing his transformation from a depressed and closed-off rabbit to the most engaging and vibrant bunny I have ever met inspires me to continue my work with animal rescue.

Quite simply, he makes me smile. I feel so very lucky to have Wiseman in my life.

Jacqui Steele, Big Ears Animal Sanctuary, Tasmania

Otis, Hospital Hero

We'd often seen a small black-and-white dog eating out of a bin at the local milk bar, but we could never catch him to see if he had a collar on. At the time, my partner and I were living and working at a large hospital complex spread out over many acres of parkland.

One cold and rainy night, my partner was visiting a ward when he noticed the same little dog huddled near the front entrance. He was still there an hour later, drenched and shaking, so my partner brought him home to dry him off. A few days later we found the dog's owner, and reluctantly returned him to her. She said his name was Otis.

'We can take him for you if you feel you can't look after him,' I offered, hopefully. But she said she wanted to keep him.

I was devastated. You see, in the short time he was with us, we had become totally smitten. He was an unusual mix – a Dalmatian–Airedale, I think – and the happiest dog I had ever known. We already had two beloved dogs – Yarkie and Pahna – and they loved his antics too.

Over the next couple of weeks we saw Otis at the milk bar again many times looking for food. We were terrified he would be hit by a car, be stolen or get sick from eating rubbish, but it was out of our hands. He was not our dog.

Then a wonderful thing happened. His owner turned up again and told us that she just couldn't care for him properly, and asked if we would adopt him. We were over the moon!

Otis soon made himself at home. Our garden, like all the other staff residences, had a low cyclone fence and our new four-legged, being a very smart dog, soon discovered that it was a breeze to escape. He actually learnt how to climb up the wire and pull himself over!

The other dogs saw Otis escape repeatedly but were never able to do it themselves. That was the beginning of Otis's daily adventures around the compound, during which he managed to scrounge every available scrap of food and attention that he could.

He began his daily ritual with a visit to the occupational therapy department across the road for morning tea. The patients would give him biscuits and have a play. He would then return home for a nap before heading off to a ward kitchen for lunch. After a nice long nap at home, he'd start on the half-kilometre walk to the staff cafeteria for his evening meal, where he would somehow manage to slip though heavy glass doors when a staff member went through. Everyone knew where Otis came from and would call us to collect him, or a kind staff member would drive him home. Sometimes he turned up with ribbons or other decorations tied to him. Surprisingly, despite all his extra meals he didn't seem to put on weight (perhaps it was all the walking!).

Otis always greeted patients and staff with cheerful enthusiasm, his little tail stump wagging. Everyone adored him.

After four years we moved to the suburbs and Otis's wandering days came to an end. However, he kept up his climbing skills. He learnt how to scale the fig tree and was able to propel himself over the paling fence to play with the dogs next door. He had bucket-loads of character and endless love to give. When he gazed at you with his beautiful dark eyes, it was impossible not to smile.

Otis was eighteen when he died, and his passing left a huge hole in our family and many broken hearts. His best doggy friend, Emi, our black spaniel, grieved for a long time – they had been devoted to each other for fifteen years. Emi died not long after, from the same cause as Otis: kidney failure. But we were comforted that Otis had lived a long and happy life and brought joy to many people, particularly those at the hospital who needed some sunshine in their day.

Ellen, Victoria

The Mayor of Paddington

That thug of a ginger cat was stealing my kitties' food again! Big and scrawny, with a head like a soccer ball, he scared the hell out of my cats. I'd never really fancied ginger cats, especially the toms. How could I stop him coming around? I should at least catch him and get those giant nuts cut off. Poor thing – I guessed he was a hungry stray or maybe a feral cat.

'Puss, puss!' I called to him one day, whereupon he threw himself down on the ground and rolled around, begging for attention.

'Oh my God,' I cried, as he went into raptures when I patted him. 'Someone has loved you once! You're not a feral, just abandoned.'

From that moment on, I belonged to him. Charlie moved in and took over the house. Now that he was 'home', he was very sweet with the other cats. He was passionate with me and would just about crush me when he sat on my lap for a smooch. When he had his trip to the vet, they pegged him to be at least five years old, so we gave him an August birthday – he was such a Leo! Charlie filled out and became an enormous beastie. At his prime he was a lean 9–10 kilograms – all muscle. And that huge head was almost as big as mine!

When I opened my eclectic gift shop, Pussies Galore, in Paddington a few years later, Charlie found his true vocation. He became the PR man for the shop and ambassador for my Pussies Galore Cat Rescue group. He thrived on being the star attraction in the store and people began to come in especially to see him. Charlie liked to lie like a giant rug right across the front of the shop. I loved hearing comments from those outside with their foreheads pressed to the window: 'Is that a real cat?' or 'Oh my God! That thing moved!'

We lived behind the shop and at night, when it was shut, Charlie and the other rescue cats would parade around in the store window, entertaining passers-by. Gradually, more rescue cats joined Charlie in the shop, diverting some of the attention from him. Not one to share the limelight, Charlie found his own solution. He began canvassing the street for the adulation he felt he deserved. He found a worthy spot in the café up the road and became a regular feature there for breakfast and lunch. Diners would become quite indignant if Charlie did not show up on time.

Charlie would always turn up back at the gift shop for elevenses; you could set your watch by him. In fact he was very strong on routines. His day would begin with breakfast at seven. At 7.30 a.m., inspection of troops and property borders would commence. By 8 a.m., Charlie would commence his first tour of Latrobe Terrace. At nine he would check on the businesses that opened at that time, and the same at 10 a.m. for the later openers, especially Pussies Galore, which often needed a hurry-up. Charlie needed to be 'in place' at the local café by 10.15 to commence his PR tasks and food-quality assurance work. After elevenses he was 'back at base', at work on the Latrobe Terrace strip, making sure he was able to make appointments with his loyal fans and then with fellow diners back at the café for lunch afterwards.

In the afternoon, Charlie liked to choose different shop windows to display himself in for a nap. Most shops loved the honour of having a 'Charlie display' for a few hours. A favourite was the bottle shop, where he would recline on top of the boxes. He really was 'top-shelf material'! Customers and staff alike looked forward to his visits, even when they had to step over his large, furry body. Charlie loved me to fetch him from the bottle shop every evening. He would cuddle into me as we walked home, deafening me with his purr.

Soon Charlie had a massive fan club. A proud celebrity, he featured in media stories and appeared on *Totally Wild*, *Brisbane Extra*, *Getaway*, *The Great South East* and in some news stories. He was in his element!

In February 2004 I heard our local elections were coming up and the senior citizens' hall across the road was our polling booth. Charlie's fans insisted that he should run for office. How could he refuse? We ran his campaign 'Vote 1 for Charlie!', with his big mug face featured in the local papers beside the other human candidates. Everyone loved it. We had flyers, T-shirts and a campaign website.

On Election Day, we had our own polling booth across the road from the real one, with a manqué, sandwich boards, balloons, ballot papers and boxes. Charlie's ballot-paper opponents were creative animal adaptations of the human candidates running in the election. A lot of our ballot papers ended up in the real election box, which was accepted with good humour. Over 250 people voted in our booth and the day was greatly enjoyed by all, especially the star.

After the counting, it was official – Paddington had a new mayor! Charlie took to his new office with gusto. Always the diplomat and a just ruler, he petitioned for animal rights. His main cause was to find good homes for his fellow kitties. Eventually, Charlie ran for a second term in September 2006 and naturally won again.

At age sixteen, Charlie was forced into early retirement when we sold the shop and moved to Red Hill. At the time he was suffering from hyperthyroidism, and he began to lose weight and look unkempt. Fortunately, he responded instantly to radioactive iodine therapy, which ultimately saved his life. He soon regained weight and looked his fabulous self again within months.

Once well again, Charlie had to face his new challenges. It was hard for him not to have hoards of adoring fans pay tribute to him daily. He kept up his good work at home, though, training the young rescue kittens we fostered in manners and respect. Charlie never lost patience with the kittens, who often pounced on him or ambushed him from around a corner. They all loved and respected him. He kept the peace in the house and was a benevolent patriarch.

But it wasn't enough. Charlie soon began canvassing the neighbours for attention. Most households were honoured to receive his visits. He even beguiled and converted our cat-hating next-door neighbour,

David. Over the years the two greatly enjoyed each other's company, looking forward to and relying on time spent together each day. As Charlie grew older and his 'range' decreased, his daily excursions were limited to David's house where, in his last days, I would need to carry him. He didn't want to let David down. After Charlie died, at the incredible age of twenty-two, I think David may have missed him more than anyone.

This story is a tribute to a remarkable cat who was loved by everyone. There will never be another Charlie. You will always be Mayor of Our Hearts.

Katina, Queensland

◇◇◇◇◇

Delilah, TV Star

To be homeless and wandering the streets one day and TV star the next? This story must be about the delightful Delilah!

A beautiful four-year-old red kelpie was spotted wandering as a stray in Queensland's south-east. Sad and lonely, she was picked up by council officers and soon made it into the care of the Animal Welfare League of Queensland. We assist a number of local council pounds with their unwanted dogs and cats in an effort to find them loving homes. While we got to know sweet Delilah, we had her desexed, vaccinated and microchipped, so she was ready for adoption.

Meanwhile, imagine our surprise when we were contacted by Channel 9's hit TV show *Big Brother* – they were after an 'Australian-looking dog' to fill the upcoming role of house-dog for the 2012 edition of the show. Did we have any suitable candidates?

The staff and I discussed the possibilities, and of course Delilah was one of the first canines to spring to mind. Calling her in, we gave her an unofficial audition at our rehoming centre on the Gold Coast, and decided that the combination of her sweet demeanour and engaging personality was a sure winner. Delilah was going to be a star!

From the moment Delilah made her first appearance in the *Big Brother* house, she became an instant fan favourite and a trusted and loving companion to the housemates. She was seen dressing up in outfits made by Stacey and playing cricket with the boys. She also made herself at home in the kitchen, where she took on the role of official 'taste-tester' for Stacey's infamous dip!

Because of her huge popularity, Delilah lived in the *Big Bother* house with the housemates until the end of the show, a total of forty-two days. When the show drew to an end, lots of people were getting in contact to learn more about the kelpie breed, and to adopt a pet from the same shelter Delilah came from. What a wonderful ambassador for rescue pets our girl was!

Delilah now lives on a large property with a loving family where she can run like the wind and swim and play with her two canine brothers. She has also been made an honorary ambassador for the AWLQ, and can sometimes be seen meeting fans and 'networking' at events held at our rehoming centre.

Delilah is just one of over 130 000 animals the Animal Welfare League has rehomed since its founding in Southport in 1959. So many other loving and deserving animals like Delilah await their forever homes at our Gold Coast and Beenleigh rehoming centres, and while they might not *all* become TV stars, they will no doubt become bright stars in their own right in their new forever homes.

Brooke Whitney, Animal Welfare League, Queensland

Our Time with Matilda

Matilda was about four months old and just starting to fur up when I found her.

As a registered wildlife carer, I always stop and check any animals I see on the side of the road, and on this particular day in September 2012, I'd noticed a wombat had been hit and killed by a car not far from our farm. It was a female, and inside her pouch I found her baby – a solid little girl weighing about 800 grams who we named Matilda. It was so sad her mum was dead, but at least she was alive.

I had cared for other wildlife before, so had all the equipment I needed, but this was my first wombat, so I contacted another carer I knew to get extra advice and some wombat formula. She told me my baby would need four-hourly feeds around the clock for the first two to three months, then they would taper off to four-hourly feeds during the day only. For the first few weeks, Matilda slept in a woollen pouch inside a heated box next to my bed. It took a few days for her to take to bottle-feeding after losing her mum, but on day five she suddenly realised what the bottle was all about and never looked back.

Now, I'm a busy mum with four kids, and I also run Maremma Rescue Victoria (MRV), so whenever I went out, Matilda had to come with me. I bought a cloth bag that went over my shoulder so I could carry her around in her woollen pouch. She slept in the bag really well (I guess the constant movement was not unlike being with her mum) and I fed her whenever it was time.

As she grew, she began to run around the house and play with everyone. She especially loved tug-of-war and, just like a puppy, she would run and leap, and adored having her belly scratched. She was a joy to have around.

I've run MRV for maremma sheepdogs over the past five years and volunteered for them for almost nine years, and it is my passion to save and rehome this amazing breed. During my time with MRV I have fostered, helped, given advice about or been involved in rehoming around 200 maremma.

Matilda made friends with two of my dogs during her stay – and we had around fourteen maremma dogs come through at that time – who were all super gentle with her. One was a rescued maremma we adopted named Duke. It was lovely watching him look after Matilda – it's just the nature of this incredible breed. He would come and sit by me when I fed her and keep himself between Matilda and any other dogs in the house. He would also sit by her custom-made pen when she was outside, keeping an eye on her there as well.

When Matilda was approximately seven months old, we built a safe pen for her outside so she could exercise properly and learn to forage and dig for her own food. At first she only spent part of the day there, but as she got bigger she spent more time outside – though she came inside for regular cuddles!

We always go camping over Christmas and New Year and, of course, Matilda came with us. Having bonded to us, she never wandered far from where we were and she slept in her basket in our tent at night. She had a great time keeping cool in the river and even had a comfortable afternoon snooze on my son's camp bed with her head on his pillow!

Matilda stayed with us until she was ten months old. By then I had found another young wombat for her to live with. There are several wildlife carers in our area and a friend told me one of them had a wombat a little older than Matilda that needed to be paired with one like our girl.

At her new residence Matilda is learning to live down a wombat hole, play with her wombat mate, sleep outdoors and forage in the bushland around the property. The duo will stay together until they are two years old and will then be released back into the wild.

We dearly miss Matilda and her wonderful antics, but it is deeply satisfying to know that we were able to save her life and help her to return to the bush where she belongs.

Jodie Cawood, Maremma Rescue Victoria

Puss the Railway Hotel Cat

'The house comes with a cat,' I told the new owners.

I'd just sold them an investment property I'd had in Middle Park, whose previous tenants had been looking after a stray (with my blessing).

The new owners promptly replied, 'We've got a dog; we don't want a cat!' so Puss's pub life began with a car ride from Middle Park to my place in Fitzroy. He didn't seem to mind the ride, but he never really settled into the Builders Arms, which was his home for about two years.

At the Builders, Puss lived upstairs and rarely ventured down to the bar. He'd found a way of getting onto the rooftops around Gertrude Street and that's where he spent most of his time.

In 2000 we sold the Builders and bought the Railway Hotel in South Melbourne, so Puss got another car ride back over the river. It was here that Puss really came into his own and blossomed as a true pub cat.

In the beginning, he was a bit timid downstairs, but as the years went on he became far more confident. If a dog happened to be in the courtyard, Puss would regard the intruding canine with disgust. He took on a few dogs over the years – Puss knew who was boss and who the pub belonged to!

During the winter months Puss controlled the fireplace. There are always two chairs in front of the open fire and one belonged to Puss, so if a punter happened to take his spot, Puss would have no hesitation in jumping straight up onto their lap.

He also enjoyed sitting on a bar stool next to staff or punters and would regularly join guests dining in the restaurant. On one occasion, a group of young blokes were celebrating a bucks night and Puss decided to join them at the table on his own chair!

Puss was such an important part of the team that many staff would commence a shift by signing on and then going straight to him for a smooch.

We used to leave a window open for Puss on the first floor, but had to lock it after a burglar used it as a point of entry. This meant that Puss was occasionally locked out, but he never had to sleep rough, as we had a nice undercover booth in the courtyard for him where he would wait until the bar staff arrived to let him back in.

The pub has a few maintenance and delivery personnel with access keys, and many of them were accosted by Puss, who would 'drag' them up the stairs (by meowing, running, stopping and then meowing again until they followed) to a space known as 'Puss's Kitchen'. Here it never took long for one of the delivery drivers to spot Puss's food supply and work out what all the commotion was about!

Puss lived at the Railway Hotel for twelve years and made many friends, not only with all the staff that came and went, but also countless customers. He appeared on the Channel 10 news and was the topic of many online postings: 'Saw the cat!', 'The cat walked past' or 'The cat's awesome'.

Old age eventually caught up with Puss. He's now left the Railway bar and is resting comfortably under the big oak tree in the beer garden, where he can continue to watch over the comings and goings of his pub.

Phil, Victoria

PERFECTLY IMPERFECT

◇◇◇◇◇◇◇◇

There are some animals whose physical wounds never really heal, but their ability to continue on is what makes them most special. It's blind dog who is the most perceptive, and the ferret with the missing paw who is the most persistent. They may be 'not quite right' to some, but to us, they are perfectly imperfect.

Magical Myron

Myron was born to an abandoned boxer mix who was suffering from malnutrition and could no longer care for her puppies. A man from Guildford had found her by the road when she was about to go into labour and took her home. There she gave birth to nine puppies, eight of which survived initially.

His family lived in a small flat and had to move the puppies on quickly as the wife was about to have a baby herself. They decided to keep the mother and find homes for her babies. We were the lucky adopters of one of the puppies – Myron.

A couple of weeks after Myron came to us, we discovered he was blind. Worse still, he would need to have his eyeballs removed due to glaucoma, and would go on to develop environmental allergies and epilepsy. At this time we learned that at least four of his siblings received similar diagnoses but were put to sleep. We were devastated, but decided Myron's incredible enthusiasm for life and readiness to learn meant he would want to go on, despite what was ahead.

As the years have passed, Myron has proven all that and more. His happy disposition in the face of adversity has been an encouragement to people from all over the world who follow his journey on Facebook. It wasn't long before we received requests from people who wanted to meet Myron. So we began visiting nursing homes, schools and disability organisations where people fell in love with him. Initially, some said they felt pity for a dog with no eyes, but once they saw Myron do his tricks and witnessed his skills with a tennis ball, they realised a disability was no reason to give up pursuing a happy and rewarding life. Myron encourages many of his admirers to do just that.

In 2008, we became involved with the RSPCA's fundraising initiative, Cupcake Day. At first Myron and I simply held a small cake stall outside Narellan Library. We had wonderful support from the local newspaper promoting our event and were surprised to raise $333 on the day – not bad for a one-dog show in a small town!

The following year, friends of Myron offered their support and also brought cakes on the day and raised a little more money. Each year the event continues to grow, and we have had special guests from the RSPCA attend Myron's Cupcake Day, including Dr Katrina Warren who has become a personal friend of Myron's. Getting to know Dr Katrina has been a blessing for our boy. Her radio show 'Talking Pets' with Dr Rob Zammit enabled Myron to receive some valuable suggestions from Dr Rob regarding his seizures, and these have now been reduced from every second day to once every two months.

Myron's other pastime is rubbing shoulders with celebrities. So far he has met more than sixty, and been photographed with all of them, including David Hasselhoff. 'The Hoff', as he is known, along with his fiancée Hayley Roberts, were really touched by Myron's story. When they left Australia Hayley kept in touch with Myron on his Facebook page. When we meet elderly admirers, they marvel at the pictures of Myron with familiar faces such as Kamahl and Ita Buttrose. School kids are in awe when we show them pictures of Myron with Bondi Vet Dr Chris and James Hetfield of Metallica. We love playing 'Guess the Celebrity' with Myron's pictures at the events we attend.

Local and international media have kept an eye on Myron's activities too. He has a YouTube video that has gone viral called 'Blind Dog Plays Fetch' and he has featured in hundreds of newspaper and magazine articles. He has also appeared on numerous television shows such as *Talk to the Animals*, *Rodders Life*, *The Kerri-Anne Show* and *Celebrity Apprentice*.

Myron is almost seven years old now and still going strong. Thankfully he has responded incredibly well to treatment provided by the

University of Sydney for his allergies. After five years of injections every three weeks of a special serum created just for him, Myron was finally able to be weaned off the injections and has been free of symptoms for the last eighteen months.

Myron's health is being closely monitored. He is on high doses of medication for his epilepsy and we expect one day for this to take its toll. To be honest, we thought that day would have already arrived. He continues to prove us wrong and his zest for living is as strong as ever. He hasn't slowed down at all, and continues to bring happiness to his friends, both local and overseas. I'm sure the love he receives from every corner of the globe helps him to keep on doing what he does best – lifting people's spirits and bringing hope to all, no matter what their challenges may be.

Raquel, New South Wales

◇◇◇◇◇

Chi Chi the Chicken

About seven years ago, I was asked to look after my neighbours' chickens while they were away. Chi Chi, an ISA Brown, was near death at the hands of her wicked sisters. I never wanted a chicken, but the sight of her withered body disturbed me. I allowed the girls to roam free during the day, as the owners did, and this gave Chi Chi some respite from her suffering – she could hide from the others. She was half the weight of a normal chicken, was losing her feathers and could not stand. Sadly, chickens can be quite brutal when it comes to removing the 'weakest link' in the group.

One afternoon I heard a commotion in their yard. When I ran over I saw a fox with one of the healthy girls in its mouth! For some reason, it had not seen Chi Chi, a more likely target, lying down in the pen. The fox made a quick getaway with a tasty meal firmly in its grasp.

After this scare, I had to lock all the girls back in the pen during the day, and I decided there and then to take Chi Chi home with me. A few more days 'cooped up' would have meant her definite demise.

When my neighbours returned from holiday, they noticed two chickens missing. I recounted the fox story and the fact that I had removed one chicken to safety. My record as a chicken minder was somewhat in tatters – they left with seven chickens, and they came home to five! They were very understanding, however, and let me keep Chi Chi, as I told them I had grown attached to her.

Only one problem – no chicken coop at my place! I quickly commissioned a beautiful steel A-frame home for her, which arrived a few weeks later. In the meantime, she stayed in a small box inside and each day she regained some strength and her feathers started to grow back. Chi Chi was still extremely ugly at this stage; however, we had bonded. Meanwhile, next door, her beautiful, plump, wicked sisters lasted only six to eight months, all being lost to foxes. Somewhat ironic.

After about six weeks, Chi Chi was firmly on the mend. But on the first day when I let her roam free in our beautiful yard – she vanished! I was distraught, scouring the area for her. She was missing for three days until a neighbour down the road asked if we had lost a chicken. The neighbour had seen her being carried down the street in the mouth of a dog! I gasped to hear this. But he went on to tell me that luckily the dog had the courtesy of not inflicting any wounds – he was simply walking down the street with a chicken in his mouth. Gotlieb had rescued Chi Chi and she was at his place, recuperating.

So, again, Chi Chi returned and recovered well. After that episode it took me three or fours years until I let her roam completely free again. We also fenced our 1300-square-metre property to keep the dogs out, which was an expensive exercise for the wellbeing of just one chicken!

Next, we decided Chi Chi needed a friend and introduced a Muscovy duck, aptly named Jemima. They have been great mates ever since.

Late last year I returned from work to find our front gate open. On entering my property, I found a young staffy called Buster standing over the lifeless body of my Chi Chi. Feathers were everywhere; a horrible sight for any chook owner to see. 'No!' I shouted. Grabbing Buster, I locked her away and called the number on the dog's ID tag. Her owner immediately came to collect her. Tears flowing, I then found a shovel and a towel in order to prepare for my little girl's funeral. Imagine my surprise when I went over to Chi Chi and noticed that she was breathing! As I picked her up, she opened her eyes. She had been so still, I just assumed she was dead. I could see where Buster had inflicted bite marks around her legs and a severe wound to her back. I wrapped her in the towel and sat cradling her. Visiting friends were shocked to see me in tears, sitting with a lifeless chicken in my arms. They might have heard me murmur, 'Don't leave me now, Chi Chi,' but that has never been verified!

A close friend of mine, Mark, a practising vet, was called for the first emergency consultation. If you have pets and don't have a vet as a friend, I highly recommend it! On arrival, he was shocked at Chi Chi's wounds and amazed she was still alive. He inspected her injuries and commented on the severity of the open wound on her back. The main concern was spinal damage. She could not stand up, from a combination of the injuries and the shock. He believed she would need an operation if there was any chance of survival, but recommended the most humane thing to do was to put her to sleep. In the pharmaceutical side of the profession, Mark did not have the necessary drugs with him to euthanise her, but added he could do it the old-fashioned way. It would be quick. My husband and friends urged me to agree, but I would not.

I called the local after-hours emergency vet service. I ended up speaking to Dr Rick Prowse from Austinmer Veterinary Hospital. It was Sunday and he advised me that a visit would immediately attract a $200 fee, which I was happy to pay. We prepared a small box with towels and a hot-water bottle for Chi Chi, and waited for Rick to arrive. As time went on, I decided to cancel the late-night visit and asked him to come in the morning. If my girl survived the night, we would take matters from there.

I spent a few extra hours with Chi Chi and although she had not improved, more importantly, her condition had not worsened. In the morning, I ran to the laundry to find Chi Chi *still* alive. We waited anxiously for Rick to arrive. Upon examining her, he said, 'We might be able to fix her!' and whisked her away.

I felt a glimmer of hope. Chi Chi was placed on a drip and crop-fed for three days. The level of care and devotion the staff at Austinmer Vet Hospital showed my girl was just amazing. She returned home with a large section of feathers missing across her back, replaced with a row of stitches that pieced her together again. She was a funny blue colour from all the disinfectant they'd used and had lost some weight. Amazingly, she had no spinal damage. Over the next three weeks we had to keep her in the house, away from other animals and all the elements. She had problems eating, but never gave up trying. That was my brave girl.

Four months have passed, and now all Chi Chi's feathers and her appetite have returned. She is back outside with her best-friend-for-life, Jemima the duck, and often waits at the front door as if to say: *Can I come in?* She quite enjoyed her time as a house chicken, it seems! Everyone who saw her after the dog attack was amazed she recovered, let alone returned to her former glory and then some, especially at nine grand years of age. Most chickens around here are lucky to reach two or three.

Being visually impaired (a legacy from her first illness), she can get lost quite easily and recently spent three nights missing in our area. How she avoided foxes and dogs again is beyond us all. She cannot roost very high because of her sight problems, so she would be a soft target on the ground. As such, Chi Chi is a legend in our street and everyone knows my famous survivor! Perhaps there is a guardian angel of chickens looking after her?

But the surprises don't end there – one week ago, we discovered she had started laying eggs again! Although small and with a soft shell, they are still as fantastic as they were before. Chi Chi has provided us with hundreds of these little gifts throughout her life.

In a nutshell, Chi Chi has survived being hen-pecked, two dog attacks and three nights lost in the wilderness. She has an amazing will to survive, second only to her appetite. Now the oldest of our three wonderful pets, my husband and I always laugh and say she will outlive all of them. We have no doubt!

Ausilia, New South Wales

◇◇◇◇◇

What Disability?

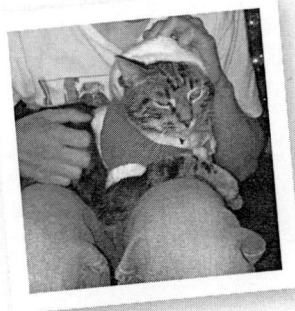

Pet-friendly rental properties are rare. My housemate Michael and I were delighted when we finally found one and gratefully moved in with my cat, Gizmo.

'I think I'd like a cat of my own,' Michael announced one day, as we watched Gizmo eagerly exploring her new environment.

I told him I thought it was a great idea, and that we should look for an adult cat to adopt, rather than buying from a pet shop. We went online to PetRescue. During our search, we saw several 'special needs' cats. This was a new and interesting idea to us . . . a cat that wasn't 'perfect', but unique. After much discussion we decided that adopting a cat with a disability was something we really wanted to do.

Our plan interested a colleague who had previously fostered cats through Homeless Hounds Rescue Victoria. She immediately posted on their Facebook foster carers' page, asking if anyone knew of a disabled cat that needed a home. The response was instantaneous: we should adopt Kevin, a one-year-old vision-impaired tabby.

With cat carrier in hand, we made the forty-minute drive to meet Kevin at the home of his foster carer, Laura. She was very open about his disability, and provided us with all the information she could about his prognosis and possible future needs. Of course he came home with us that afternoon, but with a name change to Toby.

We soon had the new arrival checked over by our vet, who thought Toby might be suffering from an acquired brain injury. This resulted in bouts of kittenish behaviour, which gave us a ton of amusement; ever watched a 6-kilogram cat try to climb the curtains?

Because his vision is so poor, we expected Toby to take a long time to settle in. But happily he found his way around our house quickly and we soon learned that he didn't hurt himself when he fell off the bed or windowsills.

Laura had told us she thought Toby was only able to sense movement. However, after he settled in we noticed he did have some limited vision, as we saw him watching Gizmo playing in the garden. He is an indoor-only cat for his own safety but has some limited outside time every day on a harness and lead. He loves his outside time and even manages to get up into trees and onto low branches!

We had hoped that Gizmo and Toby would become friends; however, Toby is far too boisterous. They have, however, come to a mutual understanding and will both happily share the same living space.

We are so grateful that we adopted Toby, and can't imagine life without him. He loves to be with us whatever we are doing. His favourite place in the world is on Michael's lap while he's playing video games. Perhaps he's trying to play too?

Because of our wonderful experience with Toby, I became interested in becoming a foster carer for other cats in need too. I signed up with Homeless Hounds and have recently fostered my fifteenth kitten. Toby loves to greet his new foster-siblings whenever there are any new arrivals. He is also the leader when it comes to any kittenish mischief, and no doubt a bad influence on them!

Many thanks to Susan, Laura and the Homeless Hounds team for all the awesome work they do. To anyone thinking of adopting a special-needs pet, go for it! It's the best decision we've made.

Kirsten, Victoria

◇◇◇◇◇

Kala – the Real Slumdog Millionaire

It all started on the streets of Bangalore. While living and working in India, my partner and I fell in love with a street dog that lived outside our office. She resembled a tall kelpie and was severely underweight. Feeling sorry for her, we started to bring her food. Soon we had a new friend always waiting to greet us, and seeing her became the highlight of our day.

We soon found out that the street dogs in India are known as 'INDogs' or 'Indian Pariah' dogs. Many are mistreated. The maintenance crew in the estate where our office was located were told that they would lose their jobs if they didn't get rid of the stray dogs. Sometimes when we arrived for work we noticed our doggy friend was limping. The security guards would tell us they saw a maintenance person hit her with a broom.

It was no surprise, then, that after we showed her just a small amount of kindness, she would look out for us, and when I came to see her and then went back inside, she would sit beneath my office window and watch me go back upstairs. She would then curl up on the mat outside the office door. We soon thought of her as 'our' dog, so when we realised she was pregnant and faced collection by the pound – where she'd probably be put to sleep, pups included – we decided we couldn't let that happen. We would adopt this lovely girl. But how to get her all the way back to Australia?

Unsure of when the pups were due, we asked the security guard at the office to let us know if anything happened when we weren't there. When we got the call that the pups had been born in a garden patch outside the office door, we raced over and, not having a car, hailed a rickshaw. Placing Mum and the hour-old babies into a cardboard box, we then travelled forty-five minutes to an animal shelter that could take care of the little group, until the pups would be old enough to survive by themselves. We named our mumma dog Kala (which means 'black' in Hindi) and visited her every weekend for the next four weeks. After an agonising month, it was finally time for us to take her home. We gave money to the shelter to help find homes for the puppies, and bundled Kala into another rickshaw for the ride back to our house.

Sadly, while she was in the shelter, Kala contracted parvovirus, a potentially deadly virus that affects dogs. As she had been a street dog, we had not been able to vaccinate her before admitting her to the shelter. So we took her straight to the vet to see what he could do. In India, a lot of vets can't hold dogs overnight, so we took her to the vet twice a day for two days to be placed on a drip. At that stage, the vet did not know what was wrong and after two days he told us she would need to be admitted to the vet hospital in Hebbal. So off we went with Kala on another rickshaw ride. Five days later, she had improved, but had lost 30 per cent of her body weight. Nevertheless, we were finally able to take her home. Slowly she gained weight, her ribs began to disappear and her coat started to shine.

By then, everyone in our neighbourhood knew Kala's story. The locals would comment on how good she looked, and marvelled at the fact that a foreign couple had adopted a street dog and planned on taking her with them when they left India.

After six months, my role changed and we going to be relocated to Sydney. We soon hit the first obstacle in bringing Kala home with us. For quarantine reasons, dogs from India are not allowed to travel directly to Australia, so Kala would first need to live for six months in an 'approved' country to qualify for import. Luckily, my brother and sister-in-law live in America and are veterinarians, and kindly offered to take care of our girl for the six months. So the next hurdle was getting Kala from inner-city Bangalore to the gorgeous countryside of Portland in Maine, United States. We arranged transport (a car this time!) to take us to the airport and walked Kala into the terminal. I imagine she is one of the only street dogs who have ever sat in the waiting area of an international airport! After thirty hours, we finally touched down in America. The next six months were an adventure for Kala, filled with outings to the ocean, lakes, walks with my nieces, deer, black bear sightings in the garden, and snow. Quite a culture shock for her!

As the winter set in, the temperatures in Maine dropped to −20 °C. It was now January 2012, and time for Kala to relocate to Sydney. So, after another long drive to Boston airport, a flight to Los Angeles, an overnight stop, final vet checks and a fifteen-hour flight to Sydney, Kala made it to Charles Kingsford Smith airport. She was finally here! But Kala wasn't out of the woods yet – the next step was thirty days in quarantine.

So, after a total of seven months since we left Bangalore, our small family was back together again. Kala now lives with us in Gladesville, a suburb of Sydney, and enjoys exploring the local parks, off-leash areas and the odd trip on the Parramatta River ferry. Over 40 000 kilometres and three continents later, our own 'slumdog millionaire' is now a much-loved family member who demonstrates just how wonderful a 'mongrel' can be.

We could not save every street dog in India, but we did save one.

Rochelle, New South Wales

Our Little Battler

When my daughter started volunteering with a small dog rescue group, Staffy and Bully Breed Rescue (SABBR), the more I learned about the amazing dogs she was meeting, the more I knew I had to help too. So I agreed to become a foster carer.

After the dogs entered my home, I would watch them gradually gain confidence, learning what love means, and happily bounce out of the door when we found them their forever homes. It was always hard letting them go, but meeting the caring families who were perfect for each of these dogs made it so worthwhile.

Around October 2011, I received a call from Bec, the heart and soul of SABBR. 'Are you ready for a special rescue?' Bec asked me.

'Of course,' I replied without hesitation. Bec explained that a few litters of staffy mix pups had been removed from a backyard breeder. The ranger had called SABBR to help find foster homes for all of the dogs and commented that one of them had a hare lip and would almost certainly need to be put to sleep. The pup was just eleven weeks old.

Bec insisted on an assessment by their vet, who confirmed that while the pup did have a hare lip, it could be operated on. However, the pup had bigger problems. Deprived of vital nutrients in those first few weeks of life because of her inability to feed properly, her development was stunted and we were warned that she would never be 'normal'.

The little one came to me for a few weeks before the surgery on her hare lip. We had to feed her puppy formula with a syringe, adding lots of water because she didn't know how to lick, lap or chew. She was dangerously frail and could hardly walk.

We knew her operation would be risky, but it had to be done to give her the best chance possible to eventually run, bark and play like all the other dogs. And she did make it through that major surgery!

However, the vet warned us she had more issues to face, and a few weeks after her operation it seemed that she might not survive after all. She was still not eating and was unable to lap milk or water. She failed to put on weight and we prepared ourselves for the worst.

We took her back to the vet who suggested putting some cream on top of baby food to tempt her to eat. It worked! The first time she picked up a mouthful of cream was hysterical, and the whole family was cheering as our little princess looked up with cream all over her face. Princess was given her name when we discovered that she expected to be treated like one. Soon she would refuse to eat anything that wasn't sprinkled with cream or grated cheese. As she finally started to gain weight and strength, we tried taking her for her first walks. Princess could not grasp the concept of 'walkies'. She expected to be carried out to enjoy the open air.

Some people were critical of her appearance and would say horrible things about her as I carried her through the park. No, she did *not* look 'normal' – but we loved her just the way she was.

I don't know that there was ever one moment in time where I decided Princess was staying with us for good – but the day she went in for her surgery, I realised just how much we all loved our little battler.

Princess now licks, give kisses, runs like a greyhound, howls like a wolf and plays crazy games with her doggy and kitty siblings. I will be forever grateful to SABBR and the amazing work they do, not only because it has encouraged me to foster and find homes for almost twenty beautiful babies, but also because it has brought Princess into our lives. She has taught us that even though she may not be perfect to the world, to us she is one in a million. We simply can't imagine life without her.

Michelle and Claire, Western Australia

Flo, Sweetie and Stumpy

If I ever needed proof that ferrets are very special animals indeed, it can only have been before Stumpy came into our lives.

This story begins in late 1992. I had two jills (female ferrets) that had given birth some weeks before, one of whom was a very eccentric and dysfunctional little beastie called Flo. Flo and her twin sister, Pip, were adopted by us in 1988 when they were only about seven weeks old. Sadly, they both contracted an infection that resulted in Flo's eyesight and brain being damaged. Flo remained neurotic for the rest of her life, and wouldn't socialise with other ferrets.

Pip was a delightful little animal but sadly she died of cancer when she was only two years old, having produced just one litter of two kits. Flo had sporadic litters of kits over the years, culminating in her final brood of nine babies in 1992. Jill ferrets were always mated after they came into season in those days, as failure to do so often resulted in death from prolonged oestrus disease, which is a type of anaemia. We didn't have hobs (male ferrets) that were vasectomised, let alone drugs, to safely take jills out of season back then.

As we might have expected, Flo wasn't much of a parent. Several of her last nine babies died. All of the survivors were very small and not growing as they should have been. They were living in a double-ended cage, with Flo and her kits at one end and a rescued stray jill we called Sweetie at the other end.

Sweetie had been found at a nursing home several months before. The staff rang me to say they had come across 'either a ferret or a possum; can you come and take it away please?' She turned out to be a good-natured little sable jill whose previous owners never surfaced, so she stayed with us for quite some months before we found her a new home.

Sweetie had also become a mum recently, and her babies, born a week after Flo's, were already quite a bit larger. We began supplemental feeding of Flo's surviving kits with full-cream cow's milk, but it didn't quite do the trick. We knew they were going to die without intervention, but it seemed they would do so regardless of our help. Specialised milk powders like Wombaroo were not readily available back then (and later, even when they were, didn't seem to work very well with ferrets).

Meanwhile, something special was happening. We could see Sweetie, at the other end of the cage, was becoming distressed by the cries coming from Flo's little ones. Nothing we were doing was comforting them. Just when I was wondering what else to do, Sweetie did one of those incredible things you never forget.

I had opened the lid of Flo and Sweetie's joint cage at feeding time when Sweetie suddenly hopped over the divider and picked up one of Flo's babies in her mouth. She then hopped back into her own cage, put Flo's kit in with her own, then hopped back into Flo's side of the cage to repeat the performance. At this stage there were just five of Flo's kits still alive. All of the babies were carefully transferred by Sweetie in this way, one by one, and Flo took absolutely no notice at all. I just stood there in dumbfounded amazement! Sweetie wanted to become the surrogate mum, and she did!

Over the next few days, with Sweetie's generous care, Flo's babies picked up considerably. Meanwhile, Sweetie's own babies found the sudden drop in rations displeasing and became very demanding. To offset this problem we began further supplementing their feeds by mixing minced beef with full-cream milk and placing this into a shallow dish in their cage. Sweetie's kits, now close to six weeks old, quickly made the transition to solid foods and developed the ravenous appetites that are usual at this stage of their lives.

Solid foods also made a big impression on Flo's surviving kits, who, despite their tiny bodies, became very aggressive towards their younger, but bigger, adopted siblings. This set the scene for the next phase, which was very distressing for all concerned.

I was teaching a drawing class when I received an urgent call from my wife, Chris. One of the smaller babies had just had its right front paw bitten off after climbing into the food dish! Could I come home straight away and put the poor little thing to sleep so it didn't suffer any more?

Because I had classes for a few more hours, I asked her whether the now three-pawed ferret was crying. 'No,' Chris replied.

'Was the injury bleeding noticeably?' I asked.

'No,' came the reply again.

'Give him a little food and see if he's still hungry,' I suggested.

'He's apparently still starving,' my wife said, after going away from the phone for a few minutes to do the quick test.

'So, then,' I said, 'he's obviously not so distressed that he can't wait a few hours before I come home and put him to sleep.' So Chris agreed it wasn't urgent after all.

When I arrived home about 6 o'clock that night, the little fellow was still doing fairly well, and managing to limp around the cage without too much trouble. I decided to stall 'doing the deed', and see how he was the next morning. The next day, I deferred any action until later that night, and so on. About five days later, the scab had dropped off the leg and the little fellow was happily stumping around on three legs without a lot of bother.

It was only natural that the three-pawed survivor should be called 'Stumpy', because for his entire life he simply didn't understand that he was missing the right front quarter of his visible means of support. (We did contemplate 'Tripod', but only very briefly). For quite some time he would try to scamper up the front of the cage like his cage mates, only to fall back to the floor when he changed legs. His pawless leg would wave in tiny circles as he attempted unsuccessfully to catch hold of the wire.

Probably because of his disability, we paid him far more attention than we otherwise would have, and he quickly learnt to exploit our goodwill. It was largely because of his antics that we began to understand that ferrets are really quite clever, if devious, creatures. Far from being smelly, savage little things that undesirables keep for poaching rabbits, they are genuinely domestic animals that can only exist with human assistance, and, when treated with similar respect to other domestics, they can become a really delightful companion animal.

Many years ago, an old breeder friend of mine said that on a warm summer's morning there was nothing he liked to do more than to sit on an old chair he had placed under the grape vines in his backyard and just watch the ferrets playing. It was better than TV, he reckoned.

Several of my ferrets were real gluttons for exclusive attention. They much preferred being picked up and spoken to than eating, so they would always rush to me at feed times rather than to their bowl. Apart from these games, ferrets have their own individual little routines that they perform, which often reflect their personalities. Some like to do laps; when they are released for a run, they will gallop at a very high speed around the yard or through the house, just enjoying the speed they can't normally develop inside the cage. Others will play ambush games with each other or the neighbour's cat, Roger, who often spent time in my yard avoiding his owner's grandchildren.

In the cage, a fellow we called Stanley liked to play the 'Turtle game'. He evicted the others from the sleeping box, turned the box upside down, got under it, then slowly walked around the cage with the box over him like a turtle's shell, his head peering out of the box's entrance. But the most active of my five ferrets at that time was Stumpy. He liked to play 'Snap', which, despite his disability, involved him scrambling to the highest point in the cage and jumping, open-mouthed, onto anything nearby that moved. Since the upturned sleeping box made a convenient launch platform for this game, he often slowed Stanley's game of Turtle down considerably.

Flo didn't indulge in games very often, although she was quite good at playing dead. I almost buried her once, believing she had expired. She would go into such a deeply comatose state that my kids often came running inside to tell me Flo had gone to God. If she could talk a bit more audibly I'm sure she would have attributed this to being like a cat, only better. Cats have nine lives, but ferrets have lots more. She's been nearly dead at least six times, yet, like some 'Groundhog Day Lazarus', she returns to the land of the living just in time. As we approach the cage, spade in hand, she will open one rheumy eye and give us the look that says, *Not so fast!*

Poor old Flo was about five years old and quite arthritic. She had lost a lot of hair since her spring moult, and had atrocious bad breath. Periodically I cleaned her teeth (a task involving a small cat toothbrush and toothpaste, which was most decidedly not a game for the faint of heart – I could not convince her it was for her own good!) and her claws often needed careful trimming as they cracked and got caught on her bedding.

Still, she insisted on 'killing' the bedding whenever it was changed, and though I'm sure this wasn't a real game to her – despite the others joining in as though it was – she was very possessive after she had 'killed' it. Once 'dead', it was hers! If anybody touched the bedding, she bit the person's hand firmly. It was a *'Get out of here!'* bite rather than a savage, skin-piercing, *'Die, scum!'* kind of chomp. Nevertheless, considering what was growing on her teeth, I was reluctant to put my hands in the way. Bites are just part of the game with most ferrets, but because they often aren't aware of their own strength they can pose a serious problem to people who are new to the species.

My ferrets often play a game called 'Sleeves'. It involves having bedding made from old clothes with sleeves or legs that they use as tunnels. Slippery lycra tracksuit pants are a favourite, as the animals can get up to a great speed in these. While one runs through the sleeves, the others all jump on top from the outside and try to stop him from getting through. Stumpy usually tried to arrange for the outlet of the sleeve to be pointing into the water bowl, so that the participant unwittingly ran into the bowl. You could see him smiling to himself as he did it, wicked boy.

Stumpy stayed with us for his whole life, entertaining us with his hilarious games to the end. He won third prize in 'Albino' class at Gawler Show in 1995 (despite protests from jealous rivals who claimed he should have been disqualified because of his disability).

His antics featured frequently in the South Australian Ferret Association newsletter, to the extent that one of our overseas members, a medical professor from a university in the USA, wrote a tongue-in-cheek letter chastising me for Stumpy's name on the basis that it highlighted his disability. Shortly afterwards, the professor received a letter directly from 'Stumpington Charlesworth Smith' denying any connection between his name and disability. The letter, by all accounts, was framed and displayed on his office wall (much to the amusement of his students). The professor and I both doubted that any other academic in America had ever received a letter from a ferret, least of all one from Down Under.

Sadly, though, ferrets have a fairly short lifespan. Stumpy developed bladder cancer and was put to sleep in 1997 at just four years and five months.

I've kept ferrets as pets for the better part of fifty years and they continue to engage me with their odd but endearing behaviour. Your local ferret rescue group would love to hear from you if you would like to open your heart and home to these wonderful critters!

Geoff, South Australia

Mr Invincible

At first sight, you wouldn't notice that Monet had no eyes. Nor that he had undergone several operations so that he could walk. This is the story of an extraordinary, loveable, cheeky pup who bounced back when the odds were against him.

Monet was one of a litter of five Shar Pei pups rescued in December 2011. A lady in Sydney contacted the Animal Welfare League wanting to surrender them. 'Pup-dumping season' was in full swing, so the AWL, being full to the brim, referred her to us, Shar Pei Rescue Inc., which could provide the specialised care that these dogs often need. Our Sydney manager Matthew Stevens went to collect the pups. They were all in terrible condition and sadly all but Monet had to be put to sleep.

December 2011 marked Monet's first birthday. When most pups would be out celebrating with their puppy friends, he was being prepared for surgery. You see, when Monet came into our care, we found that his eyelids had rolled in and his eyelashes had rubbed against his lenses, causing them to rupture. He was blind and as there was no chance of him ever being able to see again, the best option for him was to have his eyeballs removed to lessen the pain. Although Monet's move into the new environment of his foster home worried us, this amazing little guy had the layout of the house down pat in half an hour. Whenever something got in his way, he'd simply shake his head and keep on going.

Then, in January 2012, it was discovered that Monet had luxating patellas; this is when the kneecaps are not in alignment with the knee joint and can regularly pop out while running. Surgery is needed in serious cases, such as Monet's, to stabilise the knee. So we went ahead but after Monet's first surgery, he would not keep still! He was a fighter and wanted to prove that nothing would keep him down. He was dubbed Mr Invincible!

In April 2012, Monet had his second surgery. Due to inbreeding, he was genetically predisposed to the condition and prone to recurrences. After his operation, Monet had both his back legs plastered and he was told to sit down and not move. Of course that didn't last long, and he was up and about in no time, once again proving what a strong and determined young man he was.

In May 2012, Monet joined the loving Gardner family. Many people had applied to adopt Monet, but a calm and loving environment was the order of the day, and this was exactly what the Gardner family would provide for our special man.

In September 2012, Monet had his third surgery. A few days after, he was trying to scratch himself with the plastered leg! It was now clear that nothing was going to keep Monet down.

In December 2012 Monet turned two. Because his first birthday had been pretty miserable, the Gardiners decided to make his second birthday very special – complete with party hats and party food!

Monet is such a happy-go-lucky boy. Considering everything that he has been through, we think he is extraordinary. Sometimes we have to remind ourselves that he is blind, as he has totally taken his 'disability' in his stride. And he's taught us so much: about resilience, about how to love life and enjoy every moment for whatever it brings. No matter what obstacles he faces, he picks himself up and just gets on with being happy. Monet is the cheekiest dog around and all you can do is laugh and feel glad he is in the world.

Emerson Gardner and Amanda Booth, Shar Pei Rescue Inc., Victoria

WE ARE FAMILY

◇◇◇◇◇◇◇◇

Whoever says 'You can't choose your family' has never met these animals! Adopted pets who are given a second chance at life can become an integral part of family life and their new parents' very own beloved fur-kids.

TRUE LOVE
Bondi Vet star Dr Lisa Chimes with her beloved poodle–crosses Nelson and Lucas.
(Photo courtesy of the Ten Network)

BEST MATES

Right: Kala the 'slumdog millionaire' was rescued from a life on the streets of Bangalore in India for a new life in Sydney with Rochelle and her partner.
(Photo by John Jore)

Top left: Geoff with his pet ferret, Stumpy. He's kept pet ferrets for almost fifty years and loves their 'odd but endearing behaviour'.

Bottom left: Charlie, who was the unlikely 'kitty mayor' of Paddington in Brisbane, sharing the spotlight with his owner (and campaign manager) Katina.

Below: Dave still recalls meeting his rescue dog Sahara: 'I'll never forget the massive grin she had while she was nestled in my arms.'

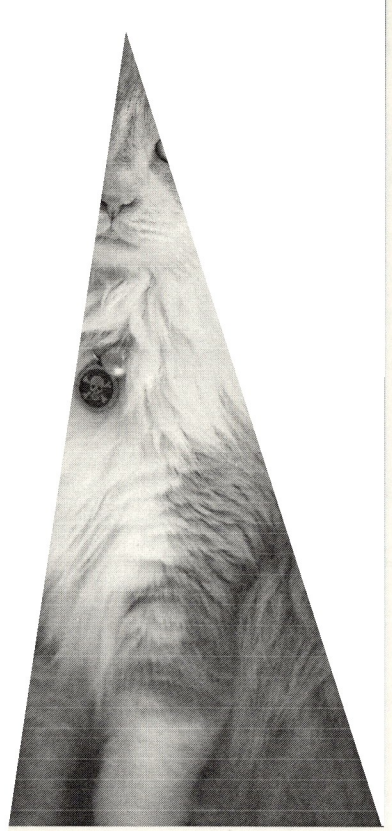

PERFECTLY IMPERFECT

Left: You would never know this gorgeous cat, Leo, is a survivor of animal testing that permanently damaged his eyes.
(Photo by Emma Turner, emmaturnerphotography.com.au)

Right: 'Even though she may not be perfect to the world, to us she is one in a million,' says Princess's owner.
(Photo by Claire Garrett, Petography)

Below: Myron the blind dog was found abandoned on the road but has gone on to rub shoulders with celebrities while helping with fundraising.

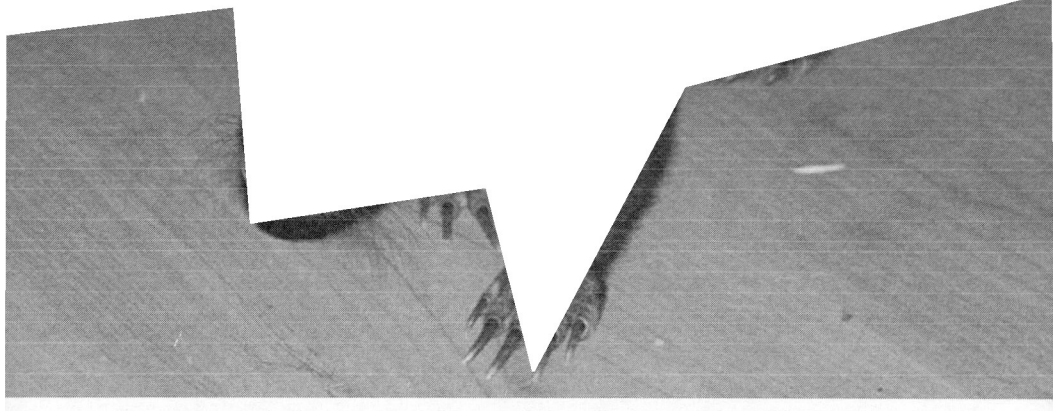

THE CUTEST CRITTERS

Above: Matilda the baby wombat spent months delighting the Cawood family before she found her forever home.

Below: Python the guinea pig (left), who narrowly escaped being a pet snake's lunch, with his 'wife', Cookie.

Above: Animal-lover Ruby shares a cuddle with her precious bunny.

Left: Fergus's scruffy charm captured the affection of his adoptive family. *(Photo by Natalie Brabham)*

Below: Lilly the Filly is a strong and proud little pony with plenty of attitude. *(Photo by Carrie Palmer)*

HELPERS AND HEROES

Above: Alby had a rough start in life, but is now the heart and soul of an aged care facility. *(Photo by Lisa Winter)*

Below: The gentle Carmella helps promote the message that 'feral' horses rescued from the wild deserve a second chance.

Above: Malibu brightens the day of all around her. 'She follows me like my shadow and always radiates such happiness,' says one of her owners.

Below: Ted is more than a beloved pet – he also assists a conservation centre to find and protect the endangered tiger quoll. *(Photo by Shayne Neal)*

HAPPILY EVER AFTER

Above: This pup overcame grave illness and injury to see another day. 'Ohlin is a fighter and has much to live for,' says his owner, Lisa. *(Photo by Jeremy Jasinkski)*

Top left: Resilient husky Shelley survived sickness and surgery, and was rewarded with a loving forever home.

Bottom left: Bailey, who was tied to a tree and left to die, is a 'true rescue dog' – he's saved his new family just as much as they've saved him. *(Photo on left by Jan Baker. Photo on right by Alvina Narayan.)*

CLEVER CREATURES

Above: What do you get when you cross a paintbrush with a pooch? Rembrandt, the German wirehaired pointer! *(Photo by Tina Louise Borg, Jet Photography)*

Below: Rescued kelpie Delilah delighted millions of TV viewers as the official house dog for *Big Brother*. *(Photo by Diana Leventhal, K9 Photography)*

The nimble-footed and sweet-natured Cocoa was rescued from the pound at the final hour. *(Photo by Ruthless Photos)*

BIRDS OF A FEATHER

Above: Chantal rescued several chickens from a battery hen farm. Now they are free to stretch their wings and lay as many (or as few) eggs as they please.

Below left: Chi Chi's been through more than your average chook, having survived hen-peckings, two dog attacks and three nights lost in the wilderness.
(Photo by Alex Olguin, olguinphotography.com.au)

Below right: This bird was part of a family of kookaburras who took it upon themselves to adopt and nurture an injured orphan kooka back to health.

ANIMAL DUOS

Above: Best buddies Gizmo and Marli make for a dashing pair on outings.

Below: Soulmates Sophie the goat and Mr Wigglesworth the pig are proof that love doesn't discriminate. *(Photo courtesy of Newspix/Melvyn Knipe)*

WHO'S THE BOSS?
This adoptee, Puss, became both the resident pet and bouncer of a Melbourne drinking spot. 'He took on a few dogs over the years – Puss knew who was boss and who the pub belonged to!' says his owner, Phil.

What Obstacles?

We had just moved to our new house after my marriage failed, and were ready to brighten our lives with a four-legged rescue friend. The kids and I headed to the RSPCA at Wacol with excitement.

Walking past all the enclosures, I fell in love with the three-year-old white-and-tan whippet–terrier mix as soon as I saw her. But she was a terrible sight. Six days earlier she'd had her left front leg amputated and had stitches running down her side. Her face was cut up and she had deep scratches along her torso and legs. The RSPCA believes she may have been in an accident on the motorway and came through the windscreen of a truck. It was horrifying to contemplate. A caring member of the public had saved her life when they found her on the Ipswich motorway and brought her in. She was named Ice Tea by the shelter staff as they thought her eyes looked like tea bags! My three older children liked the poor girl straight away, but my eight-year-old daughter was quite disturbed that the doggy only had three legs. However, after a little playtime together, my daughter warmed to her and said she was a lovely dog.

'Let's help her, Mum!' she begged.

So with all our family members happy, we began the adoption process.

We talked about how we would manage Ice Tea's recuperation, and had a special plan of attack for conquering the nine steep front steps at home: I would just have to carry her up them until her back legs were strong enough to manage by herself! Everyone was willing to help out where required – but we hadn't counted on Ice Tea having a little help of her own to give.

When we got home, I put Ice Tea down at the bottom of the steps so that I could get the house keys out of my bag. Looking up, I suddenly saw our new three-legged family member waiting for me on the top step. When I gasped, 'How did you get up there?' she looked at me as if to say: *What do you mean? How I normally do!*

It is only four months since we adopted this amazing dog and not a day goes by without me appreciating what she teaches me. On weekday mornings Ice wakes me up with kisses and a wagging tail to help me start the day. (She is so clever, she's worked out that on weekends I am allowed to stay in bed.) Every time I think I can't do something, she shows me that I can. I have my down days (especially when the kids are with their dad) when I think: *I can't do this any more*, then I look at my little survivor and how she has adapted to her own trials. The clever girl uses her tail as a rudder to help balance herself (her tail only ever stops when she is sitting or lying down). And after a few failed attempts at jumping on the couch, she devised a way around it – she's taught herself to run and jump sideways instead so her back feet land on the couch first. Brilliant!

But above all, the best thing about our special girl is that she has shown my family that you may look broken on the outside, but it's what's inside that counts. Even my daughter is now attempting things she normally wouldn't. Unfortunately, due to a bullying episode at school Charlotte had lost a lot of self-confidence. But after just a couple of months with Ice Tea, she is asking her opinion on certain matters rather than asking me. She tells Ice Tea what is bothering her out loud and a very patient Ice Tea sits and listens to the whole saga before wagging her tail madly when Charlotte articulates a plan of action that Ice approves of. Together, they work it out.

Recently, we decided that Ice Tea needed a friend for the days we are at work and at school. So we began to look for a canine pal of around three or four years of age. Once again, Ice Tea had her own ideas! She picked out her new friend herself. When we all went to visit some doggy candidates in foster care, there were four dogs in the pen together but only three eagerly awaited us as we walked towards them. A young pup was trying to hide at the back. Sure enough, Ice Tea took control of the interviews. She jumped into the pen and had a chat with the ten year old, the two year old, then the four year old. Next she tentatively made her way to the seven-month-old trying to 'blend' in with the pen. She gave him a little nudge, and slowly pushed him forward to present him to us. She looked at me, then at him, then wagged her tail and encouraged him to do the same. His name was Rajah.

I said to her, 'We can't get a puppy! He's only seven months old.'

Ice Tea looked at me as if to say: *I will look after him.*

Well, she's kept her promise. Ice Tea tells him off if he chews on anything and has shown him where to go to the toilet. Raj has found grass a scary but interesting new concept – before being rescued, he had spent seven months in a wire cage on concrete. But Ice has shown Raj that grass is a great spot to play on.

Ice Tea amazes me every day with her tenacity and her ability to know when I need her a little bit more than usual. And of course, every day that I get home there is one very happy smiling face waiting to greet me. She is a guide and mentor to us all.

Brenda, Queensland

Two Weeks till Forever

When I first saw Ohlin, little did I know this beautiful boy would steal our hearts so quickly.

As a volunteer for Staffy and Bully Breed Rescue (SABBR), I didn't hesitate to say yes when the team asked us to foster a twelve-week-old pup with mange, 'Just for a fortnight'. Apparently he was an American staffy mix who was found dumped at a bus stop. The plan was we would care for the little one for just enough time to commence treatment and get him on track to recovery. Then another carer could take over and prepare him for adoption.

I cried when I first saw him. Not only was the poor boy covered in mange, but he had a huge scab on his tiny head which had to be soaked by the vet nurses to be removed. What on earth had he been through? But despite the state he was in, the pup was a friendly, bouncy boy who craved human touch. We bundled him up, took him home and called him Ohlin – a strong Viking name.

Our existing dog Luna, another staffy mix, wasn't very impressed when she first saw the funny-looking pup, so we decided to keep them separated. Ohlin was tiny and needed to heal. Every day was a struggle: Is he okay? Can we introduce him again to Luna? Slowly we let them spend more time together, and our previously grumpy two year old blossomed into a doting mother, caring for Ohlin as if he was her own. We let them be, astonished at the new calmness that came over her. Our normally crazy, anxious Luna had found a sudden peace with her new friend.

Baths every two days, weekly injections and lots of rice, vegetables and chicken was the routine – but suddenly our little man developed vomiting, diarrhoea and loss of appetite. Concerned, I took him to the vet immediately and he was placed on a drip, suspected to have parvo, a serious virus that unvaccinated and neglected pups like Ohlin are susceptible to.

We visited Ohlin in the hospital a few days later, and as we walked into the room our hearts sank at the sight. This little dog, who had almost wasted away, was trying to raise his head in recognition at the sight of us, his two-legged friends. My partner and I sat there with him, resting his head on our open hands, letting him know everything would be okay and he would be home soon.

Meanwhile, Luna was missing her new brother terribly. On the fifth day, when Ohlin was allowed home, the moment he entered the house and Luna saw him again, you could see her happiness and relief. At this moment, we knew that Ohlin belonged with us. He was so little, weak and skinny, but he was alive and needed our help more than ever. He still had to recover from parvo, put on some weight and recommence treatment for mange.

Ohlin is a fighter and has much to live for. Thankyou to the kind stranger who found him and took him to the vet. Thankyou to the vet for contacting SABBR to help him, and thankyou to this wonderful group for the privilege of letting us have this beautiful boy in our lives. He is proof that you *can* make a difference – even if it is just for one dog. And just one dog matters.

Lisa, Western Australia

The Fight to Bring Shasta Home

Shasta places her paw on my arm and waits. I look at her and ask, 'What do you want, sweetie?' Our beautiful bull–mastiff mix just pushes down on my arm and blinks at me. Her tail wags and I know what she's asking. She wants to play, and she knows I am a sucker for her beautiful multicoloured eyes – one blue and one brown!

Last year, when we decided to adopt a dog, I knew it wouldn't be an easy task. I had grown up with canines, and always had companion animals before moving to Australia. I very much wanted a dog, but my four-year-old son Balty is a precocious boy with impulse control issues and hyperactivity. He is highly intelligent, but there is a disparity between that and his social IQ where he has deficits, including boundaries issues. I felt a dog might help. Obviously, though, we needed a calm and patient animal that would tolerate Balty's overenthusiastic love and help him learn appropriate behaviour. Was there such a dog out there?

When I found Shasta through Forever Friends Animal Rescue (FFAR), I knew she was just what we were looking for! With a lovely nature, she is gentle and good with everyone, particularly our son. Balty climbs all over her and she just lies there patiently and licks him, even when his cuddles are a bit rough. He has thrived since her love entered his life. She has become a constant companion for me and my partner, Paul, as well – we all adore her.

Choosing a name was challenging. I grew up overseas and was hoping to find something that reflected my Pacific Northwest American upbringing, so I was looking specifically at names that reflected the Native American peoples of my homeland. I thought of mountains, tribes and so forth, but Paul didn't have any connection with them until I thought of Shasta. Mount Shasta is known as a spiritual place: from

Native American origin myths and rituals, to a Buddhist Monastery at its base, to New Age traditions. The name fitted Paul's interest in spirituality and my desire for a link to home. The name of the snow-capped mountain also matched our peaceful white dog perfectly.

But right from the start, Shasta had health problems. I took her to our vet because I noticed a purple lump and some discolourations on her belly. He said it was likely to be cancerous, and she should undergo surgery immediately. He was pessimistic and told us not to get attached. We were devastated – we were already attached! We turned to Forever Friends, who asked us to take her to see their own vet, Dr Andrea. She was more optimistic and, at their expense, they removed the cancer. Dr Andrea had had cancer herself and didn't think Shasta should be written off yet! As Shasta had no secondary symptoms, Dr Andrea suggested we not worry, but just take Shasta home and enjoy her. It was good advice. She has been symptom-free ever since, though she has unrelated skin rashes for which she needs prescription food.

Just when we thought our new family of four was finally going smoothly, something horrible happened. One Friday night, Paul took Shasta for a walk. At one point, he popped into a restaurant to use the bathroom, tying up Shasta outside. When he returned, she was gone, lead and all. Sick with worry, he wandered around for hours in the dark, looking for her. He knew at once our good-looking girl had been stolen, as there wasn't any way that Shasta could have slipped free and taken the lead with her.

The next morning, Saturday, I went to the local police station and made a report. There wasn't a lot the police could do. I learned that dog theft is on the increase, and bull breeds are sometimes stolen to go into illegal dog fighting rings. I felt ill. How could this happen? Our girl wasn't a fighter! I went home, resolved to do everything we could to find our girl. I created a 'Lost' poster. Balty was very upset, wondering where his friend could be. Paul starting calling pounds and shelters and found that the large North Melbourne pound, the Lost Dogs' Home, had a dog fitting Shasta's description. She had been brought in by a ranger during the night, having been found wandering almost 20 kilometres from home, in an area on the other side of the city. This was further proof that Shasta had been dog-napped. What on earth had our poor girl been through? She must have escaped her captors, our clever girl!

We were so happy – she was safe! I was already grabbing my keys to head straight out to collect her, but our joy was short-lived. We weren't allowed to pick her up.

'What?' I cried out when Paul told me and I grabbed the phone to protest.

The pound had scanned her microchip and found our gentle family dog was listed as a 'menacing dog' on the chip registry database. They couldn't release her without discussion with the relevant councils on Monday. Our Shasta, 'menacing'? How ridiculous! She is one of the calmest dogs I have ever known. I was devastated. What could she have done to receive that label?

Just when we thought the nightmare was over and our girl, a victim of kidnapping from her loving family, could come home, the words I was hearing just didn't make any sense: 'Call back on Monday. We can't do anything on the weekend.'

Leaving our dog for the rest of the weekend in a cage like a criminal was unbearable. I phoned Forever Friends and spoke with their adoption coordinator, Lisa, who was also outraged. She called the pound, telling them Shasta was definitely not a 'menacing dog'. She never would have been released from the country pound where FFAR found her if she had that label on her record. There had been a mistake. Shasta was the victim here, not the perpetrator! What on earth was going on?

The North Melbourne pound staff had no answers: 'Call back Monday.' They would, however, allow me to take Shasta's prescription food in to her because she is allergic to regular dog food. Unfortunately, it was too late to make it across town before they closed, so I had to take the food down on Sunday morning. Lisa from FFAR said she would call again first thing Monday and wouldn't stop until Shasta was released.

Balty kept asking me when Shasta was coming home. He missed

her. I tried to explain, but his pleas broke my heart. When the shelter opened on Sunday morning, we were there, food in hand. When we asked to see our girl, I was aghast when we were refused. Our girl had done nothing wrong, apart from being so gentle to let herself be stolen – why was she being treated this way? And why were we? We were the victims of the crime and just wanted to console our family member who had no idea what was happening!

The staff member finally relented and allowed us a five-minute visit. Shasta was happy to see us but confused. She was clearly distraught when we left. It was heart-wrenching to have to leave our family member behind due to ridiculous red tape. Balty was particularly upset. At only four years old, he didn't understand why his dog couldn't come home and had to sleep in what appeared to be doggie jail. The nightmare continued.

First thing Monday morning I called the pound again to find out what needed to be done to bring Shasta home. *Please let today be the day*, I prayed. Many calls and much frustration later, the red tape continued to torment us. The staff member I spoke to said she needed to talk to the council where Shasta had been found, and until she spoke with them, nothing could be done. From her tone and manner, it was clear she wasn't in a hurry to call.

I felt powerless and had to do something, so I went to my local council. They were sympathetic but explained that if Shasta had exhibited aggressive behaviour before and had been officially listed as 'menacing,' she wasn't suitable for a family home. I would presumably get the dog back, but would probably have to make the decision to put her down. They had no idea why FFAR had rehomed her. Such knowledge should have come up as part of the temperament-testing process and the dog would have been deemed unsuitable for adoption.

I was in tears as I rang FFAR again. Lisa reiterated that what everyone was saying was a mistake; Shasta was being tried and convicted despite having done nothing wrong. She reassured me to hang in there. They would get to the bottom of it.

Lisa called the country pound that originally released Shasta to FFAR and told them about what we were going through. Outraged, a staff member there called the local council for us. The council searched their records and confirmed Shasta had never committed an aggressive act. Next, the microchip company was phoned and they revealed that they had made an error. On closer examination of their files, they found that when the country pound had faxed Shasta's paperwork to them, there was a crinkle in the paper that made the box for 'menacing dog' look like it had been checked. Instead of verifying this serious designation, the microchip company simply entered 'menacing dog' in Shasta's registration. We were right all along – our girl was innocent!

The company admitted fault and all of this was explained to the city pound over the phone, but they demanded hard-copy proof. Admission of fault for the error was sent by the microchip company, and the country council also verified they had no record of Shasta committing any 'menacing' activities. I hurried across town in peak-hour traffic to break Shasta out of the city pound and bring her home.

I was almost beyond speech when I arrived and was told there was more red tape to be dealt with and hoops to be jumped through before Shasta would be released. Why had my dog entered this place as a victim of a crime, only to be treated as the criminal to be punished? Was it partly due to the recent introduction of breed-specific legislation in Victoria, which seemed to encourage suspicion that every bull-type dog was aggressive?

When our reunion with Shasta finally – *finally* – occurred, we were overjoyed. She was too, licking our faces, wagging her tail ferociously and moaning with excitement. We gave her cuddles and Balty climbed all over her.

When Shasta first went missing, I posted a plea on Facebook about wanting her back and warning others about dog theft, which my friends and family posted on their pages as well. FFAR followed suit. Many people were sympathetic about what we were going through, and the post spread. To my disbelief, not everyone was supportive, though. One person commented that he 'had never known a pit bull that wasn't menacing', making an erroneous assumption about Shasta's breed – a dog he'd never met. American pit bull terriers are not an officially recognised breed in Australia, although there are many Staffordshire terriers that are unfairly regarded in the same negative light.

Moreover, one of the most sobering and eye-opening experiences during our whole ordeal was that many people didn't think that the labelling of Shasta as 'menacing' had been a mistake. She looked 'scary', therefore she must be dangerous. The same people chose to advise us that, once released from the pound, we shouldn't keep Shasta because of the breed they presumed her to be, never mind that she's a 'bitsa' who might be best known as a bull–mastiff mix. But they were wrong about Shasta and they are wrong about the overwhelming majority of bull breeds. Anyone who's met Shasta knows the truth about this gentle dog. And, fortunately, support for her was greater than the irrationality and fear.

Because of the publicity on Facebook, I was contacted by a reporter from our local newspaper, the Port Phillip *Leader*, who wanted to write an article about our ordeal. The article was published a couple of weeks later – the front-page story! – accompanied by a stunning photo of best friends Balty and Shasta reunited, with Shasta kissing Balty on the forehead.

If there's a warning in this tale, it is that you must never leave a dog unattended in public. If there is a moral to this tale, it is that you should never judge a book by its cover.

Even now, it is very upsetting to think about how Shasta was treated during her ordeal, and what might have happened to her if she hadn't escaped soon after being taken from us that night. We are lucky that she is agile enough to climb fences and trees! If she didn't have that ability, we might never have seen her again, and who knows what horrors would have lain ahead for her. We were delighted to hear recently from the police that the man who stole Shasta had been apprehended, and he will soon face court.

We are beyond relieved to have Shasta back. While she was away, we all realised just how much we love her, and it seems that she realised the same about us. She has settled in more deeply with our family and is even more affectionate now, perhaps even a little bit cheeky, as she is now prone to sneak into bed with her humans at night for an extra snuggle. We are all completely in love with each other. Shasta is the perfect easygoing family dog, even if she sometimes goes a little crazy around possums!

Renee, Victoria

◇◇◇◇◇

Sir Walter

I always knew I had the potential to become obsessed with dogs (a 'dogaholic'!) but had kept it hidden for years.

For over a decade my family was the focal point of my life; and anyway, my husband, Brad, told me he never wanted a dog. Then, in July 2007, when my youngest was ten years old, I finally convinced Brad to adopt a greyhound.

One of my work colleagues, Simie, had been to a dog event and had picked up a brochure from Friends of the Hound. I read up about them and was quickly convinced that a rescued greyhound would be the perfect dog for us. We checked their website and the first hound we saw was Wally. He was 'Hound of the Month' and everyone fell for him instantly.

Brad and I were sitting in our garden with a friend, who had just stopped by to admire our newly completed fence, when Lisa and Shane arrived with Wally. As we watched him step elegantly from the back of Lisa's truck, our friend casually commented, 'That's not a dog, it's a horse. And mate, your fences need to be taller!'

We were in awe of this athletic fawn-and-white creature. In the many emails the coordinator Lisa sent me prior to his adoption, Wally was described as a big, happy goofball, but not yet house-trained. To our astonishment, he settled into our home like he had always lived there. And he just seemed to know about relieving himself outside, and would inform us with a short bark that he needed to go.

And so Wally's training of his humans began. He soon abandoned the bark signal to ask to be let out as we learnt his canine body language: get up, shake vigorously, stretch enormously long legs in the downward dog pose and head for the stairs. He also trained his formerly exercise-phobic owner to walk him every day by being a perfect gentleman. He was a strong dog and could have easily pulled me around the park, but instead walked placidly beside me, sniffing the ground only when we stopped.

Wally taught my dog-hating husband to love canines, and Brad now understands how people feel about their pets. Through Wally, we also learned to enjoy sitting outside in the garden just to watch his goofy antics. He loved the fetch game, and seeing the athleticism of his 'zoomies' was awe-inspiring – running at huge speed for the sheer joy of it, usually straight at us and at the last second turning away or screaming to a halt!

Although he could easily have jumped our fences, he treated any boundary we imposed on him with respect. He liked digging in freshly tilled earth, so to protect our new garden beds we put in a knee-high barrier and he never dug in those beds again.

But the greatest lesson of all that he taught us was about unconditional love. He would brush up against our bed, like a giant cat, wagging his stiff little docked tail to greet us at the start of the day. Then there was his gentle leaning on my legs, or nudging with his head when he wanted attention.

His passing was a great trial for Brad and me. We had known for six weeks that we were going to lose Wally to cancer. I had hoped he would pass in his sleep, but his will to live was strong and right to the end he wanted to stick to all his routines – nothing would stop him going down the stairs to do his business outside, even though he had only two good legs to stand on towards the end.

His inability to walk was the defining moment for us. We knew we had to release him from this less-than-satisfactory existence. He didn't fight it, trusting me to the end.

But we are forever changed. It was a privilege to have shared over five wonderful years with our precious Sir Walter, and we will always have rescued greyhounds in our lives.

Susan, Queensland

◇◇◇◇◇

No More Dogs!

Tipsy was a Port Hedland mutt, given to me by my friend Fred when she was still a very young pup. At the time I was a truck driver and mechanic. Tipsy soon learnt to love the trucks and travelled all over the Pilbara with me.

When I married Tina in 1973, Tipsy, then around two, came to live with us. Despite her inexperience with family life, she became a beaut family dog and was great with the arrival of sons Mike and then John, who no doubt cranked her up at times. She loved the ocean and would swim for ages. As she got older, we would have to remove her from the water, as only her nose would be sticking out. She was fifteen years of age when she passed away, and her death left a huge gap in our family.

After about six months – it was time – we visited our local dog pound with the boys, then six and nine. All the dogs were jumping about and barking excitedly except one – a black labrador mix. She was sitting there quietly, just looking sad. We took her home, naming her Bindi. It took a while for us all to adjust but she soon won us over, and became a wonderful family member. It was a sad day a couple of years later when we came home and found her sitting in the yard unable to move. We immediately took her to the vet, but there was no hope for her – an irreversible paralysis – and we had to put her to sleep.

I thought, *No more dogs!* The pain of losing them is just too much.

But then, a few months later, I got home from work to find my family gathered around a tiny, furry, light-brown bundle on the lawn. She was a very young terrier mix (I'm not sure what breed) and apparently had been brought home 'on appro' (I still wonder about that!). We named her Sandi and she proved to be a very smart girl indeed. She was easily trained to learn lots of tricks and to obey hand signals. She loved water and would walk around the edge of the bricked bath each evening, testing the water. On the downside, she did not like to socialise with other people or dogs. Her only canine friend was T.D. (Tim's Dog), the elderly silky owned by our neighbour.

Sandi was a great guard dog and had no problem rounding up tiger snakes to show Tina. We loved her dearly; she had so much character. How terrible it was to have to one day decide whether we should put her down. At fifteen she had developed heart problems and tumours on her skin. I sat on the lawn with her after Tina and I had discussed what we should do. Tina called me in for tea and when I came out thirty minutes later dear little Sandi had passed away. She hadn't moved from where we had last patted her. What a sad day.

This time I meant it – *Definitely* no more dogs.

Just over a year later my son, John (JB), had started up the PetRescue website, so of course we had to check it out – including the listings. There were so many lovely dogs, some like Tipsy, some like Bindi, and even some like Sandi. It was all a bit too much for me.

Then one day a fifteen-month-old silky terrier caught Tina's eye. My first thought was, *I don't want a male*. Plus it's hard to tell his front from his rear.

He was still online the next day, near Donnybrook, about 50 kilometres away. Tina was keen, so I agreed to go and have a look on the weekend. We went. And of course we returned with this thing in a basket on the back seat.

His name is Max. His previous owner had been an elderly lady who'd found him a bit too much to handle. He still is at times!

Max is completely different from our other dogs. He's friends with nearly every person and animal in our small acreage subdivision. He has a mate, Fergus, a Jack Russell mix from whom he often borrows toys; and a little further down the road is Sage, a beautiful golden labrador he finds quite attractive. In the other direction there is Bear, a young staffy; next door to Bear is Bella, a young springer spaniel; and across the road from Bella is Millie (of unknown origins).

Such a big canine community gives Max a full social life, which is only restricted by the times he's in his enclosure (when we work) and also during the heat of the day. He knows that when Mick's truck comes home, the gates will be open and he will be able to get in and play with Bear.

Max loves chasing the cows in the paddock, perhaps because they turn around and chase him back. He also loves running after rabbits, possums, rats and mice. As John says, Max is in 'puppy heaven'. And we feel very lucky to have this very happy boy join our family.

Looks like I'll always have a dog, doesn't it?

Peter, Western Australia

◇◇◇◇◇

Get Me to the Church on Time!

It was June 2006 and I had been looking for a companion for my gorgeous one-year-old blue heeler, Ruby. She was like a child to me and my fiancé, Jamie, and we spoiled her. Ruby came everywhere with us, and we wanted the new dog to be able to do the same.

We'd trialled a dog four months earlier, but that had not gone well – Ruby was lucky to be in one piece. It was proving quite difficult to find a good match and a little bit stressful, yet I was determined to get a rescue dog.

At that time I was working in the Melbourne CBD and one lunch break I paid a visit to the Lort Smith Animal Hospital in North Melbourne. I told the staff that I was looking for a companion for my heeler girl, and they introduced me to a kelpie–blue heeler mix who was barking his head off in the pen.

They explained that Bluey was four years old and that his previous owner had become too ill to care for him. They said Bluey was used as a 'temperament-testing dog' to help gauge the temperament of other dogs entering the pound, because he was such a beautiful boy.

I said, 'Gee, he barks a lot!' I couldn't help thinking the worst, but as soon as the staff let him out of his pen my fears vanished. He was beautiful, with his dark coat, alert little ears and intelligent eyes. Bluey had already served twenty days and his time was running out – at that time in Victoria there was a terrible rule that pets in pounds and shelters were only allowed to remain for twenty-eight days before being killed.

Bluey was well known around the shelter for his beautiful nature and had won the hearts of many of the volunteers. I placed my name on him, but I was second in line – another family had already met him and were interested. My heart sank.

I told my fiancé about Bluey and how I'd put my name on him but that we were second in line. Two weeks went by and I'd pretty much given up hope, when I received a call saying the other family pulled out. Bluey was ours! I was ecstatic, but there was only one small catch – I was getting married the next day!

I called Jamie at work and told him that Bluey was ready to be collected. He said, 'Therese, have you gone mad? Can't it wait until we get back from our honeymoon?'

'No – he's been there twenty-eight days and if we don't take him now, he'll be killed.' I heard Jamie sigh at the other end of the phone.

I'd taken the day off work to prepare for our Big Day, but all that was forgotten. I arranged to collect Jamie at work on his lunch break and bring Ruby along for a meet and greet with Bluey at Lort Smith.

Well, it was love at first sight for everyone. Jamie was smitten and Ruby had given the 'paws up' in the way young dogs do: by licking Bluey's face until it was completely wet. I thought how funny it was that we were just about to have our Big Day, and our newly united dogs were acting like they were having their own Big Day!

So, just hours later, Jamie and I got married and it was a lovely day for everyone. And since Ruby suffered separation anxiety, we had already planned to take her on our honeymoon with us . . . so Bluey would have to come along too!

Bluey will be eleven this year and is still going strong. He and Ruby are now beautifully behaved with their human siblings – a three-year-old sister and an eighteen-month-old brother. As crazy as it seemed to adopt a new dog the day before my wedding, I'm so glad I did!

Therese, Victoria

◇◇◇◇◇

Fergus the Fabulous

The dogs in my life have always been chosen from a litter of puppies, their breed carefully selected or at least clearly recognisable. When that inevitable urge overcame me to find a livelier companion for my ageing schnauzer – and for me – I put in an order for a Manchester terrier pup, which would be the brother of a young male, Chuck, that I knew and liked. Unfortunately, a phantom pregnancy dashed my immediate hopes of owning Jack's brother.

In the meantime, my daughter, who volunteered with our local dog rescue group, had been quietly searching on my behalf and word came that there was a dog in a pound that might suit me. The photo of a scruffy, ginger, long-haired, short-legged terrier mix didn't quite match my vision of a sleek, black, short-haired, long-legged Manchester terrier. Nothing was known about him except that he was young, cuddly, friendly and lovable, and possibly had Australian terrier in him. They had called him Fergus.

While convinced on principle that rescuing a dog was the 'right' thing to do, I was filled with misgivings. Reassurance that 'there is no pressure to take him on permanently' did little to allay my concerns. How would I cope with the sense of failure if I sent Fergus back to the rescue group? How would he cope with another move? Did I really want a dog I hadn't chosen? How would I convince the Master of the House, who didn't see the need for another dog, that this was a good idea?

Aware that time was running out for this dog, I signed the foster care application form, promising that I could provide a safe *temporary* home for a stray. And things began to move with alarming speed! Suddenly, I found myself going to collect 5 kilograms of skin and bone and fluff.

It wasn't love at first sight. He certainly was cute, but the concept of a four-week trial period was reassuring. It took all of that month to discover the *real* Fergus. And during that time he steadily wormed his way into our affections.

He was a little timid to begin with, afraid of big cars, trams, vans, narrow passageways, solid fences and iron gateways, and he still doesn't like people to rush at him. He had to be taught to climb steps and go out through the dog door, and that he shouldn't lift his leg to mark his territory while indoors – in anybody's house! But he was a quick learner and was soon sitting and waiting on command, at home at least.

Fergus is a dog's dog. He loves all other canines and expects them to love him. Uncomplimentary remarks at the park about his short legs are quickly replaced with admiration for Fergus's speed, agility and ability to bounce to amazing heights. He springs along like a rabbit on strong little legs. He loves to fetch and will chase toys and balls for as long as anyone is prepared to throw them.

Fergus is, as promised, friendly and lovable. He is also mischievous, inquisitive, cheeky and feisty and has a doggy sense of humour. He loves chewing bones, playing with toys, going for walks, chasing birds and running in the sea. Most of all he loves being with us and, when not curled up on a lap, is usually lying on the floor just close enough to touch one of us.

And the Master of the House? The beaming smile when the little orange blur bounces down the hallway to greet him at the front door says it all!

Yes, of course we adopted Fergus! And I cancelled my order with the Manchester terrier breeder. In the end, it was an easy decision. Fergus the short-legged rescue mutt is just perfect.

Robin, Victoria

ANIMALS HEALING HUMANS

◇◇◇◇◇◇◇◇

There are incredible animals in our world who have the power to heal their humans. Whether it's a miraculous physical recovery or a soothing of the soul, pets can have spectacular, life-changing effects on people in need.

The Best Medicine

The end of 2009 saw my life change in all the very best of ways. Yet there was still a hole that needed to be filled. And the missing piece came in the form of a furry angel named Lilly.

Backtracking a few years, I had always wanted a dog. However, life for my partner and me was not stable enough for a pet, and we lived in a rental apartment that did not allow animals. But we faced a far more serious situation. I have cystic fibrosis, and I was growing increasingly unwell, having to spend more and more time in hospital. Cystic fibrosis is a genetic disorder that affects the lungs, and also the pancreas, liver and intestine. Difficulty breathing is the most serious symptom and results from frequent lung infections.

A double lung transplant would save my life – I just had to wait for it to become available. And in mid-2009, it did.

Three months later, with our future now looking bright, we bought our first house. I knew straight away what I had to do next to make our new house a home! I jumped onto PetRescue to search for our missing piece of the puzzle – a furry family member.

When I saw her photo it was not the best, and it was hard to see what she really looked like, but one thing was very clear . . . her eyes. There was something about them that I could not ignore. A week before we moved into our new house, with the intention of 'just having a look', we took a drive to Pets Haven Animal Shelter at Woodend to meet Jane, a six-month-old border collie–golden retriever mix.

As Jane was just a pup, inside the shelter all she was interested in was trying to say hello to the nearby cats, or eating food off the shelves. We took her for a walk and she couldn't have cared less about us. The big wide world was out there! But those eyes still spoke to me and we knew we could not leave without adopting her. We changed her name to Lilly right away and took her home that same day.

Lilly has enriched and changed our lives in so many ways. She has become well known and much loved at our local dog parks. We have made so many new friends in our area this way – she's made it so easy! Lilly even has a doggy best friend called Sally – a black labrador roughly the same age – and they are like sisters. They have play dates during the week and thanks to Lilly and Sally we have become close to Sally's family too. Lilly has also become a trendy café dog and wears her 'Oscar's Law' bandana wherever she goes, helping educate people on the importance of closing puppy factories and how great rescue dogs are. She's quite the ambassador!

But the best thing of all? Lilly has been a marvellous motivator for me to keep fit with my new lungs. I have to exercise – and Lilly never fails to remind me! I love nothing more than jogging next to her with her smiling up at me with those special eyes that never fail to make my heart swell. We have been so lucky with Lilly. She asks for very little but gives us so much in return.

Thankyou, Pets Haven, for rescuing Lilly; you all do amazing work and we will be forever grateful to you!

Samantha, Victoria

The Healing Power of a Tiger

Do you believe in miracles?

Recently we had a lovely lady adopt Tiger, a six-year-old tabby, from the Great Lakes and Manning Branch of the Animal Welfare League. The lady in question was soon after diagnosed with breast cancer and looked as though she might have to have a breast removed.

One of our carers rang her recently to see how she and Tiger were getting on. She reported she was absolutely delighted with her new furry friend. She said, 'One night recently there was a thunderstorm, and our terrified dog jumped into bed with Tiger, and the cat's purring calmed the poor little critter quite quickly!'

She then went on to relate how Tiger sits on her lap and purrs, and when he does this, funnily enough, 'It feels like a vibration is going through the breast with the lump in it.'

Imagine everyone's joy and amazement when she went to have her final ultrasound before the operation, and the doctors couldn't find any sign of the cancerous tumour whatsoever.

Perhaps cats really do have healing powers!

Tina Lonsdale, Animal Welfare League, New South Wales

Our Very Special Resident

From the moment Tasha entered our lives we knew she was the right dog for our house.

I manage St Joseph's Community of the Abbeyfield Society at Malvern in Melbourne, an independent living establishment for people over fifty-five, and there are usually five men and five women living here.

When I first mentioned the idea of having a dog live with us at the house, the residents' responses were overwhelmingly positive. So I searched PetRescue and found a very cute dog named Toby at Forever Friends Animal Rescue (FFAR). Unfortunately for us (but fortunately for Toby), lots of other people thought he was cute too, and when I emailed FFAR I discovered that he had already gone to a new home. However, their adoption coordinator suggested we might like Toby's companion Tasha, who had also been given up for adoption by the same owner.

A few days later, Tasha duly arrived at the house in the arms of one of FFAR's volunteers. I instantly fell in love with the little bundle of fluff, and knocked on all the doors to introduce her to the residents. All were delighted except for one, John, who told us in no uncertain terms that Tasha was not to step over his threshold under any circumstances!

We kept Tasha for the day and a sleepover that night, and soon a 'one-day' visit became a week – we couldn't bear to hand her back! The next step was to get permission to keep her from the committee that runs St Joseph's. To do this properly, I thought I should take her back to her foster carer for a short time, but we missed her so much that I had to go back and get her the next day – and she's never left since!

Tasha is a Maltese–pug mix. She has the prettiest face, with huge eyes ringed in black and long, long eyelashes. Weighing 8 kilograms, she is white with some splashes of grey on her back. She is just a fluff ball of love and will go to anybody. To her, the world is one big lap with lots of hands to constantly pat her.

Tasha is incredibly affectionate, yet is a brilliant watchdog. She barks at any stranger who comes to the house – she knows if someone is a friend or stranger from the minute they park their car or open the gate, and she is always right.

She gets walked twice a day by one of the residents, and if he goes for his walk without her the locals will stop and ask him where she is. She visits each of the residents in their rooms daily if their doors are left open, and has one special friend, Rosemary, who understands everything Tasha says to her in the secret language they share. Tasha has Rosemary wrapped around her little finger and if I am nowhere to be found she goes straight to Rosemary, as she knows she will get plenty of attention.

Tasha sits under the table at Rosemary's feet throughout every meal, and when we have all finished she is then allowed to jump up onto her lap, whereupon she leans over and licks Brian seated next to her on the cheek to say hello. This happens at every mealtime.

Prior to Tasha's arrival, Rosemary kept to herself and rarely spoke. She had a few mental health issues and was very depressed. Tasha's company changed everything, and Rosemary is now a much-loved resident. The devotion between the two is mutual and a delight to see. As Tasha's mother I could get a little jealous of their close relationship, but Tasha has so much love to give that there is plenty left over for me. She sleeps in my bed each night, so I get extra-special cuddles.

Grumpy John was eventually won over too – just as I knew he would be – and he spent a whole day trying to curry favour with Tasha to get her to jump on his lap. At first she played hard to get, but eventually she rolled over on her back so he could scratch her tummy and chase her around the dining room table.

Recently, John had a massive stroke. In the days beforehand, Tasha had spent an increasing amount of time on his lap in his room – something she had not done previously. She knew he was unwell before we did. When I found him after the stroke, she ran into the room and licked him all over to settle him down. When he said her name, we realised that he was able to recognise someone. It was the only word he said.

Tasha has become the light of John's life. He also had mental health issues that diminished once she came on the scene. He had been an aggressive and argumentative person, very unhappy with his lot, but she brought out the love inside him. I have actually received permission to take Tasha to visit John in the rehabilitation hospital where he is recovering. With Tasha to encourage him, we're sure he will be home with us again soon.

I have seen the immeasurable joy and transformation that this loving little dog has made to the lives of these elderly people, and would heartily recommend *every* aged-care facility make room for a rescue dog as a very special resident.

Leeta, Victoria

◇◇◇◇

Buddy Saved Me

Out of all the people living in my neighbourhood, I am so blessed that Buddy the cat picked me to be his mummy.

Our wonderful journey together began many years ago. I often used to see Buddy Pumpkin (as I named him) roaming the streets, looking hungry and thin, and I started leaving food and water outside my front door for him. He was very timid and I couldn't get close to him, but I still assumed he belonged to someone – albeit someone who was neglecting him.

One day I heard that one of the neighbours was phoning the ranger to come and remove Buddy from the area. Alarmed, I quickly went to the shops and bought a name tag and collar for him, so if the rangers caught him at least they would contact me. I couldn't bear the thought of him being put to sleep in a cold pound because no one cared about him. But how to catch him, and put the collar on?

After spending many hours trying to coax him near, I finally cornered him in my garage. I had put food inside it as a lure and when he came in I closed the door. Trapped! He let me put his collar on but as soon as I opened the door he bolted off again. I couldn't help but wonder if an irate person was going to call and ask me why I had put a collar on their cat!

Of course, no one did call, so then I definitely knew Buddy was a true stray in need of a home. I decided to try to tame him, and despite already having five other cats, I was determined that he would become part of our family. So many stray cats are homeless through no fault of their own: they've been abandoned by their owners who have moved on and uncaringly left them behind, or they've been abused or neglected.

It took me many months and enormous patience to get Buddy to be comfortable around me, let alone to bring him inside the house. My other cats were territorial and Buddy was very timid. Once inside, at first he just hid in my cupboard – I used to call him a cupboard cat! Because of this and other signs, it became quite clear to me that Buddy's fears came from having been abused; the poor boy had even had his tail chopped off in the middle. I also took him to the vet for a checkup and vaccination, and found he had no microchip but, unusually, had been desexed.

In 2012, I received a letter from the breast screen clinic to come in for a routine mammogram. I made an appointment, but cancelled it when one of my other cats, Rainbow, was sick. Although I took screening very seriously, I just felt it was more important for me to deal with my cat first. It was a very sad time, as I soon lost my precious Rainbow to her illness.

I rescheduled my appointment, but then Buddy started having seizures. Once again I found myself running back and forth to the vet, and put off my screening. After undergoing many tests, Buddy was diagnosed with epilepsy and we managed to get his seizures under control with medication.

Around this time, I became aware that Buddy would not stop sniffing me under my left arm and breast area. He seemed very worried and even tried to bite me in that region! I recalled hearing stories about animals having the power to sense when someone is ill, and alarm bells began to ring in my head. I decided to schedule an urgent mammogram.

When the doctors confirmed I had breast cancer, I was not surprised that the tumour was in my left breast, where Buddy had been focusing his attention. They promptly performed a lumpectomy, followed by twenty-eight radiation treatments. I am now on the mend and determined to stay healthy.

I asked the doctors if earlier detection would have affected my diagnosis. They told me that if I'd had my mammogram months earlier as planned, the cancer may not have been able to be detected at that stage. Buddy had not only alerted me to the fact that I was sick (as I well might have kept delaying my appointment for many more months), but his seizures had also made me postpone my earlier mammogram until my cancer was detectable.

Today, Buddy enjoys his cuddles as much as my other cats. He loves watching TV with me, and we share a pillow at night. He is a contented indoor cat and gets on well with his furry siblings. My children say to me, 'You saved Buddy and Buddy saved you!' I can only agree.

Esther, Western Australia

Toby the Pony and Me

He was wild and woolly with half a winter coat falling out. He gazed at me through the weldmesh of the unused chook house, wary and defiant. He was beautiful.

'What's his name?' I asked.

'Toby, after my dad's old draft horse,' replied my father.

Toby was a yearling Shetland–miniature horse mix. I knew little about his background – just that he had been bred by a local woman and he had had very little human contact. Apparently she told Dad she didn't want to deal with such an 'unruly, untrained, vicious pony', and she thought he'd be more use as meat for her dogs. That is when Dad stepped in.

I could see it would take time for Toby to accept me. My early attempts at patting and brushing him left me smarting with bruises from his nasty teeth. But I will never forget the day I went to visit him and he whinnied a greeting to me!

That was twelve years ago. Toby and I have grown up together, and the bond between us has grown stronger with each passing year.

Our early days were full of racing around obstacle courses and going cross-country on foot. Wherever I went I figured Toby could too! I decided I would train Toby, and this often led to a war of wills – we were both stubborn and very determined!

Toby had always been an escape artist, and his urge to wander has never left him. Sometimes I would find him in the next street, or in a neighbour's paddock. But on one occasion he jumped our Victorian border into South Australia! It took us days to find him and, not having a float, it was a very long walk home. One thing we always agreed on: a good adventure away from the home property was the best of fun!

When I became a teenager, Toby transitioned from childhood playmate to friend, counsellor and wingman. By this time we had moved into town and Toby was put on my grandparents' fruit property, which we owned and ran. It was a fresh place to have all-new adventures, with a creek and bushland nearby.

As we grew older, Toby and I both began to learn we weren't bulletproof. I have cystic fibrosis: an incurable genetic disease which affects mostly the lungs and digestive system. My lung function was slowly starting to decline and I was getting sick more often with chest infections. A day before I was booked to go into hospital for two weeks, Toby fell ill. He had sand colic. He was down and wouldn't get up. I remember screaming and sobbing at him to stand. I pulled on his lead with every ounce of strength I had. I was terrified I was going to lose my best friend.

Then something amazing happened. My riding pony walked up to Toby and bit him quite hard on the ear! Toby was up in a flash. I managed to keep him up until I was dragged unwillingly off to hospital. Mum stayed home with him and thankfully the vet was able to treat him. Being so close to losing Toby made me love him even more.

Despite my illness, we still went for mad runs off the property and into the scrub. Toby would buck, rear and plunge, dancing on the end of his lead, and try and drag me to the best grass. He knew if I started to cough or became out of breath it was time to calm down. He would wait quietly beside me until I recovered – and as soon as I was okay he would be back to his antics.

I must confess that, for a time, my social life and full-time work became priorities, and I started seeing a little less of Toby. But our bond was as strong as ever. Whenever things got to me, I would drive straight to his side and just hang out with him, sometimes at ungodly hours of the morning! He didn't seem to mind; we have such a connection that we can happily sit together in silent contemplation for hours.

I created a special greeting for Toby, a whistle that mimicked his greeting neigh to me. It consists of one long high note followed by seven short whistles, each dropping in pitch. I could whistle to him from anywhere on the property, and he would reply.

Whatever food I was eating was Toby's food – or so he thought! He mastered the art of pulling a cute, innocent and starving face, and I would end up sharing my food. Twisties were a favourite, along with toast with jam, Vegemite or peanut butter! And a slice of fruitcake was never refused. Living on a fruit farm also meant he often got apricots, loquats, peaches, apples and oranges. He knew to spit the seeds out, too!

But even Toby's love of food came second to his love for me. My partner once carried a delicious-looking bale of lucerne hay past Toby and me, and threw out the question, 'Who do you love more, Toby – Jess or food?' Toby looked at him for a few seconds, gave a rather smug snort, and turned his attention back to me. Question answered!

Toby and I remain inseparable and still get up to mischief. We are about to embark on our next big adventure, when Toby comes to live with my partner and me on the property we recently bought. I've been waiting for so long to spend each morning having breakfast with my best mate – although I have a feeling I'm going to have to share it!

Jess, South Australia

◇◇◇◇◇

My Warrior Queen

When I was twenty-one, I moved away from my family to live with my grandmother and to look for work. I loved being with Nana and had just started a job I enjoyed when I was involved in a bad car accident. I sustained multiple bilateral fractures of both legs when I lost control of my car and hit a pole late one night. As a result I spent a couple of months in hospital before I could come home, as Nana worked and there was no one else to help look after me.

My whole world was turned upside down. I was unable to work, and had difficulty walking. Stuck at home, Nana could see I was lonely. So she and my uncle put their heads together, and he turned up one day with a beautiful red kelpie pup. I named her Teela after the warrior from *Beast Man*, my favourite movie at the time.

Ultimately, Teela helped me recover. When my walking improved, we did everything together, venturing out for a couple of kilometres every day. I grew physically and emotionally stronger, with her help.

But unfortunately, Teela always had more energy to spare! When she was six months old she attacked Nana's ducks and killed one of the drakes. Nana was very upset and, although heartbroken, I thought it was best to find Teela a new home on a farm. Being a kelpie, she was a working dog and needed more exercise and stimulation.

Some friends of our family owned a farm about 400 kilometres away, at Mildura. I rang them, and as they were willing to help me and adopt Teela, I said I would drive up and drop her off that coming weekend.

All the way to Mildura I told Teela as I drove that this was for the best and how much fun she would have chasing sheep. But I couldn't convince her or myself – I cried the whole way while Teela sat on the seat beside me, listening with her head close to my knee.

When we arrived, I had a quick drink and left as soon as I could. I knew if I stayed I would have given in and taken Teela home with me. It was a long, sad trip back, but I was glad Teela would be working and enjoying her new life.

Nine days afterwards, I received a terrible phone call. Teela was missing.

When the new family had taken Teela to work in the paddocks on her first day, she had disappeared. They spent two whole days looking for her. They were really sorry, but there had been no sign of her since. She was gone.

I put down the phone in tears. I couldn't bear to think of my girl lost and alone in a strange area. I discussed it with my uncle, who suggested I go down to the farm and look for her myself. Maybe she would hear my voice and come running?

I didn't need to think twice. I jumped into the car and drove the 400 kilometres back to Mildura. Imagine my joy and surprise when I pulled into the farm's driveway and there Teela was: sitting, waiting! Although not sighted for almost ten days, I believe Teela knew I was coming back for her, and turned up to meet me.

As soon as she saw my car she started wagging her tail. Even before I had jumped out to greet her, her whole body became one big wiggle, and she was barking and whining. I was so happy I was laughing and crying at the same time. All I could do was tell her she was mine and I would never leave her again. I sat on the dirt driveway for ages just holding her, taking in every detail, and telling her how much I loved her too.

I just had to take her home again. We needed each other – that was clear.

Teela and I went on to spend many happy years together. She was eleven when I had my first child. Everyone warned me that she would resent the baby – maybe even be dangerous around him! I didn't believe it, and did the only thing I could – I told her to guard little Alec shortly after he was born, and walked a short distance away to watch them together. She looked at him, licked his hand and lay down beside him.

When Alec was older, Teela helped him to stand, and later to take his first steps – even when she was so arthritic she had trouble standing herself. He would crawl towards her then grab her fur. Teela would then stand up and drag Alec up on his feet, then she would start to walk slowly, with him attached, as he took his baby steps. If he fell, she would lie back down and wait to help him do it all over again. It was magical.

If I was ever looking for my son I just had to call Teela, because they were always together. And to think some thought she might harm him.

When Teela finally reached fifteen, she broke a disc in her back. My vet advised that though her heart was still strong, my girl was now blind, deaf and so arthritic her joints were failing her. It would be kinder to put her to sleep. It was the hardest day of my life when we said goodbye.

For many years, I could not even think of adopting another dog. No one could ever replace my best friend. But now, almost twenty years later, I have a beautiful staffy called Jill. Unplanned, I got her as a puppy when I was suffering severe depression. My marriage had ended after eighteen years, I had allowed my husband to put us so far into debt we were going to lose our home, and the kids and I were facing living on the streets. To cheer me up, a friend asked me to go with her to a neighbourhood party. When we arrived, I spotted a litter of young pups playing together. I stopped to look at them and one came over to me. The owners were amazed – they said that particular pup didn't usually go to anyone. Jokingly, after a few drinks I asked if they 'did layby'. The next day I was surprised by a knock at the door – it was the pup's owners with 'my' little girl. They said she was meant to be mine – I could pay what I could afford.

Jill fits into my slower lifestyle as if born especially for me, yet when I look into her eyes I behold the same love that I used to see from Teela shining back at me. She loves my boys but has a special bond with my eldest son Alec, and I like to think Teela was reincarnated to help us through more of life's difficult times. She is always there for me, and I will always be there for her.

Janette, New South Wales

How One Cat Healed My Heart

I was never a cat person. We always had dogs, and as far as I was (and still am) concerned, the bigger and goofier they were, the better. Cats were just small, wicked little creatures that used you for what you had, then ignored you. Who would want one of those?

My opinion stayed the same for nineteen years until I looked after a friend's cat for a few weeks. One purry little headbutt later, and I was completely hooked. Afterwards, convincing the rest of the family that we needed a cat was easier than I thought it would be. So the first little kitty soon joined us – a grey ball of fluff named Kahlia. Kahlia was quickly joined by Clawedia (named for the cuts she ripped into us on the journey home) and, six months later, Shiba (because she liked sleeping on my Toshiba computer).

Kahlia was a bright ball of energy – hysterically funny and a pure joy to have around. Tragically, she was taken far too soon when, at barely one year old, she slipped out a door that was accidentally left open and was killed on the road. I was beyond devastated. I had lost animals to disease before, which was heartbreaking, but the agony I felt at losing my little grey angel was horrible. I declared to my family that day, '*No more cats!*' I could not possibly fathom ever going through such grief again. No way were any more cats entering our house.

My declaration lasted less than a week. Kahlia left a giant hole in our lives. Clawedia and Shiba are gorgeous cats, but they're quiet and keep to themselves – Kahlia was lively, loud and demanding. I missed being followed around and meowed at every two seconds. I decided that, okay, we could *probably* look at getting another cat, and pretty soon. I had to admit we had room, and could offer a loving home to a cat in need.

We started looking on PetRescue for a rescue kitten. My next new rule was *'No grey cats!'* Kahlia had been my Lady Grey, my angel, and another grey cat would be an insult to her memory. One cat soon became possibly two kittens – so they had each other to play with. The older cats probably wouldn't want a little kitten hassling them to play, right?

We enquired online about a few kittens, but none were right for us. Some were too skittish for our household, others a little older than we wanted, and some just didn't sound like they would be a good fit for our lifestyle. Our next step was to check with different vet clinics. Perhaps they had kittens for adoption? We struck out – none had what we were after either. Almost giving up, we made one last phone call, to Baldivis Vet Hospital. Yes, they had kittens! Three bottle-raised babies, in fact. They had been tossed away at a local tip, found and rescued. Gorgeous, lively babies. Ready to be rehomed!

'Wonderful – what colours?' I asked.

'Grey and white,' came the reply. Oh dear.

My parents and I decided to 'just go and have a look'. When we arrived, a vet nurse led us to a back room where three tiny balls of fluff were let out of their cage. And really, that was it. Five minutes with those little ones, all spindly legs and fur, and the decision was made.

'So, which one will you be adopting?' the nurse asked when she returned.

'All three,' I said. Yes. All three. In our infinite wisdom, we decided it wouldn't be fair to take only two and leave one lonely sibling behind. So three it had to be!

The little souls who came home with us that day are Silvia, a short-haired female; Gidget, the tiniest thing on earth; and Spike, the biggest kitten, a furry demon child. I admit, my favourite at first was Miss Gidget. She required more attention than the others – I gave her extra food and fattened her up. She had a urinary tract infection and a hernia, was unwell after being vaccinated, and the fur on her back end took ages to grow properly.

Fate had other plans, though. With five cats in the house, there was one cat who, early on, decided he was having none of me picking 'my' favourite cat. So Spike picked me. I was chosen as 'his' from around four months of age. He followed me everywhere, constantly cried for attention and always had the spot nearest to me on the bed.

Spike became a very special piece of me – my big, fluffy, grey boss cat – and the household bully. Spike is vocal, sits on command, walks on a lead and frets when I'm not around. He takes up my attention on a near-constant basis. He is incredibly jealous of my poor dog, who he will torment if he feels it's necessary! Spike also likes a good chat – his big, loud meow bursts through the house whenever he is called. Spike is also the king of accessories – he owns far too many collars and bowties, and has to wear a different one every day.

Spike's next 'trick' will be as a lifesaver, hopefully. He is going to become a kitty blood donor, along with two of his sisters. My mother came home from work one day where she had been told about a woman who had tragically lost her cat. The kitty had become ill very quickly and needed a transfusion. The only compatible feline blood donor was over an hour away. Unfortunately, the cat just wasn't strong enough to survive the trip. Saddened, I looked online to see what made cats suitable blood donors – size, age and health were the major factors. Spike and his sisters are the ideal age, are up to date on their vaccinations and are indoor-only kitties. They will go into the vet soon for some blood tests, to make sure they're completely healthy, and will be 'blood typed' – the same way humans are – so that their type can be kept on file. If a cat gets sick at our vet, and one of ours has the matching blood type, we will get the call that our kitty's help is needed and in we will go!

It's been almost two years since my gorgeous Kahlia left me, and nearly two years since a grey fur ball forced his way back into my heart. I still miss Kahlia; she was a once-in-a-lifetime cat. But Spike, and all the other furries I share my home with, keep me going. I never regret bringing the three siblings into my life so soon after losing Kahlia. Adopting them was, and still is, the best decision I ever made. Some may say it was too soon, but it was exactly what I needed. What better thing to treat grief over one furry friend than with the love of another?

Spike isn't Kahlia – he is no replacement for her, and never will be. He still has the best spot in my bed, and is jealous of any other man in my life. But Spike will always be my number one. Just don't tell the dog that!

Krissii, Western Australia

A Dog Left to Die

In January 2011, a very underweight, dehydrated German shepherd mix was found by a ranger in bushland in western Sydney. The dog had been tied to a tree and left to die.

From Blacktown Pound, where the dog was first taken, he was immediately transported by a volunteer, Jan, to German Shepherd Rescue NSW. Jan named him Hope because she could only hope that he would survive. Volunteers were shocked by the dog's condition. He had extreme hair loss and his dry skin was covered in callouses. His tail was badly docked and there was a large growth on his side. He was not desexed and covered in fleas. It seemed probable that he was another unwanted car-yard security dog left to perish – an often hidden tragedy in Australia.

The emaciated boy was taken to a vet, where he remained on a drip for several days. But being deprived of food and water in Sydney's fierce summer heat had taken its toll and Hope teetered between life and death. Even when he was released by the vet and relocated to kennels, the dog did not thrive. It was as though he no longer cared about life. He had given up.

'There's a perfect family out there somewhere looking for you,' Jan promised Hope, desperately trying to give him the will to live. 'Soon they'll come and take you home.'

In December 2010, our German shepherd, Toby, died after a battle with cancer. Our family was devastated, especially our youngest daughter Jacqui. Toby was Jacqui's dog and had been with her for more than half her life. Jacqui decided that we would not own another large dog for at least six months, but she did agree to foster a dog, so I contacted German Shepherd Rescue.

Within days I was told about a shepherd mix, Hope, and a young purebred male, Ace. I could choose either to foster but was left in no doubt that Hope's need was desperate. They sent me two pictures: the first one stunned me; the second one broke my heart. Hope's eyes spoke volumes to me.

At the kennels, our first sight of Hope filled us with horror and sadness. He couldn't stand or even lift his head to eat. This beautiful big dog, just a bag of bones, had lost the will to live. We had made our decision. They asked us to think it over and come back, but we refused to leave without him. He needed a chance to be shown that the world could be a happy and loving place. As he was unable to walk, we carried him to the car and he travelled home with his skinny head resting on Jacqui's knee.

For the next week, we helped Hope eat and drink and carried him out to go to the toilet. Jacqui slept by his side every night. Eventually, he was able to walk a little further every day; his eyes shone and the boy we first met who had lost all hope had come alive. His coat began to grow thicker and shinier, and his little docked tail would wiggle constantly. Soon he was able to go outside by himself and started playing with toys. His appetite returned and we had to be careful to continue small regular meals so as not to damage his organs during recovery, and for him to not gain weight too quickly. To give him some exercise and to help build up his wasted muscles, we would take him to the local off-leash park where he would chase and return balls to our hands. We discovered he knew the commands 'sit', 'down' and 'stay', and he walked extremely well on a lead. Sadly, this indicated he was probably not an abandoned car-yard dog after all, but possibly once a family pet.

One day, Jacqui announced his name would be Bailey. We knew this was the name she had been keeping for a new puppy once she had come to terms with the loss of Toby. Smiling, I then knew that Hope-now-Bailey would be staying with us forever.

Bailey weighed just 12 kilograms when he was rescued from Blacktown Pound. He now hovers around the 30-kilogram mark. Today Bailey is a happy dog who constantly smiles, wiggles his bum and loves company. He is obsessed with water, which my vet feels is quite normal for a dog that nearly died of dehydration. Despite his starvation, he has never shown any signs of food aggression and is very gentle with people and other animals. Bailey's first official day out in public was at the RSPCA's Million Paws Walk in May 2011. We did the short walk and he behaved impeccably.

Despite the suffering humans put him through, Bailey is the most loyal, loving and gentle dog we have ever known. We still foster other dogs and cats in need, and he has always been welcoming to all animals coming into our home. I know, however, that he would protect Jacqui with his life if he had to. After the grief of losing Toby, the utter joy and love she feels for this boy has also given new meaning to her life.

Bailey has rescued our family as much as we have rescued him. He is our true rescue dog.

Sue, New South Wales

CLEVER CREATURES

◇◇◇◇◇◇◇◇◇

Animals aren't just loving and loyal, often they're talented too! The pets in the following pages – be they TV stars, brilliant artists, exceptional performers or caring therapy dogs – have tapped into their inner prodigy.

Rembrandt the Master Painter

What do you get when you cross a paintbrush with a pooch? The answer is Rembrandt, the German wirehaired pointer!

Last year, an 'impossible' dog was surrendered by his owners to Animal Aid in East Gippsland. Having a tendency to destroy things, he was reported to be a 'juvenile delinquent' and wasn't considered rehomable by many, unless he received significant rehabilitation.

But as Animal Aid's East Gippsland Shelter Manager and a seasoned assistance-dog trainer, I could see that this dog was capable of great things. I was going to *work* with this energetic young boy, not put him to sleep.

I had an idea this canine could become a great therapy dog, but I had to put him through some tests first to make sure. He really excelled with a couple of tests in particular – they included 'targeting' (touching a person or object, with either mouth or paw, in a specific spot as directed), and connecting with children. This showed me that this dog had great potential, and it was a natural progression to teach him to paint using targeting. It also helped me think of the perfect name for this talented boy: Rembrandt, of course!

Rembrandt soon learnt to touch the paint on the canvas with his mouth, and then move his head up and down and left to right, resulting in a beautiful work of art. He manages to spellbind children as well as the elderly, as they all love to watch 'the artist at work'!

Fast forward twelve months and, in addition to creating masterpieces on canvas, Rembrandt plays a toy piano and puts smiles on the faces of everyone he visits in his community. This amazing dog is now also the star of two children's books – *Rembrandt* and *Rembrandt Finds a Friend*. The story of his arrival at Animal Aid is told in the first book, while the second book tells the story of Monkey, a rescued cat who is now Rembrandt's 'brother' in real life.

Rembrandt has since been adopted by Metung couple Mick and Lorraine. They take him regularly into the local retirement villages where he and the residents create works of art together.

At one nursing home that he visits regularly, Rembrandt has a very special friend called Bob. Some time before they met, Bob suffered a stroke that left him unable to speak, and he became increasingly withdrawn and depressed, rarely communicating at all. Miraculously, on Rembrandt's first visit to the home, Bob became very excited and animated to see the four-legged guest. At last Bob was interacting with someone – a dog! Tears rolled down Bob's face as he patted and hugged Rembrandt. Now, Bob looks forward to his friend's weekly visits with joy, and he is always the first person that Rembrandt approaches when he walks in. It is a beautiful friendship, and is the perfect example of how a therapy dog can change people's lives. There is never a dry eye in the room when Bob and Rembrandt greet each other.

Rembrandt generates such happiness wherever he goes – his zest and enthusiasm for life and his presence create an electricity that is palpable. He has given so much pleasure to so many people.

And to think Rembrandt could very well have been put to sleep at a shelter or pound that didn't care. After all, his previous owners said he was unmanageable. But pet ownership is a partnership. Rembrandt just had the wrong owners, and was waiting to show the world everything he had to give.

Luis Marquez, Animal Aid, Victoria

◇◇◇◇◇

Not Another Statistic

Just before Sahara was due to be killed because 'her time was up', foster angels Colette from Victorian Dog Rescue and Karen from Rural Rescues went to visit Mildura Animal Shelter.

Sahara, a little brown-and-white koolie mix, had been found wandering near the Victoria–New South Wales border and taken to the local pound. She was put up for rehoming, but was unfortunately too frightened for anyone to be interested in adopting her.

Colette remembers first meeting her: 'I peered inside the pen and saw a small, mostly white dog slumped against the side mesh. When we made eye contact I was struck by her one piercing blue eye (the other was brown) and her perfect, gleaming face. She moved closer to me and extended her paw, trying to touch me. I moved away quickly because there were so many other dogs to visit, but I couldn't get her out of my mind.'

Colette arranged to foster the timid Sahara, and a couple of weeks later they both came to visit us at one of our herding workshops. These workshops are for working dogs that live in the city, to give them a shot at what they were originally bred to do. We also test working dogs that are rescued from pounds for their suitability to be rehomed in a working situation.

Colette took Sahara into the herding yard to introduce her to the sheep. Sahara was very nervous and didn't want anything to do with these big woolly monsters. She sniffed the ground and looked away, as if she had no interest in herding at all.

I decided to jump in with her to see if I could spark a little bit of her herding instinct. I ran towards the sheep and with a little encouragement she was soon rounding up sheep with a look of sheer enjoyment.

I'd never seen such a transformation! All of a sudden this little dog took on a whole new personality. Her energy and joy were infectious and I couldn't help but sweep her up for a cuddle. I'll never forget the massive grin she had while she was nestled in my arms. This moment was pure magic and captured by a photographer who was visiting that day.

For the next few days I couldn't get that little dog out of my head and decided to apply to adopt her. Within a week, Sahara and I were driving home to her new life.

Everyone who met Sahara loved her, and not a day went by without her making me laugh. She was definitely a special little dog. I felt honoured to be her guardian, but at the same time felt that she was way too special to keep all to myself.

We kept up her training and socialisation to help build her confidence and overcome her fears of people, children, other dogs and cameras. We worked her very hard but she thrived on the challenge. She loved doing anything you wanted her to: if you asked her to swim or dive into a pool, hop on a horse, learn a new trick or round up sheep, she would do it, with a smile, every time.

Sahara's love for life never ceased to amaze me. We even started her own Facebook page to share her experiences and show the world how wonderful a rescue dog could be. Sahara was now a rescue ambassador!

About six months later I was approached by Jetpets Animal Transport to help them find a dog that would be suitable as their mascot. It didn't take me long to decide to put Sahara forward. Even though she was still a little timid, I knew she could handle it. Once the Jetpets crew met Sahara they fell in love with her, just like everyone else. Now Sahara had a job!

Her first of many photo shoots proved she was a natural in front of the camera. Thank goodness we did that training. Whenever a camera was aimed at her, she posed like a canine version of Marilyn Monroe. She loved the attention and would go through her repertoire of poses like true star.

Soon after, Jetpets had a great idea to produce a fun video that would give some insight into travelling with pets, as well as raise awareness of rescue animals around Australia. The plan was to travel around the country to visit shelters, rescue groups and a couple of celebrities along the way. Sahara was incredible. She performed every task with ease to the amazement of the film crew, the producer and even me. Within a few months the 'dogumentary' film *Tour De Woof* was released on YouTube. What a hoot!

Over the next year Sahara attended many events to publicise animal rescue. Sometimes we would not be able to move for the flood of people that wanted a photo taken with Sahara, and she was always very obliging.

Being a dog trainer and behaviourist, I have met many wonderful dogs, but no other canine has touched me like Sahara has. And to think she almost became another pound statistic.

David Higgins, Diggers Herding & K9 Education, Victoria

Compassionate Karma

I was blessed with Karma just over a year ago. She was just two-and-a-half, and had been rescued from Sandown Veterinary Clinic by the dedicated people at Greyhound Safety Net. Karma had been taken in there by her racing owner to be 'put to sleep' – we assume because she had started to lose races. She'd had three different racing names and her front long teeth had grooves in them, probably from chewing her cage wire in stress.

Fortunately, Karma soon realised she was safe with me. The colour of a tiger, dark brindle with a light-brown stripe, this gorgeous girl came to work with me, slept with me and eventually, after about three months, was able to walk within close proximity of my two ageing Abyssinian cats. (I call them the Aby*ssassin*s – they rule the roost and she knows it!)

One of our regular outings is to visit my Great Aunt Lucy (who is ninety-two years young) at her nursing home. Aunt Lucy adores Karma. They just look into each other's eyes as Karma rests against her. This brings so much peace to my aunty, whose health is declining rapidly.

One day at the nursing home, an old gentleman asked if Karma would visit his bedridden wife. They had had to give up their beloved dogs due to their weakened state, and missed them terribly. Karma is not always reliable with strangers, men or women, and actually growled at the man when he bent down to say hello to her. I explained that this was her way of saying she felt threatened and wasn't comfortable with him just yet. Perhaps her previous owners or trainers had yelled at her, close to her face; her troubled past is all so unknown.

I took Karma into his elderly wife's room. She was in bed and unable to sit up. When she saw Karma, she smiled weakly. I felt confident that Karma would recognise that this lady was very ill and so I allowed her to walk up to the bed.

Karma is a tall dog, so she was able to rest her face gently on the old lady's outstretched arm. They looked into each other's eyes and then Karma gently nudged the lady's cheek with her big wet nose. We all had tears in our eyes at this touching moment. The old lady was too overwhelmed to speak.

Her husband was deeply grateful and asked us to visit again. We have since been to see his wife a couple more times and on each visit I know Karma brings her some comfort in her final days.

I am amazed by Karma's compassion. I've watched her nestle up to a tiny chick that was injured; she allows babies and toddlers to hang onto her while they find their feet; and she even shares her bones with other dogs. I have taken her to Buddhist blessings and she lies still beside me and listens to the monks. I meditate with her by my side and she never moves until I am finished.

I cannot imagine my life without Karma in it. Each day I wake to see her sweet face and feel happiness to witness her eagerness and constant joy in everything she sees. I look at life through her eyes and see wonder everywhere. She runs to me when I come home, she welcomes all my guests and I laugh so many times each day at her antics – especially when I see her creative sleeping poses.

Several times I have come close to adopting another greyhound – they are such smart, low-maintenance beings and every day I learn more about this kind and unique breed. Greyhound Safety Net does such a wonderful job – thankyou, all, for my Karma.

Annie, Victoria

◇◇◇◇◇

Shadow the Dancing Dog

'And the winner of the "Starters Heelwork to Music" section is . . . Shadow!'

Little did I think when I first met Shadow – almost three years earlier – that together we would be winning dancing awards! Me, dancing with a dog?

It all began with a phone call and the familiar words: 'Is that Husky Rescue? There's a black-and-white male at the pound. Can you take him?'

Sighing, I replied, 'Bring him down on your next trip, and I'll find a home for him,' while I did a mental shuffle, trying to work out how to slot another lost soul with an unknown history into our household without too much disturbance.

On the day Shadow arrived, when the transporter pulled up and the car door opened, out bounced a Siberian husky–border collie mix. To our absolute amazement, this dog was gorgeous, with bright, inquisitive eyes of vivid blue. He bounded over with a wagging tail to meet his new people. We were instantly taken aback by his optimism and love of life.

While Shadow was in foster care with us, on a whim I took him to the Beginners' class at the Queanbeyan and District Dog Training Club Assessment day, where he was placed third. I would have loved to keep Shadow, but the pressure of conformation shows and obedience trials with our own special huskies meant that Shadow would have to move on.

Soon after, the perfect adopter applied to meet Shadow – David, a distinguished but disabled Vietnam War veteran. David was looking for a '24/7' dog, a role that Shadow was very enthusiastic about. It brought both of them companionship and many happy times as they took their daily exercise around the beachside neighbourhood near Newcastle, stopping to chat with old and new friends alike.

As David was on crutches and with limited mobility, Shadow learned to press against his side to help him remain upright, and was reliable about providing this assistance wherever it was needed. This special dog became his human's constant bedside companion, sitting or lying close beside David with his gorgeous blue eyes fixed on his face – willing him to get up and out as their days together progressed to months and the bond between Shadow and David grew.

Tragically, and with little warning, David died in his sleep after Shadow had been with him for almost a year, and again he was without a home. However, it gladdened me that David had known the devotion and companionship of this special dog for his final days, and that Shadow was by his side when he passed.

I too had recently suffered a loss, with the passing of my very special performance husky, Taxi. There was, however, a silver lining to these two unhappy events – Shadow and I could be reunited.

From the first day that Shadow returned to us, I threw myself into grooming, exercising and training him. Shadow was grieving for David, and me for Taxi, so this daily therapy helped us both. Shadow was a willing and able trainee, and soon I decided to enter him for a doggy Endurance Test, comprising a 20-kilometre run, with willingness tests prior to and after the run. I accompanied Shadow on my bicycle, giving him encouragement and guidance as we went. After successfully completing the test, Shadow is now able to append the special letters 'ET' to his name!

And so on to our next adventure – Dances with Dogs! This is a relatively new sport, with the objective of showcasing the dog to its best advantage, 'performing to music in a creative and artistic manner'. Together we learned tricks like doing circles, leg weaves, spins and rapid changes of direction, as well as walking sideways and backwards – in time to the Del Shannon tune 'Runaway'. We entered our first competition towards the end of 2012, and were described as an 'Astaire with an ageing hippy'! Regardless of whether or not that was a compliment, earning two first places together and Shadow's first Dance title was a wonderful surprise!

But the result of any competition or trial is not what matters to me. What is important is the journey that Shadow and I take together to reach that level, and how we have helped heal each other.

Shadow the Dancing Dog is home at last, and is staying forever!

Mara, New South Wales

Mr Charisma

The Animal Protection Society (APS) has had many wonderful success stories over the years, but one of the most unusual would have to be the remarkable rags-to-riches tale of Shadow the cat.

Shadow came to APS in late 2011. We really do not know very much about his previous life, but what we do know is quite sad. It seems that he had been living on the streets for some time, possibly most of his life. A kind elderly gentleman had been feeding him whenever he could. However, he realised that Shadow could not live rough forever; he clearly needed medical care and was in constant danger from dogs and cars. Eventually, his guardian angel bought Shadow in to our shelter.

Shadow was probably only about three years old at the time and soon became a favourite of all the cat carers and volunteers. With his distinctive big, boofy head, he was not only much loved but also well known by all at the shelter.

Of course, not being desexed, he needed to be neutered. He also required some urgent dental work on several chipped and broken teeth, and a course of flea and worm treatments. In short, Shadow exhibited all the signs of having lived a very hard life. But that would soon change.

After a month or so, Shadow was in good health and in no time was running the shelter – well, the cat section. You never really needed to look for Shadow because he was always lying on the table under the tree, holding court with the other cats and keeping the carers and volunteers in line.

Then, in 2012, we received a rather unusual request. A film crew was in Perth to make a new Australian movie called *Ragtime*, and they needed to find about thirty cats for a night scene. Well, wouldn't you just know it, Shadow turned out to be the star. Somehow he knew how to find his way into every single shot. The film crew and actors all fell for him. In fact, the female lead in the film would have taken him home if her apartment had allowed animals!

The movie is still in production and we cannot wait for it to be released. We are hoping that Shadow's scenes don't end up on the cutting-room floor, although it is hard to imagine they'd edit out such a handsome boy with so much charisma.

Then, not long after his brush with stardom, Shadow found a new home. A lovely couple came in to the shelter, sat with him and were soon smitten with this charming softie. Shadow's days of going hungry and being alone are well and truly behind him. He now spends his time curled up on his owners' bed or bathing in the sunshine, all with a full belly. We will have to wait and see if he gets any more movie offers, but until then he will just kick back and enjoy the good life.

Lynn and Sandra, Animal Protection Society, Western Australia

Ted Helps Save a Species

Though thin and abandoned, the bull–mastiff mix smiled his droopy-lipped smile, wagged his whole body and folded into the arms of our four-year-old daughter, Tess.

'He's so brown and cuddly, I think his name is Teddy Bear,' she said, stroking him.

We'd spotted this big dog with a wrinkled brow and sad eyes on the Geelong Animal Welfare Society (GAWS) website, and we just had to meet him.

The staff at GAWS told us he had been found abandoned and starving, and wandering the streets of Lara. Brought in to the shelter, Ted was nursed back to health and put up for adoption.

It was love at first sight, and we knew that Ted had found a home with us.

Our family is a little unusual. We run the Conservation Ecology Centre (CEC) at Cape Otway on the Great Ocean Road and this has all sorts of implications for a new dog like Ted. As well as fitting in with two existing canine family members (a regal old border collie and an enthusiastic eighteen-month-old German shepherd), Ted also had to learn how to deal with a mob of wild kangaroos (don't chase); orphaned koala joeys (keep quiet and give them space to recover); visitors (welcome politely and don't see them off the property); snakes (stop whatever you are doing and sit down); and a little girl (keep her close but don't squash her, and let her go to kinder).

The challenges and opportunities this environment presents for a dog are immense, but in the two months since we adopted him, Ted has done incredibly well. Already we can't imagine the place without him!

One of the CEC's major programs is the conservation of the tiger quoll, the largest remaining marsupial predator on the Australian mainland. Though once common throughout the Otway Ranges, tiger quolls have become increasingly rare and are now in danger of extinction in this region.

For nearly a decade, there was no confirmed evidence of their presence in the region, until last year when the CEC team found scats (droppings) in two sites and undertook DNA analysis with CESAR, a genetics laboratory in Melbourne. This analysis confirmed that the DNA was from tiger quolls and provided evidence that, though facing many challenges, they are still surviving in some areas of the region. Hooray!

Scat detection provides important information about where the tiger quolls are still surviving, so we can better target conservation efforts. However, finding the scats in the first place is quite a challenge. To solve this problem, the CEC has developed the Otways Conservation

Dogs project, a team of community volunteers and their dogs (of all breeds, shapes, sizes) on a quest for tiger quolls. The dogs and their handlers are being trained by specialist instructors from South West Victorian Dogs to move quietly through the forest, detect tiger quoll scats, and then alert their handlers to the find by lying down silently alongside them, thus having minimal impact on the wildlife and the environment.

Ted has begun training with the team and is proving to be a natural and intelligent pupil. His obedience instruction is coming on in leaps and bounds – quite literally! As his bottom enthusiastically hits the ground for a 'sit' or he searches through a range of scents to find 'tiger quoll', Ted's zest for life and eagerness to please is truly heart-warming. He is particularly helpful at events, happily meeting great crowds of people and other dogs to share the conservation message (and the occasional sausage!).

Despite his shaky start in life, and though it is only two months since his adoption, it feels as though Ted was always destined to be a part of our family. He has folded into our lives just as he folded into Tess's arms on that first meeting. Ted seems to completely understand the importance of his role as the newest Otways Conservation Dogs member. His body is no longer bony but muscular and strong, his brow no longer wrinkles in worry but in deep concentration, and his droopy lips now constantly smile. And his smile is widest when he is lying on the grass in the sunshine, with his very own little girl.

Lizzie Corke, Conservation Ecology Centre, Victoria

My Horse, My Teacher

I started Horses Helping Humans six years ago quite by accident.

As a child, I'd spent all my spare time with my horse, Lady, attending pony club and then show jumping and eventing. In my twenties I began a long career in the fitness industry on the Gold Coast, which left me no time for horsey matters.

In 2001, I was busy running a fitness centre, instructing and delivering a program to help instructors recognise eating disorders and exercise addiction when I was diagnosed with early-stage breast cancer. It was a huge shock. I opted for a double mastectomy and took a long, hard look at how frantic my life had become.

It was time for a change. I decided to move to Tallebudgera in the Gold Coast hinterland, and to go back to my previous love – horses. Mindy was the first to join me – a beautiful white miniature pony, almost big enough to be classed as a Shetland (and as an extra surprise, she was in foal).

I was thinking of going into competition again and began looking for a riding horse when I saw a demonstration of natural horsemanship. This includes 'working at liberty', where all interaction with the horse is done with no ropes or halters in sight. I was so moved by seeing the beautiful connection between horse and human that I ceased my search for a competition horse and found Sunny, my quarter horse, to begin learning natural horsemanship.

It wasn't long before I began to notice changes, not just in the horse, but within myself. I became calmer, more patient and more assertive, and learned how to use my body language to gain respect and establish boundaries. I learned how ineffective negative emotions are when working with a horse, as the horse will reflect them right back at you, and that if you settle your frustrations it settles your horse. It occurred to me that these insights would also work beautifully with people.

At that time, I was still working part-time in the fitness industry, instructing and running a course for women on self-esteem, body image and boundaries. I was scheduled to conduct a workshop at a local café in the valley when at the last moment I decided to take Sunny with me. I made a little round yard with tape under a beautiful old fig tree and as the women were arriving I could hear them saying, 'Why on earth is there a horse here?'

When I got to the boundaries component of the program, I asked them to join Sunny and me under the tree, as I wanted to show them what saying 'no' looked like. I proceeded ('at liberty') to ask Sunny to back away from me simply by adjusting my body language.

As he began to quietly back away from me I said, 'This is what "no" needs to look like. It's not just a word, it needs to be a projection of your body language,' and some of the women started to cry.

One of them said, 'We've been told over and over that we need to learn to say "no", but this is the first time we've ever *seen* what it looks like.' They were amazed to learn that people who lack confidence often introvert their body language as they say no, which can give a message that they can be talked into saying yes.

One of the ladies attending the workshop was the head of a big organisation that works with disadvantaged youth. She commented that this demonstration would be a powerful tool for teaching students effective communication skills. Within two weeks she had every youth support coordinator from local high schools enrol in a workshop with me. From there I have never looked back.

Word quickly spread to other youth organisations and, to fast forward, our 'Horse Whispering Youth Program' is now a registered charity and can only operate with the support of funding, sponsorships and donations. In addition to working with young people, we are now hosting family-focused workshops to help improve communication within families, as well as team-building workshops for corporate groups.

Of course, none of this would be possible without my amazing horses: Sunny, Mindy, Yogi and now Larry. I adopted tiny Larry two years ago from a wonderful woman who rescues horses from the abattoir. I named him Larry as we were both 'happy as Larry' that his life had been saved.

Larry is our heart-melter, but his gentleness means he copped some bullying from the other ponies at the start. Yet his confidence continues to grow. It is truly beautiful to watch him interacting with students who are at odds with the world, showing them how being calm and gentle generates so much more respect.

Sunny is the dominant one, and the head of the herd. It's common to see him following students around the yard and nuzzling them gently. He happily works at liberty and is great at teaching students who lack confidence to set clear boundaries.

Mindy's favourite pastime is standing under the tree while the students brush her long mane. Her expression of disgust when she is led out to the round yard for some exercise is hilarious. The students have to ignore her manipulative 'poor me' expression and let her know gently and firmly that it's time for some work, but that she will be rewarded afterwards with a mane brush.

Yogi, the escape artist, can pick most gates and shed bolts and is easily bored. He amuses himself by stealing hats, sunglasses, paperwork, you name it – if it gets left around, it's his. When Yogi works at liberty with me, everyone has a giggle as I enter the yard with my little chubby brown pony to do the same things I have just demonstrated with majestic Sunny. Yogi demonstrates beautifully that it's okay to be different – we just have to find something we are good at and channel our energy into that.

Successful communication depends on appreciating that everyone is different. Teaching children about personality differences is made so much easier with the horses, as I can ask them which one they are most like. This is much less threatening than asking, 'Do you get frustrated easily and can flare up quickly?' or 'Do you feel uncomfortable around aggressive people?' or 'Do you have a problem with focusing, keeping still and staying out of trouble?'

We use the ground skills of natural horsemanship to teach calm assertiveness, focus and respect. It's not long before students are circling their ponies, popping them over jumps and backing them through obstacles.

We finish all our courses with an agility show and presentation of ribbons, trophies and certificates. It is so touching to see students who have been bullied in the past proudly receiving a trophy for directing big Sunny through the agility course. And equally moving to see a student with anger and aggression issues gently coaxing little Larry through the obstacle course.

I love my beautiful ponies. They have taught me so much about trust and respect in communication, and it has been a privilege passing this teaching on to so many people.

Sue Spence, Horses Helping Humans, Queensland

A Port in the Storm

When I first saw a photo of Storm the cat in the Mildura Animal Shelter, where he had turned up as a stray, I knew it would be difficult to find a home for him. This big, boofy boy wasn't the prettiest of felines, and his ripped ears suggested that he'd been involved in multiple brawls. I've been a cat rescuer for several years, and I'm well aware that the smaller, daintier and prettier cats are almost always favoured by adopters. Black cats aren't popular either, the old superstitions still withstanding. But I also knew I couldn't leave Storm to die in the rural pound just because he wasn't cute. I had to find a foster carer for him.

Enter the wonderful Chloe and her partner John. As Storm had not yet been desexed, he was a handful at first, but his testosterone soon settled down after 'the snip'. As soon as he was ready, I listed him for adoption on PetRescue, but had no response. A couple of weeks later, PetRescue contacted me to say they were having a special promotion for barn cats, and asked if I had any suitable cats needing homes. Did I ever! Storm would be perfect as a barn cat, I realised – he clearly needed a home where he wouldn't come across too many other cats, and he could freely exercise his feline instincts and keep the mice and rat population under control. So I put Storm forward as an ideal candidate, and he was soon starring on the home page of PetRescue!

The universe spun its magical spell, and an email arrived, from Jenny, in rural Victoria. Her old barn cat was ready to retire inside, and between the horses and the chooks, the mouse population had escalated uncomfortably. A kitten wasn't going to be right for the role. It was a job for an independent spirit – a tough, brave, outside cat. 'Would Storm fit the bill?' she wrote.

My heart leaped. Storm Boy would be perfect!

But as Jenny was about to discover, what we really need and what we think we need are often two very different things!

What I didn't tell Jenny was that Storm liked his creature comforts – the bed and couch – and he wouldn't want to sit outside on his own all day in a barn. (Never let the facts get in the way of a good adoption!) But I did tell her that he loved people and she assured me he would have plenty of company, even if he was an outside cat, so I thought we had nothing to lose and crossed my fingers. Despite the distance from Storm's foster home in Richmond to Jenny's place, a two-hour drive east of Melbourne, I was determined to get him down there, so I spent hours on the phone, email and Facebook organising his transport.

Within a week of arrival at his new home, Storm had taken possession of not only the barn, but the back verandah, the dogs, the people, the farm workers, their caravan, the backyard, and, yes, inside the house too. Storm Boy had arrived!

But what he really took possession of were Jenny's riding lessons.

Jenny teaches a very unique approach to horsemanship at her home. When she is teaching people, one of the first things that she does is take the rider off their equine friend and gets them to do an exercise on a static vaulting horse, set up in her hay shed. It can be pretty intense work, Jenny tells me. How does Storm fit into all this, though? Our boy has decided to take it on himself to be the comedic relief that brings balance to these riding sessions whenever it's needed. On the first day of Storm following Jenny and her student out to the hay shed, he jumped up on the vaulting horse with the young woman – to much laughter and surprise – and made himself at home there for the rest of the lesson. Jenny also reports that, months later, whenever anyone is taking themselves too seriously during a lesson, Storm appears in the shed, leaping up onto the vaulting horse with the student, reminding everyone to lighten up.

And while he is a very smart cat, Storm is obviously quite geographically challenged. He gave Jenny a bit of a fright the other day when he went wandering down to the back paddock with one of the staff and didn't come back. She had to call the neighbours, hoping someone had seen him, only to be told that Storm had 'knocked' on their back door earlier that day, asking to be let in! Maybe that's how he got lost in the first place?

No more wandering away from your barn from now on, Storm Boy – you've found your forever home, and have helped me prove, yet again, that there is a home for every rescue pet.

Vivienne, Victoria

SPECIAL SOULMATES

◇◇◇◇◇◇◇◇

Humans and animals often form lasting bonds. A cuddly guinea pig can be a beloved pal, or a troublesome donkey can turn into a true friend. As any loving owner can attest, pets can be much more than 'just' pets: they can be the closest of mates too.

Bruce the Black Labrador

When I was a little girl, my mother would tell me wonderful stories of her childhood on the Mornington Peninsula by the sea, growing up with a garden full of 'all creatures great and small'. Between the flowers, fruit trees and leafy vegetables scampered the large family's four-legged and feathered friends – dogs, cats, chooks, ducks and many a coastal bird.

My mum, Peggy, and her four younger brothers and sisters thrived in this garden and invented many an escapade. But the most extraordinary always involved their black labrador, Bruce, who strayed into their lives as a scruffy lost puppy and promptly became one with Mum.

The little black bundle of fur was handed to ten-year-old Peggy by some friends: 'Do look after him, won't you dear.' She looked into his eyes and he returned her loving gaze. The two were soon described as 'the girl with her tail-wagging shadow' and as long as they were together, they were happy.

The hardest times were when Peggy had to go to school. Bruce would be locked in the garden, barely comforted by his other furry friends, and Peggy would shuffle sadly off. But by the afternoon Bruce had somehow wriggled out and would be waiting by the front gate for her return.

But the daily separation of school was nothing compared to what poor Bruce would go through should Peggy wish to board a bus to go shopping. Somehow Bruce *always* escaped from the garden, bounded down the street after his 'mum', and would then attempt to get on her bus. Peggy could not find a way to tell her darling boy to stay home, so it was up to her younger brothers and sisters to devise the solution. As Peggy got on the bus, her siblings would 'round up' the dog into the nearby phone box and quickly shut the door – as if he was a sheep and they farm dogs. After the bus had disappeared from view, a sad Bruce would be safely released into the children's arms.

Bruce might have adored Peggy, the love of his life, but all boys need their mates. For Bruce it was his brother-in-antics, Colonel Percy – a magpie, of course. Poor Percy had been injured as a baby bird, and Peggy, with the growing puppy Bruce by her side, had nursed him back to health.

To everyone's surprise, Colonel Percy decided to stay in the garden after he had recovered from his early misfortunes. For him the friendship he had forged with Bruce was better than freedom, and their hilarious skit 'Dog Kills Bird' drew crowds. The play was performed frequently to Peggy and her family and their gobsmacked guests.

The plot would start with dog and bird confronting each other – dog barking, bird fluttering. Dog would overwhelm bird. Bird would pretend to be in horrified shock and fall on his back with claws stiff in the air. Then the labrador would wrap his great wet mouth around his co-star and drag him around the garden, with the poor bird cawing piteously. There would be one last terrible cry, and Percy would pretend to be utterly dead. Everything would go quiet and Bruce would hold the moment as the audience began to cheer, clap and holler. Colonel Percy would then emerge unharmed from Bruce's mouth like Houdini from a trap!

But there came a remarkable day when Bruce's outlandish ability to escape captivity and create havoc exceeded everyone's imaginings. Maybe Colonel Percy was distracted for a moment – learning his lines for a new show? – because Bruce's attention was again on his beloved Peggy.

The day had finally arrived. Peggy was to be bridesmaid at a wedding! She put Bruce securely in the back garden, rubbed his tummy and wished him a lovely day. Then she dashed inside to change into a frothy dress of rose-pink taffeta and, flushed with excitement, left for the church.

It was as exquisite as she hoped it would be. The organ played uplifting hymns, the vicar was ready with prayers, and the candles were shining. The bride blushed, the father beamed. Each of the six bridesmaids shyly hoped that they would be a bride soon themselves, and the sweet flower children – with their tiny bouquets – tried hard to behave.

Then silence fell. The vicar began, 'Dearly beloved,' and was moving to 'Who gives this woman in marriage?' – even though it was completely obvious – when a commotion at the church door made him hesitate. In bounded Bruce the black labrador, full of life and love. Maybe if he had been searching for the blushing bride things would have been seen a little bit differently. But no, he was not. It was a bridesmaid he was looking for! His shock appearance affirmed that the day's love story should be about him and his one-and-only, Peggy.

There were gasps from the congregation and little squeals from the flower children. Bruce leapt about, scattering the bridesmaids in all directions. He found Peggy and, as if they had been separated for years by war and tempest, jumped lovingly and frantically all over her. Of course his paws were dirty; yes, saliva dribbled from his panting mouth.

'Who owns this dog?' gulped the vicar, red-faced and eyes popping.

'I do,' whispered Peggy.

And then dog and girl stood to the side, breathed deeply and regained composure. Years later Mum told me that her friends had a very happy marriage. It hardly surprised me for the young couple's nuptials were blessed by the most vivid example of love . . . a dog reunited with his beloved.

Rosemary, Victoria

The Jaz Connection

I'll never forget the day that Jaz came into my life.

I'd always loved kelpies, but could never have pets due to rental restrictions. When I finally acquired my own home, I was determined to adopt a rescue pet. I searched the Saving Animals from Euthanasia (SAFE) website for five months (they have eleven branches all over Western Australia), and while I saw some lovely dogs, one adorable face kept coming back to me: it was Jasmine, a kelpie mix.

So in June 2012, with the help of Gail, Amanda and Sue from SAFE Broome, six-month-old Jasmine made her way from sunny Broome to wild, wet and windy Perth to start her new life.

I remember Jaz's little face when I picked her up from the airport. I opened the travelling crate and she emerged with a cautious tail wag and gently licked my hand. I popped the lead on and guided her to the car. Without hesitation she jumped right in, positioning herself on the back seat so she could see through the windscreen.

When we got home, I let her out of the car, gave her some water (she was very thirsty from the flight), and let her roam around her new backyard. I joined her after I'd made a pot of coffee, and just sat outside quietly sipping my drink and watching as she slowly became accustomed to her new surroundings.

After about an hour, something magic happened. Jaz walked slowly towards me and sat facing me. Without a word, I quietly put my coffee cup down and leant towards her. Her (still baby) dark-blue eyes looked straight into mine and the connection was instant. I felt my heart contract and my soul begin to tingle. I reached out, cupped her face and gently massaged her soft ears. Jaz closed her eyes and sighed a deep, doggy sigh. In that moment I realised that not only did this beautiful little creature need me, but I needed her.

One of the first things I noticed about Jaz was her incredible fearlessness. It wasn't bravado or aggression – simply no fear. On her first weekend in Perth, the city experienced one of its wildest electrical storms in many years, with howling winds, pelting rain and the kind of thunder and lightning you'd expect from a tropical storm. Jaz just looked up at the sky, watched the sound and light show for a moment, let a few raindrops fall on her face and then went to back to chewing her bone. I couldn't believe it. Most dogs I'd known had hidden under beds and been terrified of thunder.

Once, at our local park, a large dog hurtled towards Jaz, pulled up and began barking aggressively in her face. I was just thinking I might have to jump in and rescue her when I saw her response. She looked at the other dog, looked at me, then looked again at the other dog as if to say: *What the . . . ?* Being a young dog I thought she might be submissive, but she simply ignored him.

After two months, my fiancé moved into my home (now our home) and brought with him Sophie, a gorgeous pugalier who is also a rescue dog. Twelve-year-old Sophie is a genteel soul and has been teaching Jaz some beautiful manners, in particular not to 'round her up' as if she were a sheep! They get on so well – they play together and even sleep in the same kennel. They are great company for each other and have become firm friends.

Jaz is now over a year old, and a precious member of our little family. We are so blessed to have found her, and to have met the lovely team at SAFE Broome. Thankyou Gail, Amanda and Sue. You are truly amazing people. You've brought such joy into our lives and for that we will always be grateful.

Pia, Western Australia

Saving Each Other's Souls

I will never forget the shock I felt when I first saw Layah.

I initially found out about the suffering of dogs in the pet-shop trade when I heard about Oscar's Law, a campaign to end puppy factories. Horrified, I had to help. I started spreading the word in any way I could about boycotting pet shops selling factory-farmed puppies, and encouraged my friends and family to adopt from rescue groups instead. I got to know a lot of local organisations in Perth, and I fell in love with and adopted an old gent called Basil from Staffy and Bully Breed Rescue, or SABBR, as it is affectionately known.

Basil was a ten-year-old, pure white, deaf boxer that had been surrendered to the group by his owners due to neglect and health issues. Sadly, not many people want to adopt the oldies, but I already had an older dog of fifteen years, Hollie, and I thought they'd make great companions. I also have four rescue cats and eight former battery hens – a very busy, happy home of saved souls!

Sadly, dear old Baz only lived for three months in my care due to a bad fall and the years of neglect that had taken a toll on his general health. I knew the best way to honour his memory was to open my heart and home to fostering other homeless pets. So when I received a call from SABBR soon after Basil's death, asking me if I could foster a rescued pup, they didn't have to ask twice. The next day, Tuesday 22 May 2012, was a date that would change my life forever.

A few days earlier, a young boy called Brandan-Lee had seen a sign: 'Puppies, free to good home' outside a house on his way home from school, had gone in, gotten one and taken it home. After seeing the terrible condition the puppy was in, his concerned mother, Melissa, spoke to a friend who she knew fostered for SABBR.

SABBR's founder, Rebecca, stepped in and, along with Melissa, managed to negotiate with the owner's grandmother to relinquish the rest of the amstaff–kelpie mix pups. The parents were never seen, though the grandmother revealed she'd only been feeding them boiled white rice. The pups were too young to be away from their mother, but with the owner refusing to hand her over, we had to do what we could to save her young.

Equipped with puppy food, blankets and a few toys, I was in no way prepared for the shock of what was waiting for me when I went to collect my foster dog. At just four weeks of age, my puppy was so undernourished that every little vertebra on her spine was exposed. She weighed a mere 1.5 kilograms. She was very tiny, very ill, and had no idea what food or even water was. How was she even still alive? If we were to save her, she would need round-the-clock care over the coming days.

From the moment I brought my pup home, still in shock at the neglect of the small angel in my arms, I swore to her that she would never want for anything again. I taught her how to eat and drink and made sure she had everything she needed, with the help of SABBR and its amazing volunteers.

And as the days turned into weeks, and weeks into months, I realised there was no way that I could ever let my little girl go. I had named her Layah, after Princess Leia in *Star Wars*, but with a spelling all her own. Layah looked to me for everything and only felt secure when I was around. She was terrified of life. Any new piece of furniture (even a simple tablecloth) would frighten her, as would strange or new people, the rustling of leaves and the world outside the front door. All of these things would have her shaking for hours, the hideous effect of her four weeks of neglect and deprivation.

I knew then that she had come to me for a reason. I was the one who promised Layah she would receive everything she needed, so I decided there and then I would set the wheels in motion to ensure her daily life wasn't filled with fear. This is when Danielle Brueschke's K9 Positive Works came into our world.

With Danielle's positive behavioural counselling, Layah is now learning that not all people are bad, and the world isn't as scary as she once thought; most important of all, she has learnt doggy manners! We have a long way to go . . . many things still frighten her, but she is not alone. We will deal with these demons together.

So from a scared, sick, emaciated pup that weighed 1.5 kilograms at a mere four weeks of age, Layah has blossomed into a happy, healthy young lass, who now weighs a healthy 25 kilograms and is about to celebrate her first birthday. I may have rescued her, but she ended up rescuing me. Don't all rescue animals end up rescuing us? Rescuing gives me a feeling I find hard to express. To know you have given an animal a second chance at life and a voice that can be heard is a feeling like no other.

Layah is the beat to my heart, the light of my life and the saviour of my soul. I wouldn't change her for the world and it's both a gift and privilege to now be able to walk this road with her by my side.

Ju Netto, Western Australia

◇◇◇◇◇

The Girl with the Rat

'Sorry, we don't take rats,' the pet shop assistant explained kindly. I'd been looking at fish in my local pet shop when I overheard a teenager asking the staff if they could take her pet rat Ruby for her.

The young girl sounded upset, so I wandered over to say hello. My brother had owned mice when I was younger, and I had a soft spot for tiny, furry critters in cages, but I'd never planned to get any. Still, I found myself asking if I could hold Ruby – so-named because of her enormous, dark-red eyes – and as the girl passed her over to me, the little one instantly ran up my arms and snuggled into my neck.

Fifteen minutes later, I walked out of the shop fishless but with a new furry friend, a little house and all the accessories I would need to keep her healthy and happy.

It was only when I got home that I realised I now had the perfect recipe for disaster: a rat, a cat and a dog. But the introductions went surprisingly well – everyone sniffed each other and then got on with their business.

I was still living at home at this stage, so I guess I should have asked Mum first. She turned out to be less than thrilled about having a rat, but we talked about it (well, I got a talking-to after letting Ruby run up her arm!) and Mum eventually agreed.

I soon realised that Ruby didn't much like her cage, preferring to be out with me. She would just sit on my shoulder or curl up in my jacket pocket. She went everywhere with me. And when I discovered that she was happy to come with me on a tiny lead, we even went for little walks. People loved it!

I became known as 'The Girl with the Rat', and my mum began to warm to my little friend. Ruby had a lovely personality so it wasn't hard to see why Mum started liking her. Every time we watched television, Ruby would be on the couch with us. We were a great little team with the cat and dog as sidekicks.

For about eight months Ruby amazed the people she came in contact with and converted a lot of people into becoming rat fans – especially me! I was smitten with my little girl and I knew she loved me too.

One morning, Ruby did not pop her head up to say hello as she usually did in her cage. I found her shivering and looking very frail. I rushed her to my vet who was close by. She took her in and said they would give her some fluids and see how she responded, but that they didn't know what was wrong with her. I said goodbye to Ruby and went into work quite upset. My boss understood my distress, as I always talked about my funny rat and had taken her into work a few times.

I rang the vet on my lunch break to see how Ruby was going. 'It's not looking good,' the vet said.

I tried to concentrate on work, but after an hour I just had to see my little girl. My boss kindly let me go.

Twenty minutes later I walked into the clinic and the vet nurse had a big smile on her face. She said Ruby had made a sudden recovery and was up and walking around! I was shocked. She took me in to see her and sure enough, there was my little mate standing on her hind legs saying hello. She still had a drip in, so I was extra careful when picking her up, but she ran straight up my shoulder and snuggled into my neck. I gave her a kiss and she licked my nose, then I put her back in her hospital cage. I was so relieved my Ruby was going to be okay.

I said goodbye to the delighted staff and told them I'd be back after work to pick her up. I started to drive away and was on the road for about a minute before my phone rang. It was the vet's number. I thought at first that I must have left something there.

'Nat, I'm so sorry – but Ruby just died.'

'What?' My mind raced. I was so confused. 'What happened?'

'As soon as you left, I went back to check on her and she had curled herself up into a little ball and passed away. She must have waited for you so she could say goodbye.'

I was devastated. But deep down I felt very blessed and grateful that Ruby had given me the chance for a final cuddle.

I buried her in the garden and we planted a rose bush on top. Ruby's rose is still going strong. Even ten years on, I still miss my little mate.

Natalie, Victoria

My Travel Companion

The old cats stared at me aloofly, treating my attempts to coax a friendly response from them with disdain. I had come to the local shelter convinced that an older cat was what I needed; a cat that I would care for, and who, in return, would brighten up the dull, chilly, English winter days. My home, Beauvale Lodge, was beautiful, but I was missing the clear blue skies of my native Western Australia.

'Puss, puss, puss!' I cooed, and finally evoked a response. Not from the older cats, but from a kitten in a nearby enclosure. I turned to see a white belly pressed up against the bars of his cage, all four limbs clinging on at shoulder height. A soft but shrill 'Meow!' emitted from the disproportionately large head of this small creature.

I was told that the malnourished kitten had been wandering alone in neighbouring fields, and had evaded rescue attempts for days. He looked barely five weeks old, and kept meowing at me. He was impossible to ignore, and soon in my arms. I had come to the shelter to adopt an older cat, and left with a tiny kitten.

At home, he spent his first day in hiding. By the second day, I had decided on a name for him – Kato. I am a big Bruce Lee fan, and Kato's distinctive symmetrical tuxedo markings made him look like he was wearing a mask, like his namesake in *The Green Hornet*.

Poor Kato was so weak he couldn't balance well enough to wipe his face with a front paw. Gradually, however, he grew stronger and became more outgoing. He loved tearing up and down the stairs and sitting in the bay window, watching walkers and their dogs go past. He was quick to learn, coming when called, particularly when the call was 'Kato, would you like some brushings?'

Kato soon became the close companion I had wanted, and when I decided to leave England and spend time with my parents in Singapore, there was no question – Kato was coming with me! Fortunately Kato had already decided he was an indoor cat, and was happy in my parents' ninth-floor flat. Just as well, for he was far from impressed by the stark contrast between the cold English snow and the heat and humidity of Singapore!

There were no more walkers and their dogs for Kato to sit and observe, but my dad became an acceptable alternative. Each day I'd emerge from my bedroom to see Dad on his lounge chair reading the morning paper, and drinking his breakfast cup of tea. Kato always sat watching him on the next chair, and would not move until Dad had finished his cuppa.

After six months in Singapore I moved to Perth – and of course international jetsetter Kato accompanied me! However, due to quarantine laws, he had to spend a month in Byford Animal Quarantine Station. I visited as much as I was allowed, and spent the entire two hours of the visiting period sitting with him on a mat in his enclosure. It was a relief to bring him home.

We have travelled more than 15 000 kilometres together over the decade we've known each other, and Kato has been a great friend to me in all our journeying. He remains my sweet and sensitive fur kid, possibly the most kissed cat in the world. He has grown to love my husband as his new dad and is purry-smoochy towards him too. Kato now lives with his little cat brother, and doggy brother and sister, but there is no doubt who the boss is – Kato!

Ju, Western Australia

Puny Paw Prints on my Heart

I'm a rat lover from way back. At the time I adopted Pixie, I had an ageing male rat called Aerian and a young male called Alchemy. I had picked out my first rat, Pilgrim, for my eighteenth birthday; having previously kept mice as pets I needed a more interactive choice. I love rats for their personalities: each rat is an individual, but they are always friendly and happy for human attention. Their intelligence and ability to learn new things intrigues me.

I searched PetRescue and found three lovely females needing a home. I contacted Porsche's Rescue about adoption and was referred to Kristen who was fostering the girls. It was love at first sight. There was Rania, the cinnamon rat (Rani for short, or lovingly Rannikins); Tina, a black berk girl I renamed Baghira or Baggy for short; and Kinka, a beautiful buff self. Of course I adopted all three of them!

Kinka had a kinky tail from maltreatment in her previous home, but her name just didn't seem to fit her quirky personality, so she became Pixie.

From the beginning, Pixie was a real character. She'd climb right up on top of my head to make sure I knew she was there, and every night during free-range time she would sit under my knees while I was in bed on my laptop and groom my ankles with the occasional climb up to my face from under the doona to give me kisses.

One night I was making a cargo net for the rats to climb on and was attaching ropes to the top bunk of my bed when Pixie spotted me. She'd been doing her own thing until she realised that what I was doing was much more fun. She decided to 'help' by chasing whichever rope went in her direction. This led to a whole new world of play, where I taught her to chase things and bring them to me (fetch) and to play tug-of-war.

Another night I had my friend Bernie over and noticed a rubber wristband on his key ring attached to his belt. Pixie was out on her evening adventures so I tapped on the band and told Pixie to get it, and said to Bernie, 'Now watch her chew it up!' My friend looked at me in disbelief, then at her and said, 'Don't even think about it!' He was attached to that band; it held some kind of meaning to him.

She ducked behind me and watched Bernie, whiskers twitching, while she plotted her attack. When he turned away, she darted out, grabbed the band and started chewing. She's such a smart cookie. I thought it was hilarious, but Bernie was far from impressed! Of course, he would have laughed if he'd seen Pixie's next trick. She'd noticed the cord to my laptop-cooling fan was excellent chewing material, and had gnawed right through it!

Pixie was great with the other rats. She was always cuddled up asleep in a pile of her friends, and never got involved in any arguments or food stealing from others.

After a couple of years with my special girl, I learned that she had developed an inoperable cancer. I wasn't sure how much longer she had. I came home from work one afternoon and she was very lethargic. I looked into her lovely eyes and she met my gaze. It was her way of telling me it was time.

I took her to my vet Sharon immediately. She was so gentle with little Pixie. She agreed with me that it was kindest to let her go.

I was blessed with Pixie for just two years, from May 2010 until June 2012. To remember her forever, I had her paw prints tattooed on my arm. She was and always will be my Pixie-bubba.

Julz, New South Wales

◇◇◇◇◇

SPECIAL SOULMATES

Copper and Me

Where I grew up in the Middle East, dogs were always hated, but I never understood why.

As a teenager I'd had a dog named Fox. He was so loyal, and I loved him heaps, but one day my father took him away from me. He said the dog never listened to anyone but me. I missed him terribly, and dreamed of getting my own dog one day.

When I came to Australia in 2001, I realised I could make my dream come true. I was planning to buy a dog from a pet shop, but a friend told me it would be better to adopt a dog and she told me about the PetRescue website. I searched online for a while until I found a dog that looked just like Fox from my teenage years.

He was a ten-week-old shepherd mix at Hawkesbury Animal Welfare League. Called Copper, he had a shiny, golden coat like Fox had had. I felt very excited as I drove in to see him. But when I got there I found that I was not the only one wanting to meet this beautiful dog. Still being a pup, there was a lot of interest. My heart sank.

We all went into an open area where they let the puppy out for a run and then an amazing thing happened. He ran straight to me and sat between my legs! From that moment, he stole my heart. I bent down and stroked him and he looked up at me and I felt a special connection. Of course, the other people were not very happy, but when they saw our instant bond and that I wanted to adopt the pup, they wished me luck.

He is four years old this month, and is my soulmate. We completely understand each other's body language. I know when he wants to play, when he is upset and when he wants affection. And he knows when I want him to go to bed and when it is okay to start eating just by looking into my eyes. He even gives kisses to people I like and growls at people I don't feel comfortable around. He just *knows*.

Copper understands almost fifty commands and hand signals, including 'under', 'over', 'up', 'sit', 'drop', 'stay' and 'speak'. I trained him myself, after I learnt how from online classes. Because of the bond we have, he will do anything to please me.

An example of Copper's trust in me is how he learned to like the water. For a long time, he was afraid of it and wouldn't go near it. Then one day my friend and I took Copper to a dog park where they can swim. All the dogs were playing in the lake and having such a good time – all except Copper! I wished he could swim too. It was the middle of winter, but I waded into the water to encourage him to come in with me. Despite his fear, he trusted me so much that he followed me in and was soon paddling around. He now loves the water so much that I can't get him out of it!

Copper grew to become a social and charming dog. Like Fox of my childhood, I love him dearly. Not only does he look after me, he also looks after my wife and children.

Omar, New South Wales

Little Boy Blue

It's hard to believe that someone would surrender a pet on Christmas Eve, but that's what happened to the beautiful British blue shorthair at Cat Haven in December 2010. Not only that, but he had been given up because he was 'too shy'!

On 28 December, my mum and aunty visited Cat Haven and later told me about the little ball of fluff that was hiding behind his litter tray. It had been his first birthday, and I decided I had to meet him. It had been two months since my beautiful adopted cat Muffin had been tragically run over and killed, and the house felt quiet having only one little furry face in the house – my lovely rescued boy Tiger, a shorthaired grey tabby (part Abyssinian breed). Tiger also seemed to be missing the presence of another feline in the house, so we were all ready to adopt a new fur baby.

I went to meet the shy little boy the next day and fell in love with him straight away. He was beautiful with his blue–grey fur and amber eyes. The fur on his back had not been brushed, so he looked like a cuddly sheep. And even though he was timid and stayed wedged behind his litter tray, he still let me tickle his chin. I saw this as a good sign.

At first my mum and I were worried about how Tiger would react to another male cat in the house, as he was used to a female, so we decided to think it over for the night. The next morning, we drove straight back to Cat Haven – we knew we wanted him.

When I got to his pen he came out from behind his tray and sat there, as if he was waiting for me. And he even let me cuddle him. That first cuddle was so lovely – he's very soft.

I named him Ollie, and he is certainly not shy now; he just needed love. After a good brush his thick double-layer coat was gleaming. It's been wonderful watching him come out of his shell and blossom into a happy, confident cat. He brings so much joy to our house every day with his cute little face: the way he plays soccer up and down the passage with his ping-pong balls (and hides them in odd places); how he jumps around in the garden trying to catch butterflies; and the way he gives me boofy nudges and taps his food bowl when he wants me to hurry up with his dinner preparation (blues love their food). But his special trick is getting up on the toilet and flushing it!

He doesn't 'use' the toilet – he just sits on the lid (which I leave down all the time now in case he falls in!) and presses the button a few times and listens to the water run! He has either learnt this himself or his previous owner taught him. He's such a clever little boy – he thinks it's great fun.

Ollie and Tiger do enjoy each other's company, although they will never admit it because each one likes to think he is Top Cat! But we have no problems with them fighting or clashing.

I couldn't imagine life without my little Ollie. I am so glad we adopted him. I now volunteer at Cat Haven WA, and I love seeing cats and kittens find their fur-ever homes just like Ollie did.

Alicia, Western Australia

◇◇◇◇◇

A Lover, Not a Fighter

I knew from the moment I saw her in the pound. She had big, soft brown eyes and chocolate-coloured fur. And she wiggled her bum so much she was hitting her tail against each side of her kennel, over and over again until it bled.

I was at the pound to put up posters for a rally I was organising against breed-specific legislation. I had been intensively volunteering for animal rescue and advocacy groups for a long time, specifically working with bull breeds and pit bull types. I've met hundreds, if not thousands, of them, but something about this chocolate girl spoke to me straight away that day, more than any other.

She 'roo-rooed' at me to get my attention and I could see that she was stressed. I spent about twenty minutes with her. When I found out she was a microchipped stray I felt relieved and sure her owners would collect her. Since breed-specific legislation was introduced, pit bulls are often not microchipped by their owners, to avoid detection. Surely the fact that she had a chip meant someone loved her and would come for her!

Two weeks later I received a text message that her owner had been told that she was in the pound and would be 'put to sleep' if no one came for her because she was assumed to be a pit bull. They never showed up. The pound knows me well and knows my love for these dogs. The staff said if the rescue group I was associated with could take her on and have her breed and temperament assessed through the official channels, they'd release her to us. They knew that we found great homes for these types of dogs where they could shine.

The rescue group wanted to help, but there were no foster homes available. I was living in an apartment, which wasn't ideal, but couldn't bear the thought of her being killed purely for her appearance, so she came home with me. I was terrified she'd have separation anxiety and bark all day, or be destructive, but from day one she was calm and relaxed. We named her Cocoa. She didn't destroy one item of mine (and still hasn't, eighteen months later), she just collects my clothing, particularly shoes, and builds a 'nest' with them that she curls up in! The only issue was her tail, which she'd been wagging so much against the side of her kennel in the pound: it was a bloodied pulp by the time she was released. I had blood-sprayed walls for weeks until it healed. But she just couldn't stop wagging it when I came home from work, even though it must have been hurting her.

My partner at the time did not want a permanent dog and he told me from the start that we weren't keeping Cocoa; she was a foster pet only. Two months later, we broke up. We'd been together for four years and it was a sad time, but I knew this was my opportunity to keep this beautiful girl, if I could only figure out the logistics. How could I keep Cocoa in the apartment when I worked eleven-hour days and would have no one to give her toilet breaks in the middle of the day? I had a small amount of savings, and thought the chance was slim, but I decided to see some banks about the possibility of a loan to buy a house.

To my shock I was approved, and soon after found a house that would be perfect for me, Cocoa and my two cats. I can honestly say that I basically bought a house at that time *for my dog*. It was the best decision I've ever made.

My girl has been with me for eighteen months now and I just cannot imagine life without her. She makes me laugh hysterically every day with her antics – she really has a sense of humour. She gives me new bruises on my legs constantly by wagging her tail so hard against me, and she still 'roo-roos' at me when she's happy to see me. She loves everyone and everything and – to my annoyance – doesn't even let off one bark if people or other dogs come to the door. She just stands there, wagging that ridiculous tail of hers! I know someone's here because I hear it thudding against the wall. She canoodles with my cats on the rug and she loves nothing more than meeting up with her doggy buddies and having a play. She accepts foster dogs into my home (begrudgingly – it means she doesn't get *all* the attention!) and even when they have left scabs all over her neck from playing too roughly with her, she has never left a mark on them in return. She is the best couch snuggler and you couldn't get a better bed warmer in the winter.

People are *shocked* when I tell them Cocoa's probable breed. They imagine a pit bull to be what the media has told them they are – a snarling beast in a spiked collar on the end of a chain leash with a tattooed bikie on the other end. Instead they see me, a 4-foot-11-inch-tall female with no (visible) tattoos, and they see Cocoa's soft eyes and wriggly bum. We change perceptions wherever we go and I love that.

Adopting Cocoa was the best thing I've ever done, and my heart is already breaking for the day I lose her. She's a lover, not a fighter. She is a waggy, happy dog with soft brown eyes and a chocolate-coloured coat – and she deserves to live just like any other dog. The most dangerous thing about her is her wagging tail!

Melanie, New South Wales

Sheba, My Heart Cat

The very first night Sheba came into our care, I knew I wanted to adopt her.

Sixteen weeks old, she was one of many felines rescued from a house of almost forty. A few of those cats, including Sheba, were suffering from severe cat flu, and obviously had been for some time.

I've been a foster carer for Homeless and Abused Animal Rescue Team (HAART) in Western Australia for twelve months. We started fostering because we wanted to help the many homeless cats and kittens in Perth. Giving them a second chance at life by simply opening our hearts and homes to them for a short period of time is very rewarding.

As soon as one of my colleagues dropped Sheba off to me that August night, she immediately climbed into my lap to sleep as if to say, *Hello, here I am – all yours!* She'd chosen me.

Although Sheba had lived through many months of suffering due to human neglect, it had no impact on her love for people. But she was going to need a lot of help. Her first of many medical visits was an examination by an ophthalmologist. Sheba was infected with the herpes virus, a strain of cat flu. Due to many months without treatment, scar tissue had formed on her eyes and her third eyelids (yes, cats have three!) were fused in place, which made her eyes appear constantly swollen and red. Alongside this, her tear ducts were blocked, causing tear staining. The ophthalmologist sadly revealed they would be blocked for life and her corneas were scarred. Sheba had surgery to remove much of the scar tissue, however, which dramatically improved her vision. Her eyes may never look perfect, but at least she isn't blind.

We officially adopted Sheba only two weeks after she came to us, and still continue to foster cats and kittens for HAART. Sheba warmly welcomes all the foster felines that come through our home, and we have been woken on a number of occasions as she and the newbies play and run laps around the house at all hours of the night!

Sheba also has a very strong bond with two of our other cats, both of which are also rescues. One of them is gorgeous Angel, who came from the same house as Sheba, and was our very first foster fail. He's a white seven-year-old cat who is deaf, and once Sheba joined our family they immediately bonded – perhaps they remembered each other from their previous home, even though they had been separated for a number of months. The second of Sheba's feline friends is Rupert, a three-legged rescue, who was found dumped by a passer-by with his other siblings in a skip bin when he was two days old. They were handed in to a local vet where one of the nurses bottle-fed him. He had an infection on his front right leg that was so bad the only option was to amputate it when he was four weeks old. He came into our home a month later.

Our special Sheba has a number of quirky behaviours, one of which is her love for her little bell ball, which she carries around in her mouth while expressing strange muffled meows. We always know when we hear those that Sheba is not far away, playing with her special toy.

I see Sheba – and all our cats – as proof that abused or neglected animals can overcome the odds and become great companions – maybe even the best. Sheba has a wonderful nature despite her many ordeals. I struggle explaining to people just how much Sheba means to me, as many don't understand how you can have so much love for simply an animal. The best way to describe how I feel about her is that some people talk about having a 'Heart Dog'. . . Sheba is my Heart Cat.

Candice, Western Australia

⋄⋄⋄⋄⋄

Little Johnny

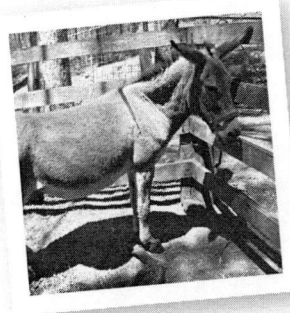

'It was a nightmare loading him onto the truck!' Jim told me over the phone from the Gold Coast.

When Jim's elderly mother could no longer care for her beloved (read 'spoiled and untrained') donkey, Jim had arranged for our sanctuary to take him. But Johnny was surprisingly strong and displayed much resistance to being loaded onto the coach.

'If this fella knew where he was going, he'd run into the truck and tell me to step on it!' mused the driver from East Coast Horse Transport.

Finally, they got Johnny inside with the other passengers, including a well-trained mule and many upper-class horses who seemed to be looking down their long noses at this common, disruptive hooligan.

At the border, the animals needed to be unloaded as all livestock and the truck had to be sprayed before entering New South Wales. Unruly Little Johnny was a perfect example of how badly an untrained animal can behave. He objected to everything and when it was time for him to be reloaded, he wasn't going back on that truck without a fight! Johnny tried every trick in the book: sitting down, laying down, kicking, charging and sprouting toes in the shape of grappling hooks! After several attempts, the driver called for back-up. In the end it took six strong men to get Little Johnny into the truck (mostly by lifting him!).

Next was the overnight stop where all the animals were unloaded to spend a comfortable night in fresh stables and have a rest from travelling. The driver would then clean the truck and prepare it for the next day. Little Johnny, however, was going to be left on board – no way was he coming off until he reached his final destination – and was tied up while the truck was cleaned. Then the driver gave him fresh straw and hay, unlatched him and opened up all the bays so he had the whole truck to himself. These are huge trucks, so Little Johnny had about four times the space of an overnight box stable on land.

Before departing for the last leg, the driver phoned ahead and told us when to expect our 'dear little pet'. We thought, *Gee, he must be a tiny little fellow*.

To our surprise, on Little Johnny (LJ)'s arrival to the Good Samaritan Donkey Sanctuary, he turned out to be a big, strong adolescent boy with appalling manners. Accustomed to getting his own way, he demanded attention and treats, pushing us if we didn't have any. And he was by far the largest donkey we'd ever had. This was going to be interesting . . .

The first week was horrific: LJ demolished stables, kicking in every wall and bending barriers. The vet had to sedate him so our farrier could trim his feet in safety without being hurled into space. While LJ was drowsy he was fitted with a heavy-duty collar, de-wormed, microchipped and given his shots.

Over the next few weeks LJ had to become very good friends with a huge corner post. You see, as we began handling him and carrying out his lessons, because of his strength we needed to tie him up to ensure he didn't break away. He learnt that when he was tied up he had to stand quietly and patiently, then he would be praised and released. But progress was slow. At only seven (donkeys can live well into their forties) he was powerful and intelligent and needed something to do – a goal in life. Although he had learnt plenty in his young years, most of it was bad. We knew it would take time to re-educate him and teach him to respect humans and accept them as the boss. He was actually a sweet animal, not mean at all, but just needed a firm hand to discipline him. Once trained, he would be a perfect example of just how lovely and practical big donkeys can be.

My daughter Sandy was determined to train LJ to stand patiently while being brushed, and to be led without getting overexcited and dragging his handler. However, his strength and pushy nature wearied her, and for safety reasons she only handled him with someone else present. Yet she persevered, and after several weeks we noticed positive changes. LJ was responding favourably to patting, cuddles and sweet talk and he was not squashing you between him and the fence when you didn't have treats. He had also given up arguing with the corner post, finally realising the post would win every time.

Things were looking up, and we felt confident that we would find a forever home for LJ. I spoke to Alan, who was already fostering two of our geldings, and asked him if he would be interested in a handsome big working donkey for treks. I explained that LJ was not the kind of donkey who could stand around in a paddock all day doing nothing. He needed a challenge, a job to do, and loved interacting with humans.

Alan has owned and handled horses all his life and has had donkeys for many years; he certainly did a great job training the two young geldings he got from us previously, both of whom had performed beautifully in their local Christmas pageants and other public outings. We were thrilled when Alan agreed to take LJ; however, we told him that there was only one hiccup – loading him into Alan's float.

'Not a problem!' Alan said.

I wasn't so sure; LJ was not your ordinary reluctant donkey, but I kept my concerns to myself.

Alan arrived late and not very happy. He'd had to load someone's uneducated horse onto a float all by himself. Meanwhile, our back-up helper had had to leave, which just left Alan, Sandy and myself to load LJ. *The poor bloke now has to load a donkey much worse than the horse*, I thought.

Alan went into LJ's box to introduce himself and 'have a little chat'. After a few minutes I opened the door and Alan walked a polite, well-behaved LJ right through the stables to the float. Sandy hitched the rope to his collar and, with a couple of firm pulls and a few words of encouragement, a hesitant but willing LJ followed Alan straight into the float and stood quietly while we closed him in.

I do not know what Alan said that day, but whatever it was, Little Johnny responded beautifully. What a great team they would be – Little Johnny and Alan, the Donkey Whisperer!

After Alan sold his trekking business, LJ went to live the life of Riley in Far North Queensland on a sheep property of 30 000 acres. He has a very important role there as a 'guard donkey', protecting sheep from dingos, wild dogs and other predators. If he has anything near as much 'attitude' as he once did, he'll be the best guard donkey anyone's ever seen!

Jo-Anne Kokas, Good Samaritan Donkey Sanctuary, New South Wales

MAKING A DIFFERENCE

◇◇◇◇◇◇◇◇

When an animal is granted a second chance, often it strives to return the favour. Rescue animals are the best advocates for those still in harm's way. Here we have a collection of pets who were lucky enough to escape cruelty and neglect and are now working hard to prevent other creatures from suffering a similar fate.

A Very Precious Cat

Each year, around seven million animals are used in Australia for research and teaching. Primates, dogs, cats, sheep, pigs and birds are all subjected to procedures ranging from observational studies to major physiological challenges.

When I tell people this they are shocked. But when they learn that most of the animals are either killed after the experiments are complete, or are on-sold to other labs for further research, they are truly horrified.

One of these animals, Leo, first came to our attention in August 2010. He had been part of a study aimed at improving surgical techniques for vision correction in humans. His nictitating membranes (third eyelids) had been surgically removed but, unlike several other cats in the study, he was not implanted with contact lenses, as he was part of a control group. Prior to this, he had been used in vaccination studies at another facility. After the closure of the research lab that used him, Leo was to be sold to another facility; however, fate stepped in and he was offered to a cat rescue group who then contacted us.

We met Leo on a cold, windy night in the freight section of Melbourne's Tullamarine airport. His sweet little face peered out at us through the crate and we were smitten. Approaching four years old, we couldn't imagine what this innocent animal had gone through. We could only promise that from that day forward he would be safe.

Most people are aware of the ethical argument against using sentient animals as mere 'research tools', but there are important scientific arguments, too. Animals differ anatomically, genetically and metabolically from humans, which means that any data derived from animal experiments cannot be applied to humans with sufficient accuracy. Because there are now new methodologies that can provide more predictive outcomes for human health, we believe what happened to Leo is outdated and should be consigned to the history books.

Following his ordeal, we placed Leo in foster care before beginning the search for his forever family. We wanted to ensure that he ended up in a home where he would be safe, loved and most importantly, valued as the precious individual he is – not a laboratory tool. We could not have hoped for a better outcome. Leo's foster parents Rhianne and Marty were so charmed by this little man that they soon fell in love with him and have now included him as a permanent member of their family.

Rhianne recently wrote to us:

> *Right from the start, Leo was so well behaved. He never made a mess outside his litter tray, never begged for food (despite his hearty appetite), and never climbed on counter tops.*
>
> *He loves his food and always acts like he's been starved for days at meal times. The cats have to be fed in separate rooms because Leo wants to help others finish their bowls. If given the chance, he approaches Alfie (a Devon Rex) and casually stretches out a paw into his bowl to hook some of his biscuits onto the floor. He loves parmesan cheese but will never beg or push. He just sits nearby and waits politely in case I want to give him some. He's such a good boy.*
>
> *Despite what he's been through, Leo has no fear of anyone. He stomps down the hallway to the front door to greet all visitors, slightly lowering his head and bracing for the full-body strokes that he just expects any stranger will dispense. He also loves children, and will jump up and sit on the couch next to young ones. He always tries to sniff my ten-month-old nephew's hands as he sits on the blanket next to him.*

Leo rarely meows, but uses his paws for communication. If you're standing near him and he wants something, he reaches out and either paws the air ineffectually, or literally taps you for attention. He stands on the kitchen bin and taps the door handle when he wants to go outside.

To Leo, the world is always friendly and interesting, which is remarkable considering his start in life. He has never killed in the garden. He sits and watches the doves with fascination but will never stalk or hunt. He's happy to watch nature and feel the breeze in his fur. He's also been an angel with all the foster cats that have passed through this house. Lacking in social skills, he immediately walks up and sniffs feline guests in the face, so has been walloped a few times by a stressed newcomer. He never bears a grudge, though. He will wait and try again later, ending up loving all the newbies, cleaning them and cuddling with them (especially Alfie who is permanently looking for warmth).

When we first fostered Leo, he was the cat that all my friends considered adopting. He has such a sweet, funny, curious, naive nature, and loves his routine and cuddles. No cat since has won so many hearts – even the hearts of sworn dog-lovers. No one actually took the plunge, though.

After we'd had him for six months, it hit me that a call could come at any moment from a stranger wanting to adopt him, and I knew we couldn't let him go. I had a distinct Leo-shaped impression on my heart!

In our work at Humane Research Australia, we spend our time speaking to politicians, researchers, students and the general public about the dangers of extrapolating data from animals to humans, and advocating for more humane and scientifically valid methodologies. We write letters and submissions and generally lobby for a change to the current system that is so heavily invested in animal suffering. Meeting Leo put a face to our purpose and reminded us of why we do what we do.

To this end, we're looking into producing small Leo toys to raise funds and awareness of animal experimentation. Keep your eyes open for him!

Leo is a very precious cat. He might only represent a tiny percentage of those animals who suffer every year, but that just shows the enormity of the situation. Each one of those seven million souls is just as precious and deserving as Leo.

Helen Marston, Humane Research Australia Inc., Victoria

The Race to Save an Old Soul

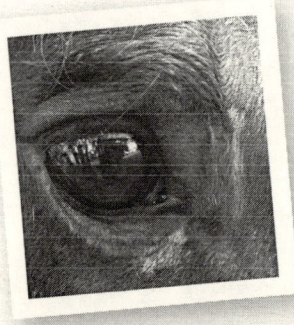

The sign on his pen read 'My name is Mate. I've served the family well and it's time for me to move on.'

He was at the Pakenham Horse Sales in extremely poor condition, old and forgotten. I watched sadly as people looked into his mouth, noted the condition of his teeth, and walked away.

I went into his pen. He hung his head low for a pat and followed me around. I noticed his front teeth were missing and realised, sadly, that he would probably end up with the men who buy horses for dog food.

I'd just walked over to look at another horse when I heard Mate being sold to a knackery for just $200. I was too late. With a heavy heart I watched him being loaded into the meat truck. He walked with dignity and grace.

That night, I could not sleep. I don't know if it was his sad eyes or his gentle demeanour, but I could not stop thinking about Mate. The thought of him being left to die made me feel sick. I had to do something.

The next day I began calling the knackery in the outer west of Melbourne that had bought him. After two days of persistent calls, I finally got through. I told them I wanted to buy Mate.

'He's dead,' the man replied coldly.

I couldn't believe he was dead already. 'For $400, is he dead?'

'Still dead,' he said smugly.

Almost in tears, I hung up. What now?

I did the only thing I could. I rang back. 'Six hundred dollars.'

A brief silence. 'He's alive. Hurry up and come get him.'

It was now Sunday lunchtime, and Mate and the other horses at the knackery were due to be killed the next morning. I called my friend Helena and asked her to help me get Mate out of there. We left at around 7 p.m. that night in a wild storm, not knowing how we could find him in the dark or even if we could get him onto Helena's float.

Around two hours later, we pulled up at the knackery. The smug man I'd spoken to on the phone was waiting. He took the money and pointed towards a nearby gate.

Heading over with my small torch, I opened the gate and walked into the darkness of the paddock. It was full of horses waiting to die. It was a chilling experience, and I felt sick to my stomach. And how was I to find my horse? Feeling overwhelmed with anxiety, I called his name. Did he even know his name? In less than a minute, a shadow moved towards me out of the darkness and put his head on my shoulder.

Mate.

It was a moment I will never forget. He had been waiting for me.

Without delay, I lifted the halter and he let me put it on with no resistance. Next, he walked straight onto the waiting float in the darkness, through the wind and pelting rain.

Driving home, the relief swept over me. Thank God I went back for him, as not doing so would have haunted me for the rest of my life. I'm so grateful to my dear friend Helena, without whom I could not have saved him.

Once home, one of the first things I did was change his name to Archer, after a brave, strong and wise toy soldier in a movie I'd seen. Those who had called him 'Mate' had let him down. He deserved a new, proud name and a new start with people who cared.

Archer was a pleasure to have around – a kind, gentle old soul – and stayed with me for two months. As I already had several horses of my own, I knew I could only be his foster carer and would soon have to find Archer a forever home.

My friend Catherine, who runs Harmony Reins Animal Haven, helped me by listing Archer for adoption on her website. We soon received a phone call from a group of friends who were dog and cat rescue volunteers, but who had always wanted to adopt a horse of their own. Could they meet Archer?

The day Liz, Lynda and Saskia arrived to see Archer, within minutes they knew he was 'the one'. He now spends his days on a picturesque small farm in the Yarra Ranges where he has blossomed. Gone are the protruding ribs and other signs of neglect; in fact, you might even call him a tad tubby these days!

His adoring new mums wrote me this moving note about Archer recently:

> *From the second we met Archer (now fondly known as 'Archie'), we knew that the only place he was going now was our farm. He resides alongside his other rescued friends: Roger the Ram; Gertie the Goat; his two girlfriends, Polly, the black thoroughbred; and Crystal, a beautiful white mare who was also in need of a peaceful safe haven.*
>
> *Archie will be surrounded by loving carers for the rest of his days. The day we gave him his first bath, he had no less than five women shampooing him all over! Quite the Romeo. He is*

a beautiful, gentle soul with a cheeky personality we all adore. For a senior citizen in his late twenties, he seems to be looking younger every day and sometimes gallops around his paddock with sheer joy. What a sight to behold!

He has certainly brought much joy to our lives, and helps complete the picture of serenity here. Everyone who meets Archie comments on how you can see his unique 'old' soul in his eyes.

Thankyou, Nadine, for your bravery and perseverance in saving Archie's life, and bringing him home to us.

Nadine, Victoria

◇◇◇◇

The Secret Cat

Three Christmases ago, my husband and I moved into a new house with our three dogs. Unbeknown to us, a secret cat that lived under the steps came as a free furry housewarming gift.

When we rang the previous owners, they said she was an outdoor cat and were concerned that she would run away if they moved her. As a seasoned rescuer and director of PetRescue, I knew she was right, so I agreed to let Secret Cat stay as long as she wanted.

Secret Cat wasn't feral, but she wasn't exactly tame either. She was somehow straddling the divide between wild animal and pet. I had her desexed and chipped, and for the rest of the summer she happily took up residence under our front steps.

I have no doubt her life became easier once we moved in. Over a period of time Secret Cat evolved from an untouchable, bitey thing to a meowing scratch-seeker who was happy to just chill with us.

She'd emerge from under the steps to greet me every morning, and I could even flea dot her without drama. But I overstepped the mark when I bought her a beautiful pink collar with a lovely pink bell. Secret Cat immediately took it off and flung it into the bushes. I found it and invited her to pop it back on, at which point she grabbed me by the scruff of my shirt, slammed me against a wall and hissed at me in a way that clearly said, *I'm not going to be wearing a collar, thanks very much!*

The day I stuffed Secret Cat into the crate for her first trip to the vet, she was equally disgruntled. Upon arriving back at her favourite spot under the steps, she flew out of that crate as if it were on fire, pausing only briefly to flip me the bird before vanishing.

I wondered if maybe that would be the last time I'd see her. But when I stood outside that evening and gently *tink-tinked* on the side of a can of cat food, there she was, throwing me daggers.

But maybe she did love us. Secret Cat did us a huge favour when our suburb became overrun with rats, keeping the areas she could access completely rat-free. It probably wasn't an intentional act of thoughtfulness on her part, but I appreciated it. So when the first really cold and wet winter nights rolled in, I took pity on Secret Cat in her box under the steps and bought her a dog kennel. Or was it a cat kennel? After a few days she stopped glaring at it as if it was going to eat her and began sleeping in it.

Over time I was hearing of many more semi-owned secret cats around Perth, and I stumbled on a study showing that 40 per cent of cat owners are secretly feeding a cat they don't own. It was heartwarming to know that compassionate cat-lovers across our country are giving outdoor kitties extra help. Wild, stray or homeless, whatever you call them, they're Community Cats. Inspired by the compassion of the community and my very own Secret Cat, I launched PetRescue's awareness campaign 'The Secret Cat Society' as a humane alternative to the common 'catch and kill' programs.

We launched the campaign in every vet clinic in Australia, and so far it's been a huge success, with councils also wanting to get in on the action, contacting us to request dozens more posters.

Sadly, Secret Cat is no longer with us to see the success of the program named in her honour. She had been moping around for a week and was off her food, but I'd assumed she was simply sulking about the wet weather. I called the mobile vet, as it was less stressful than a car ride, and he advised that I take her in to the clinic.

That day, I had no problem bundling her into the crate, which itself spoke volumes about how she was feeling. Our local vet confirmed that her liver had failed and advised that we put her to sleep.

It was only once she had gone that I realised just how big a part of our family life Secret Cat had become. We miss her cheeky greetings on the front balcony, and thank her for helping us discover the joy of being the caretaker of a Community Cat.

Shel, PetRescue, Western Australia

◇◇◇◇◇

The Great Escape

They named it 'Chicken Run', the largest farmed animal rescue operation undertaken in Australia. I called it 'The Great Escape'. For three particular chickens, it was the escape so few are fortunate enough to ever experience, and one that changed their lives – and ours – forever.

On 4 July 2012, Edgar's Mission Farm Sanctuary undertook the enormous task of rescuing 2000 battery hens. A farmer had decided to close down and didn't want his hens to go to slaughter. The situation was desperate – basically, the more hens they could rescue and find homes for, the more lives they could save.

Not long before that I had rescued my beautiful chicken, Ester, from dire neglect in a school, and her recovery had taken months. I knew that giving a home to ex-battery hens was not going to be easy, but I had to help.

My husband and I decided to make the trip to Edgar's Mission at Kilmore and give three of these warriors a home of their own. I'd known the chickens had been in a factory farm their whole life. I knew they'd bear the scars of living in a cramped cage. But as I walked into the shed housing hundreds of newly freed birds, I couldn't stop myself from crying. When you see animal cruelty up close, there is no denying it. Nothing can prepare you for the despair and helplessness you feel.

These were not your everyday, happy-go-lucky hens – these were prisoners of war. Everywhere I looked, I saw the brutality of a fierce battle. This is a species known for its preservation instincts, yet there were no winners here.

Many of the chickens' feet were deformed from standing without respite on a 45 degree-angled wire floor. Others were completely bald with bone-like stalks of damaged feathers poking out of their skin. Most had bright-red bare throats from having their necks constantly rubbing against the bars of their cage to reach food, water and air.

The signs of suffering were all over their bodies. Not even their beaks were left untouched. It is standard industry practice to trim the beaks of young chicks using pliers or hot saws to stop the chickens from pecking each other to death in their enclosures. Often the chickens go insane being in such cramped spaces; they attack each other out of boredom, lack of mobility and sheer madness. This had left several of the chickens with barely more than a centimetre of beak, while others' mouths were twisted and unable to close properly. These poor creatures stumbled around aimlessly, bumping into each other as they stared around the large shed. Some scratched in the straw for the first time, others flapped and stretched their wings, while many simply laid immobile in the small glint of sunshine that splintered through the window.

All this misery for the sake of an egg.

Three skinny, fearful chickens were gently placed into our pet carrier and we tenderly prepared them for the ride home. On the way, I peered into the faces of these little souls. Defeat stared back at me: sunken eyes, bowed heads, deflated bodies.

We were devastated for them. You hear stories about battery hens, but seeing their withered little bodies and how broken they appeared made it all so real. The entire trip home we were silent, thinking of all the millions of battery hens trapped in sheds around the world – never to find freedom; only knowing pain and misery.

That night we sat and watched as our little warriors became accustomed to their own special 'chicken rehabilitation unit', previously known as our bathroom. This was where the scars of the first eighteen months of their lives became the most obvious, and this is where they would begin to heal.

Queenie was the first chicken to be crowned with a name. She had an oversized comb, which looked like a giant crown, that covered the entire side of her face. *Queenie the Bantam* by Bob Graham is one of my favourite children's stories about a chicken who escapes from a farm and is taken in by a loving family. It seemed to suit her perfectly.

Like all the chickens, Queenie's throat was completely bare and red – it looked as though it had been scrubbed with dry sandpaper. Broken shards of tail feathers protruded angrily out of her skin, while several broken wing feathers dangled uneasily as she quietly walked around the bathroom floor.

Then there was Belle, named after the Liberty Bell to represent her newfound independence on the 4th of July; she was more confident and self-assured than I'd expected. Belle's awkwardly trimmed beak left her with a crooked grin and a mouth than didn't close properly.

The last little chicken was Ruby. Named after the ruby slippers in *The Wizard of Oz*, she had finally found her way home, but not before tearing around the bathroom in fear like a tornado. Dramatically underweight, her beak was severely short. She seemed to have trouble drinking. Aside from a few young feathers on her wings and back, she was almost completely bald. Her throat was stained red and dimpled with the buds of new feathers hoping to burst out.

The next day was a momentous occasion for all of us. This was when Queenie, Ruby and Belle would experience the most important moment of their lives – the moment they touched grass for the first time.

We set the carrier on our lawn and opened the door, moving out of the way so the girls wouldn't be intimidated. But the three hens dared not. Their eyes were wide and wild, their hearts beating with urgency and trepidation. Darkness, wire and constant noise had been the only home they'd ever known; this was the big open world, one they had never seen.

It was Belle who first lifted her head and took to her feet. Tempted by a bowl of fresh food placed at the entry of the carrier, she lifted herself cautiously and left the dark, cramped space behind. Ruby soon followed, tiptoeing up to the food dish, her feet touching the soil and grass as she ate hungrily.

Queenie remained silent, lowered in the back corner of the carrier. Her fear broke me, and we sat on the lawn looking in at her with tears streaming down our faces.

Confinement was an enemy she knew well; freedom was something new and frightening. Her eyes remained on the ground, her body completely still. We held our breath. It took Queenie over an hour to finally gain the courage to leave her cage and join the others.

Eventually all three hens stopped eating and started to soak in their surroundings. With each new gust of wind, they would all freeze – startled by the sudden sound and rush of air. They flinched at every movement or sound: branches swaying in the breeze, leaves falling from the trees, birds flying overhead. Everything thrilled them with terror and filled them with curiosity.

Queenie, Ruby and Belle all began to walk around with fresh eyes, taking in every detail of their surroundings. Their senses overloaded, their minds racing; with each cautious step the girls grew more curious and less afraid. And for the first time, Belle began to scratch with her overgrown nails in the dirt – using her natural instincts to search for grubs and bugs in the grass.

After all that time in a cage, all those days and nights in an artificial world, devoid of stimulation and unable to express their normal behaviours, these amazing creatures knew exactly how to behave in their natural environment.

A few hours later, we found the girls huddled up under our crepe myrtle. Covered in dust and soil, they had their first dust bath. Scratching, rolling and flapping in the freshly raked dirt, they savoured every inch of soil – getting it under their wings and soothing their dry, red skin.

It was a sight I will never forget. I silently promised them that they would never be deprived of such simple pleasures again and I would work to raise awareness for all chickens used for human purposes.

Over the next months, Queenie, Ruby and Belle's feathers began to sprout from their bellies and backs, and eventually over their necks. Each day, more brown-and-white speckled feathers emerged; their combs grew redder and stronger, and their eyes brighter and wider. It took over four months before they began to look like real chickens rather than shredded up, ragged dishcloths.

Egg laying has become a very special event in our household. The first egg wasn't laid for several weeks after the girls started living outside. One morning, Queenie and Belle were huddled up together; they'd been quietly clucking and making a fuss in their pen. I went to investigate, and there before me was a perfectly formed egg sitting on a mound of straw. It was such a wonderful moment because it was the first egg any of them had laid outside of a cage, and not on a wire floor.

Each hen has her own special nesting space in the garden. Belle likes to gently cluck to herself and dig a cosy hole under the magnolia tree where she leaves her eggs. Ruby prefers to hide under the azaleas and only lets Ester, our other chicken, come near her. Ester will flap around and cluck near Ruby while she's laying, letting us all know that something special is taking place. She then goes to check Ruby's egg once it's been laid. Queenie loudly and proudly boasts when she's laid under the bougainvillea vine and gets the dogs all excited. I often hear the dogs howling while the chickens crow in unison.

Watching these sacred rituals has made us realise how special egg laying is to a chicken. Belle, Queenie and Ruby have earned the right to keep their eggs. They now enjoy eating eggs by breaking the shells and scooping up the albumen, yolk and shell. It is nature's way of providing chickens with an extra source of nourishment, which they'd only occasionally receive in the wild, as they wouldn't lay that number of eggs naturally.

Being able to lay eggs was Queenie, Ruby and Belle's burden – the very reason why they were deprived of sunshine for so long. It's why they didn't know how it felt to roll in the dirt and have wind blow through their feathers. It's why they now suffer ongoing health issues: Belle has needed a hormone implant to stop her laying. Her reproductive organs have started to fail because her body had been unnaturally forced to lay so many eggs from a young age. Ruby, on the other hand, has respiratory issues caused from months of living in filthy, dusty, ammonia-filled air in the factory farm shed. We have spent a great deal of time trying various treatments, but are yet to see her recover completely.

Health aside, Queenie, Ruby and Belle now rule the backyard – even our vegie patch and occasionally the dogs' beds. When it's cold, they like to come inside and hunt around for treats – especially in the kitchen when I'm chopping up vegies. They often race us to the back door to get inside, and if we happen to leave it open we discover chickens strewn across the whole house – from the bedroom to the couch to the fireplace!

With their crazy antics and surprising mischief (such as jumping on my knee to pinch my lunch), they remind us every day how special and amazing chickens are. Queenie, Ruby and Belle each have a unique and quirky personality of their own.

I cannot imagine that they once lived in total fear and misery, in a place where they were seen as commodities – egg-laying machines to be discarded as 'pet food' or 'chicken nuggets' when they could no longer produce 'enough' numbers. I shudder when I think of the fate of their brothers who never made it past a day old after hatching in an incubator, instead of under the loving wing of their mother.

Belle, Ruby and Queenie are no longer seen as 'just chickens'. Instead, they are loved and appreciated for all the wonder and mystery they bring to our family. Seeing them stretch out those wings, roll around in the straw and magically lay their eggs in a place reserved especially for them is such a reward, one that I won't take for granted, no matter how many eggs they lay.

Chantal, Victoria

◇◇◇◇◇

Never Take No for an Answer

When I was a little girl, I always had pets. One of my first memories was watching our possum climbing up our curtain. My mum had rescued him before I was born, after a car had hit his mother.

Animals always found their way into my heart. Twice during my childhood I found dumped kittens and brought them home and screamed and cried until the family let me keep them. That was the other trait I had: I never took 'No' for an answer. I simply thought hearing 'No' meant I needed to keep going until the answer changed to a 'Yes'! How I must have vexed my parents!

As I grew up, I still adored animals but naturally my interests changed. I saved up for a year and took a suitcase and every dollar I owned to live in the UK. There was an emptiness, though, in my selfish years without animals in my life. Fashion and friends didn't feel right after a while, and soon family life began. I got married, had a daughter and bought a little dog called Ruffles. Returning to Australia with all the family, two- and four-legged, I discovered the problems of our quarantine laws. I had to run around submitting paperwork and making sure that Ruffles had everything she would need to be able to enter the country.

When Ruffles was finally on the plane I thought with relief: *Thank God I will never have to go through this quarantine process ever again!* How wrong I was.

In May 2011, my life changed forever. ABC's *Four Corners* aired a report on the slaughter of cattle in Indonesia and, like so many others, I was horrified by what I saw that night. I could not believe the way these beautiful creatures had their lives ended – shaking in line, waiting to be hacked to death while they watched their friends dying one by one in front of them. I decided to educate myself on the plight of animals around the world, and the sufferings they have to endure.

On my new journey of awareness I stumbled across an organisation called the Soi Dog Foundation (SDF). SDF is a charity based in Thailand that cares for street dogs and cats. It has a shelter in Phuket with a hospital and sterilisation clinic. They also operate a cat hospital. SDF also supports many monasteries and government shelters that are caring for Thai dogs and cats, and they provide them with food and medical aid.

I was horrified to read that many of these dogs are victims of the dog meat trade in the region. In parts of Asia, millions of dogs are killed every year for human consumption in the most brutal ways, as it is believed to make the meat more tender. In Thailand this is illegal – Thai people do not eat dog, it is not part of their culture. But there are some Thais who will smuggle dogs across the border to neighbouring countries such as Vietnam. Many of these dogs are stolen pets, but most are street dogs.

I had never heard about this before and felt I should learn more. I found that SDF has a wonderful YouTube channel, and I watched the inspirational stories of many different four-leggeds. I felt a connection to this work and decided I would make a difference and adopt one of the dogs that had been rescued from the smugglers. They had little chance of finding homes.

I met Cindy of SDF via email; she was a wonderful help. She explained it was possible to adopt a rescued pet, but it would be extremely difficult due to Australian Quarantine rules and regulations – something I already knew a lot about. A dog from Thailand cannot come directly to Australia, because there is still rabies in parts of Thailand, so the dog must live in an approved country for 150 days before it is allowed onto our shores. It also needs to pass quarantine blood tests. Cindy reminded me this was costly.

Understandably, most people would give up on learning they would have to spend approximately $5000 *and* find a foster home for their dog in another country for almost four months. In fact, as far as SDF could tell me, no other Australian had ever done this. I knew I still had that little girl inside me that would not take 'No' for an answer and decided to prove that I was going to make this happen. This was going to be a 'Yes', and I was going to adopt a Soi dog.

I have never been afraid of a challenge. Being dyslexic always meant I struggled at school and had to work harder to be just a below-average student. Dyslexia has been the biggest gift to me in my life, however – it has given me such drive and ambition and the ability to be persistent and not follow the crowd. When I was presented with the problem of adopting a Soi Dog, I thought: *Well, how hard can it be?* I thought I would just contact anyone and everyone to find a foster home overseas and make it happen. I also have a background in sales, and that helped immensely. I thought: *This is just a numbers game – most people will not be able to help, but if I keep contacting people, eventually someone will be there for my new dog and me.*

I did what we all do in the modern world – I Googled. I contacted animal rescue charities from around the world, because without a foster home, I could not adopt. Most could not help as they had plenty of problems in their own area to worry about.

I made myself a rule. For every one who said 'No', I would contact three more people until I got a 'Yes'. (Sound familiar, Mum and Dad?) Then I came across a charity called American Dog Rescue and emailed the founder, Arthur E Benjamin. I nearly fell off my chair when I received a reply the next day. Arthur said he could help me. He had previously visited the Soi Dog Shelter in Phuket, so he understood and knew exactly why I wanted to go the extra mile to find an amazing forever friend.

Arthur told me that the Education and Animal Rescue Society (EARS) in Dallas had found me a foster home. I was impressed by how thorough they were. They asked numerous questions and I put together a ten-page document about the quarantine process and what needed to happen for a dog to enter Australia. It was a big commitment and required a number of vet visits and blood tests.

Finally, everything seemed to be coming together. Now all I needed to do was find my dog! I had done all this work with no particular canine in mind. My husband Robin and I decided we needed to fly to Thailand for this important mission. I couldn't just select a dog from a picture – we needed to meet him and understand where he came from and what he had been through. We also knew we must adopt a four-legged with the right temperament to fit our family.

Soi Dog Shelter in Phuket is like one big family, a family with 400 dogs! I could sense the love the staff had for these animals and knew that those I was meeting were the lucky ones: they had love, food and shelter. I thought to myself: *How am I going to pick just one? This is impossible.* Each day in Phuket, I fell in love with a different dog. My husband Robin thought I was crazy; I would say, 'This dog is the one!' and then thirty minutes later I would change my mind. I realised I was not making a real connection, because if I had, I would not keep changing my mind! Robin told me to be patient. I was attracted to all the timid dogs and I knew they would not be the right fit for my home environment, which is busy with two little girls.

By day five I was thinking maybe the right dog wasn't even at the shelter. How would I tell the Soi Dog people that none of their dogs were right? They would think I was crazy. However, there was a little voice in the back of my mind saying 'my' dog was definitely not there.

The next day I had booked a day trip to Bangkok and during this trip I was to visit Soi Dog's sterilisation clinic. When I arrived, I noticed a little girl about the same age as my own daughter playing with a gorgeous brown puppy in the sweltering heat. The puppy could not walk properly and was dragging his legs. There was something different about this dog, in addition to him being in clear need of medical attention. He did not seem to notice his troubles – he acted like he didn't have a care in the world.

When I picked him up, held him in my arms and looked into his eyes, I knew he was 'the one'. This special boy had found me and I was going to do everything to give him a home and the medical treatment he needed.

As I later found out, 'Sea Lion', as he was known, was tiny and suffering. He was dubbed this as he has severe deformities in his hips and his knees, which cause him to drag his back legs along the ground like the sea mammal. SDF had come across him in a government shelter. His mother had been rescued from the illegal dog meat trade, apparently found among already perished dogs packed into chicken crates, on their way to Vietnam where they would be killed and eaten. During this time she was pregnant, and Sea Lion and his siblings did not get adequate nutrition because their mother was malnourished herself. Sea Lion's deformities were the result of this, plus he may have been injured from being squashed in her womb inside the chicken crates. He and his sister were the only survivors from her litter of many.

There were 1800 dogs rescued from the dog meat trade by Thai authorities early that year, and Sea Lion (pronounced *Nam Mow* in Thai) was one of only eighty who were still alive by August. Being a puppy, the despair of the other dogs did not affect Sea Lion – this was the only world he knew. He didn't know having a tummy choked with worms instead of food was not how it should be. The smell of death was all around him; he had hunger and thirst; he was covered in ticks, slowing feasting on his blood; and he knew his mother's sadness. He dragged himself around on the dirt and rocks, but still his tail wagged.

The day they picked him up from the government shelter, Sea Lion slept like a puppy should – deeply – all the way back to the shelter on the lap of Soi Dog's founder, John Dalley. Sea Lion had already escaped death and now I had to ensure he would have the best life possible. Before I left Bangkok I made Sea Lion a promise. I told him his luck had changed. He was going to have a warm and safe home for life, a belly full of food and the medical treatment he needed. I promised him together we would make a difference and, through his story and his happy and bouncy nature, we would work together to bring awareness to the illegal dog meat trade. We would ensure other people got involved and helped the friends he was going to leave behind to start a new life.

One month later, I sent Sea Lion to America to spend his first Christmas in a real home. He has since been on local television in Dallas, bringing awareness about the Asian illegal dog meat trade to the people there, and recently won 'Best Personality' in the US Humane Society's 'Pet Pageant'. He's quite the celebrity now!

Very soon, my daughter and I will spend ten days with Sea Lion in Dallas. He will stay with us during this time so we can bond as a 'pack'. We also have a very important vet visit planned, as he is seeing a top orthopaedic surgeon and having numerous X-Rays and MRI scans so we can work out the best treatment for him once he has fully grown.

Two months after that, he will finally arrive in Australia where he will spend thirty days in quarantine. Then he will finally come home with us.

I will not fail in my promise to Sea Lion, and I think he trusts I will never take 'No' for an answer. That is why we are together. Sure, there will be tough times ahead of us, but there is one thing I definitely believe: Sea Lion and I were destined to meet, and to bring awareness to the horrific dog meat trade. His foster carer, Linda, told me, 'Don't underestimate Sea Lion – he is a very tough little guy.' He is a survivor, so I know he will bounce back from the numerous operations ahead of him.

> *This story is dedicated to Sea Lion's mother and sister, who may no longer be alive, and to the millions of victims of the dog meat trade. Together, Sea Lion and I have a story to tell the world.*

Ellie, Victoria

◇◇◇◇◇

The Brumby Spirit

'I am so sorry. As much as I would love to help out, I am not taking in any more horses,' I told the person on the phone.

'He isn't more than a week old,' they said. 'He's pretty wild; we're trying to find him a home.' Some local blokes had gone 'brumbying' and a little orphaned foal had followed them and their entourage of horses and vehicles out of the mountains. (Brumbying is a loose term often used for the hunting, shooting and/or capturing of our wild horses. Many of those captured are headed for the abattoir, but thankfully a few are taken in by brumby rescue organisations for training and rehoming.)

My heart went out to the little fellow, separated from his mother and herd, finding himself part of the harsh human world, where brightly coloured plastic buckets replaced the warmth of his mother's belly and teats. But I was not set up for such a rescue as I already had my hands full with my herd, my property and my students.

A few weeks went by and I heard more stories about the little colt – 'untrainable', 'dangerous', 'crazy', 'will eventually kill someone', 'should be put down', 'no use to anyone'. Nobody seemed able to handle this foal and connect with him.

I received another desperate phone call from the local vet who had taken him in. 'He's in a covered steel yard behind the building. But no one can get near him and he keeps knocking the bucket of milk over – can you come and help us with him?'

Of course I'd go. My heart strings were being tugged in directions I couldn't resist. I'd been thinking about him every day, wondering what he was feeling, how he was being treated, and what would become of him.

I was over there in a flash. The little colt stood with his hind legs splayed, as far away from me as he could get, ready for instant flight as I quietly unlatched the gate. Once inside his pen, I was careful not to stare at him or intimidate or scare him. He looked so small and lonely, his dark bay coat all fluffy and his forelock sticking up like a fledgling Mohawk. He surveyed me with a curious, wary and yet soft eye.

Observing 'herd rules', I stood still, and waited for a sign of acceptance from him. It came quickly: he shifted his weight towards me and lowered his head. I started to walk around his yard, seemingly ignoring him, yet alert to his demeanour and his efforts to accept me in his space. He watched, then started blinking, and licked his lips. I moved into his space a little. When I was close enough to touch him, I did nothing except breathe and sigh, looking at the ground. As he took a tiny step in my direction, I walked away. He took another step in my direction. *Bravo, little boy,* I thought.

I asked for a bucket of milk to be brought over. This caused a bit of excitement from him, and he became animated and pushy so I gently yet firmly asked him to respect my space by using a stick with a thin rope attached to the end of it, sweeping it in front of me like a tail and waving it gently to create some energy that indicated to him that he was not to charge into me. When he understood the boundaries, I allowed him to come in for a drink. After he had a little, I took the bucket away. He followed, and so I allowed another small drink, holding onto the bucket, and then touched him on the forehead. And just like that, we were friends.

I gave the vet staff some tips on going into the yard, offering his milk and how best to touch him. Then I went home, and for the next week, they did their best to connect with the little brumby foal. Then another call came. They needed me again. It wasn't working out. He was feral! So off I went to the vet's clinic, feeling (not for the first time!) the stirrings of fate.

As soon as looked into his deep brown eyes again I felt a clear message that he was desperately sad and lonely. No company, no friends, no reassurance, no feeling of safety or comfort was coming his way. Like any young animal, he was scared and defensive. The carers were obviously frustrated and not confident about things at all.

'How about I take him home to my place for a while,' I suggested, as I stroked his neck, 'just till I can help him build some confidence and get him accustomed to being handled?'

The idea was met with an enthusiastic smile and a huge sigh of relief from the young vet who had grown quite fond of him. I asked her what the plans were for his future. 'Not sure,' she replied. 'If he continues like this, well . . .' She shrugged her shoulders and shook her head. My heart wrenched.

That same afternoon I loaded my beautiful Anglo–Arabian gelding Olé in the float and off we went to the vet with a student to help. Olé was a gentleman and a strong leader and would offer benevolent guidance for the foal, as well as comfort and security. I was right; the colt was drawn to the older horse, and while he was nervous about the float (pointing to possible negative experiences with it), I was able to help him overcome his fear and after a short time, using patience and gentleness, we all went home together.

The vet had named him Spirit, which I liked, and it suited him, so it stuck. Safely accommodated in a very securely fenced, treed paddock near the house and within sight of the other horses, he was so scared that for the first twenty-four hours he didn't move from a tiny space between one of the eucalypts and the fence, peering out with big wide eyes at the new world he found himself in.

The little guy fascinated me, and I spent hours sitting on a log in the paddock with him that first couple of days, just observing and making notes as he wandered about and explored his new home. Eventually he approached gingerly to sniff my boots, then my clothes, then my hair. He was such a woolly, wild-looking little thing, with lightning reflexes and a bold defiance.

I felt an overwhelming gratitude for his trust as we got to know each other, and our first tentative touches turned into hearty scratches and rubs. We nuzzled each other constantly, and he followed me around and ran with me as we played 'chase me' around the trees. It was blissful to be a part of this transformation, and Spirit's confidence grew in leaps and bounds. He was irresistibly adorable, and I'd fallen in love with him.

The day came to introduce him to my herd. Arriba (my Arabian gelding) took Spirit under his wing, protecting him, guiding him and teaching him as well as any parent; it was beautiful to watch. Spirit bloomed in this natural environment, and my all-boy herd provided him with exactly what he needed to grow into a balanced horse mentally, emotionally, spiritually and physically.

Before long I felt it was time to take our relationship to the next level. The foundation of trust and confidence was solid, so we began our education sessions in earnest. I spent hours with him, focusing mostly on touching him all over, desensitising him to as many things and situations as I could, and ensuring he understood and respected my space and learned some manners.

Everything about Spirit epitomises what a horse really is: curious yet wary, brave yet flighty, strong yet soft, fast yet patient, powerful yet gentle, tough yet tender.

The whole herd and I took walks through our 750-acre bush property, everyone loose, including Spirit. People were surprised and dumbfounded when they heard this. 'What, he doesn't run away, back to the wild?' Why would he? More than any other member of my herd, he's hard-wired to *stay* with his herd; it was the opposite of what people expected.

I loved how he ran through the bush, crashing through marshy gullies, tea-tree forests and the undergrowth, his solid little body fearlessly taking nature by storm. It was hilarious and wonderful when my mini pony, Poncho, became Spirit's protégé and mimicked his bigger friend, the two of them playing brumbies in the wild!

I may have saved Spirit and given him the life that he has, but I also feel that he was the catalyst for the discovery of my life's mission, which is to help as many horses as I can to live natural, happy lives of dignity where they are understood, respected and loved.

I am a supporter of the preservation of our brumbies, and encourage others to respect the heritage of our feral equines, and their rights to a free existence. Brumbies make beautiful, loyal friends, pets and mounts. Thankyou, Spirit, for everything you are and everything you are teaching me.

Wrangler Jayne, Victoria

◇◇◇◇◇

From Racetrack to Ambassador

Where do we start with one of our true favourites, Buster? A big striking fawn greyhound, Buster came to Greyhounds As Pets (GAP) in Sydney in November 2012, after being a much-loved boy throughout a successful racing career. (It is hard to believe now, though, as he is such a lazy boy!) GAP is an initiative of Greyhound Racing NSW and involves the assessment, fostering and rehoming of retired racing greyhounds and those who are not suited to life as a racer. With the assistance of foster carers, we transition greyhounds into becoming much-loved family pets.

Buster was a hit with GAP staff from day one, easily adapting to new environments, readily smooching up for cuddles or simply conking out wherever there was room on the floor for him. Buster spent his early fostering days at Dillwynia Correctional Centre, where female inmates work with the greyhounds and simultaneously undertake training courses in animal care and husbandry. A win-win situation for all involved!

The girls in the facility did a wonderful job with Buster and were filled with mixed emotions when he left. They were satisfied, happy and excited to see him start his new life after all their training efforts with him, and saddened to see one of their treasured boys go . . . but not without a big bear hug and kiss!

GAP started their involvement with the Dillwynia Correctional Centre in western Sydney in 2010 and has seen countless greyhounds graduate from the program to become family pets. Female inmates work with the greyhounds (currently six dogs at any one time) through a minimum six-week fostering program. The program involves basic training and getting the dogs used to things they often haven't been exposed to previously, such as different household noises and surfaces, as well as basic handling and conditioning. Among the program's many benefits to all involved has been the improvement in relationships between Corrective Services staff and the inmates working with the greyhounds.

Buster excelled in his behavioural assessment, leading to him being the first dog to enter a joint program between GAP and Assistance Dogs Australia (ADA). Buster underwent his remaining fostering period with ADA, and has been chosen as their inaugural Greyhound Ambassador! This means that Buster will be on show at any events or community engagements that ADA participates in. His role will be to demonstrate to the broader community that greyhounds make wonderful pets and companions.

In addition to Buster's coveted new role, he has also passed his assessment to be a 'greenhound'. This means that Buster is exempt from wearing a muzzle in public, which goes a long way to further educate the public on this placid and loving breed.

Buster is a true gentleman and loyal companion who has taken everything in his varied life in his stride. We have no doubt he will bring much joy to anyone who meets him and provide much-needed positive awareness for this wonderful breed.

Lori McKern, Greyhounds As Pets New South Wales

Calming Carmella

I've been around horses all my life, but when I first saw three-month-old Carmella, I knew I had to take her home.

Considered by some to be a 'feral horse', she had been removed from the Guy Fawkes River National Park in December 2009 by park staff through their ongoing passive capture and removal program, but, unfortunately, they had been unable to capture her mother.

I grew up on Guy Fawkes Station, which borders the park. When over 600 horses were slaughtered in the Park during an 'aerial cull' in 2000, I decided I had to step in and do what I could to stop it happening again. I became a founding member of the Guy Fawkes Heritage Horse Association (GFHHA), set up in 2004 to take care of the horses removed from the national park – selling them to the general public and raising public awareness of their plight in the process.

Horses had been bred on lands near the Guy Fawkes River National Park since the 1830s and had been present in a wild state since the 1890s. As direct descendants of Australia's wartime cavalry horses known as walers, these horses had significant historical, military and cultural value.

After I watched Carmella being unloaded off the National Park truck, I took her home and found her to be very frightened and quite wild. I put her in the yards for a few weeks until she quietened and I could make friends with her. She was such a funny little thing, full of character and lots of spunk. She had a serious worm infestation that was dealt with, but she would only eat hay or grass – horse feed of any description was a foreign object and she wouldn't touch it. I used to count out pellets and mix them with chaff and grass, but by morning she would have cleaned out her feed bin and left exactly the same number of pellets I'd started with. Eventually, I had to trick her into eating feed by wrapping pellets in blades of grass, and the clever little thing didn't take long to work out that pellets tasted pretty good after all.

After four weeks I took her to live at a friend's place for six months, to be company for a thoroughbred filly of the same age. The filly was literally twice her size because she had been raised on good feed and grass. When that filly went to the sales, Carmella came home to start her education and begin her show career.

She settled very quickly and we found that she loves the company of people, especially small children. At one horse show a lady came up to us with a disabled boy in a pram. The little boy was squealing and laughing with delight at being so close to a horse. I thought Carmella would be frightened, but no, Carmella was curious. She bent down towards him to get closer. The boy's mother was a little concerned, but I told her I wouldn't let my horse frighten him. The little boy continued to giggle and squeal with happiness, but the pram's hood was up, so Carmella got in a bit closer, putting her head right under the hood of the pram to very gently brush the boy's cheek with her muzzle. It was like she was kissing him. He was overjoyed! The boy's mother and I were totally amazed by this display of connection and gentleness. I wondered if Carmella instinctively knew that the boy had special needs and how much this moment meant to him.

Today, Carmella lives in a paddock behind our house, but we also use her as a lawn mower – she is very good at doing the edges! She spends a couple of hours a day in our yard grazing. Besides, it is good for keeping her quiet and she likes being close to me. But if someone goes out the back door and leaves it open, Carmella will invite herself inside! To do so, she has to walk across a small verandah and through the back room to get into the kitchen. The first time I found her in there I thought she would panic about being in such a confined space, but she wasn't the slightest bit flustered – on seeing my surprise, she just turned around and walked calmly out the way she came and looked back at me as if to say, *I was just seeing what you were doing!*

I have now just finished breaking Carmella to ride. She is going very nicely, having been out for two bush rides, and just loves it, striding along happily with confidence. Now that she has turned three I am also starting to teach her some tricks. She is learning to stand with all four feet on a pedestal (like an elephant at the circus), walk on an elevated narrow plank, bow, lie down, play soccer with a big ball and carry things in her mouth. She is exceptionally intelligent and always ready to learn something new. She has been quite successful in the show ring as a led horse too, having won ten champion ribbons and numerous placings at local shows.

Carmella's beautiful nature and character has made her an important part of our family. My two kids call her my third child! She is a case in point of why I have dedicated the last twelve years to the plight of these horses, and will continue for however long it takes to get them all out of the Park or for the rules to change, so we can leave controlled mobs in the Park in their natural state. Because these horses have been there long enough for natural selection to take place, they are, in general, good, hardy, intelligent animals – as Carmella has proven – who can adapt to be anything you want them to be. They actually quieten and 'break in' much more easily than most people would expect, because they haven't been spoilt by human interference from day one and are very submissive when they are young – after all, they've been bought up in a mob where they have to abide by a hierarchy and the rules set by the older horses.

Carmella will continue to help me promote the cause of the Guy Fawkes River National Park horses through our open days, and by showing as many people as we can what special, clever friends they can be.

Erica Jessup, Guy Fawkes Heritage Horse Association Inc., New South Wales

How William Helped Save 1000 Animals

There is nothing more fun than adopting a kitten, and four years ago my partner and I decided it was time. We wanted to adopt rather than go to a pet shop because, to be honest, a kitten from a responsible rescue group has all their desexing and other vet work already taken care of and paid for while pet shop kittens do not. Why would you go anywhere else? We looked around on the internet and discovered Wagga Animal Rescue (WAR), a small private organisation in our town. Little did I know that this experience was about to change my life forever!

We visited Kellie, one of WAR's foster carers. Going into her home was the first time I was introduced to the world of rescue and so began my four-year-long passion. There we met Molly, a mumma cat, with her five kittens. Molly had been dumped while she was pregnant. Kellie rescued her and helped raise her babies, all of which later found wonderful homes. We fell in love with 'our' kitten, William, at first sight and came back two weeks later to pick him up when he was ready to leave his mum. I was very intrigued about foster care, and asked Kellie a lot of questions, admiring the work she was doing.

We took William home and have been smitten with him ever since. His name has always suited him – he is so regal and King of the House! Everyone who comes to visit comments on how handsome he is. Within two weeks of adopting him, I received a call from WAR asking if I would be interested in fostering a three-week-old kitten. I jumped at the opportunity!

My first foster kitten was called Chippie, as he was found in a wall at a construction site. The builders at the industrial area out the back of Wagga heard small cries coming from a wall. After investigating, they decided to make a hole in the wall, through which they could hear the mournful noise coming. They pulled out a tiny, wet orphan kitten. Not being able to find a mother cat or any other kittens, they assumed the mum had taken off when work started on the site and this little kitten was left behind.

The builders called WAR and Kellie came and got him straight away. She showed me how to bottle-feed and toilet him, and so Chippie became the first of over one hundred orphan kittens I have raised. From then I was hooked!

William lovingly accepted every kitten or cat we fostered – he even nursed several orphan kittens back to health! Our special boy would lick clean every kitten that came into our care; he loved the formula milk we fed the babies, so maybe this is why he loved the kittens! As soon as he saw their bottles being prepared, he was there, ready to 'help'. He cleaned the new arrivals, kept them warm, slept with them and taught them how to be a proper cat. The kittens followed him everywhere; some of them even started to suckle on him, thinking he was their mum! I believe William is the reason so many of these orphans survived and went on to find wonderful families.

Next, when we also started to foster puppies and dogs, William became our temperament-testing and socialisation cat; being so calm, his role was to see if a dog was going to be friendly or aggressive when introduced to him (carefully, of course!).

Time moved on, and I soon took on the Cat Coordinator role with WAR, fostering up to twenty kittens at a time in our converted shed cattery. I was elected Vice-President after that, and took on the additional areas of publicity, education and fundraising for the group. We continued to rescue animal after animal and busily recruited more foster carers.

Later, I took on the role of President when our founder, Linda, retired after ten years. She taught me everything I needed to know to run a reputable, successful rescue. The people I have met through my time with WAR have since become my best friends – all very passionate and caring people.

In 2012 we adopted our second cat, Johnny. He was surrendered to our group as a purebred female Burmese, but in fact he was a *male* ragdoll! William and Johnny quickly became the best of friends and it was obvious we could not give him up. They are the best cats we have ever known and show how amazing rescue pets can be.

After four wonderful years of working with Wagga Animal Rescue, the group will sadly be folding, as myself and numerous other members are leaving the area. By the time we officially close, we will have rehomed over 1000 animals. This is an amazing achievement for a small group, and so rewarding for all involved to know they have given so many four-leggeds the chance of life.

While running WAR I was also studying, and have recently graduated with an Honours degree in Animal Science, and start work soon as a Companion Animal Management Officer in Sydney. I aim to make positive changes within the companion animal management and welfare industry. I will always help rescue and rehome animals – I doubt I could ever stop!

Looking back at my time with Wagga Animal Rescue, I know it probably never would have happened if I had not adopted dear William. I now have the best memories and experiences that I will cherish for the rest of my life. I encourage others to consider volunteering with their local rescue group. There are so many worthy lives to save, and wonderful new friends to make.

Emma, New South Wales

◇◇◇◇◇

Inspiration in a Box

Peering over into what looked like an old shoebox full of wood shavings, I first saw Rella the rat. She was a friendly girl from the start, but when she arrived from her previous home, she was suffering from a range of medical issues. Terribly underweight, she was also displaying severe symptoms of an untreated respiratory infection; wounds on her skin from scratching; and dry, itchy skin.

A volunteer with Perth Rat Rescue & Rehab, I was almost too scared to pick up the tiny one because of how little she weighed. Rella was so emaciated I could see that being handled caused her pain. I tried picking her up within a blanket to give some padding to her small frame, and she seemed to enjoy this.

We took Rella straight off to the vet and it was confirmed that she had a serious respiratory infection, which had resulted in her lungs being full of fluid, and that the reason her skin was so dry was possibly due to the lack of essential oil in her diet. It was flaking away with fur when rubbed backwards. Rella was placed on antibiotics and we added omega-3 and omega-6 oils to her diet. Within days this little miracle was starting to improve, and our hopes were raised that she would survive and maybe one day find a home.

Our work was soon rewarded. Rella went into foster care and continued to progress. She went to visit the vet again to get another check-up: her lungs were clearing well and her skin was all healed and not dry any more. Then cheeky Rella decided that she did not want her antibiotics any more! Her carers Lynne and Joe were forced to hide them in soy milk every morning.

The vet told us that because Rella's respiratory infections had been left untreated for some time before coming into our care, she would have permanent lung scarring, which caused her breathing to be faster and deeper than normal.

Rella was stronger and more determined than we all gave her credit for. Soon, beyond all our expectations, Rella was able to be adopted, and a very special person came forward wanting to offer her a forever home. Our girl was going to have one of the happy endings we strive for!

It takes a compassionate and special person to accept a pet will have (possibly expensive) medical issues for the rest of their life. The woman who adopted little Rella not only offered her a forever home, but also a promise that the rat would always be loved, unconditionally, with all the medical treatment she may ever need. Her name was Peta and she said to us, 'It isn't her fault that she was left with permanent health issues!' She told us she felt the little one deserved so much more than what life had already dealt her. We couldn't have agreed more!

At first, it was thought that Rella may not be a friendly rat due to her lack of socialisation with her peers. So Peta prepared herself to have a 'loner' rat, but with much human time and cuddles to make up for it.

As it turned out, Peta wanted to adopt another rat, Merlin, at the same time as Rella. I felt these two would have to live apart, with a view to getting Merlin a buddy soon after. But it was decided that after a few weeks of the two being in Peta's care, she would attempt careful socialisation between them. 'Needless to say,' Peta reported, 'there were two nervous rats and one very nervous "Mum"!'

Our group guided Peta with the 'tricks of the trade' to introducing the little ones, including 'masking' their scents, providing yummy treats and conducting the meets and greets in a neutral and supervised territory.

It went well! I am ecstatic to report that Rella beat the odds of being a loner rat for the rest of her life. She accepted Merlin and he, in turn, accepted her. It was the most heart-warming sight to see the two of them snuggle up together, like they were always meant to be pals. Rella learnt how to groom Merlin and let herself be groomed, and found out what it was like to 'rat pile', even if it was only the two of them sleeping on top of each other! Rella got to experience all the things ratties should be able to, and to just be a happy and loved rat for the first time in her life.

With her background of neglect and deprivation, Rella was a miracle in two ways: that she survived as long as she did; and secondly, that she was such an affectionate and beautiful little girl.

Rella passed away due to complications with her lungs at the age of twenty-seven months, the last eight of which she spent in Peta's loving care. We will never forget her amazing survival and spirit. Thankyou, Rella.

Aimee Samuelson, Perth Rat Rescue & Rehab, Western Australia

◇◇◇◇◇

A Pebble in the Pond

I look at Daisy every day and wonder: *How did I get so lucky? Why did the powers that be bless me with this dog?*

Every day my dog changes lives in so many ways. She brings smiles to the faces of patients in the hospital that we visit as a Delta Society Certified Therapy Dog Team; in malls we're mobbed by children while we raise awareness of this fantastic non-profit organisation; and to puppies she teaches lessons of politeness in their puppy classes. Daisy inspires the average Joe on the street to believe that their staffy mix can be polite like her and walk on a loose lead, and when they ask me if she can be bred, I turn it into a conversation about why desexing is more important. Daisy reaffirms every day with her actions that her appearance really shouldn't matter. Finally, like me, she's not from Australia: she is my family, my rock, my friend.

Daisy is no ordinary dog. Well, maybe she could have been. Her remaining sibling back in Canada, where we come from, does pretty chill, everyday doggie things with his family too. But maybe I saw back then (like so many others see in her after only a few moments) that she's destined for more. Daisy's mum was pulled from a cruelty situation into rescue – severely emaciated, forever mentally scarred – and poured all her strength into her litter, and Daisy came from that.

I took Daisy on as a foster dog. I already owned a pedigreed American Staffordshire terrier, and seeing the plight of the non-show dog versions, I had to get involved. In Canada we consider all these types of dogs – American staffies, staffies and pit bulls – to be one and the same: 'pit bull–type dogs'.

This mischievous little puppy peed everywhere, chewed everything and went everywhere with everyone. And I fell in love with her. Because I didn't fear her being stolen away by government authorities she went to puppy classes; she learned bite inhibition and appropriate play around other dogs, and that strangers equal goodies and pats. She came to markets and cafés and street fairs and learned all about the weird and amazing things that humans do. She met horses and slept with cats when she stayed over at her aunty's. She did ordinary doggie things. But I saw how she oriented towards humans – as an adolescent she would pull me down the street to greet someone – and all these things set her up for a great adulthood. While never titled in obedience or agility, she is reliable with her manners both on-lead and off-lead, even with kangaroos bounding around in our local State Reserve, and constantly receives praise for her behaviour, particularly from people who 'normally don't like those kinds of dogs'.

When moving to Australia, Daisy was loved and adored by the quarantine kennel staff. Starting out in nursing homes, she now visits hospitals and has been short-listed for a children's reading program. At her current hospital she started out visiting just one man, as the facility staff and even some patients were initially quite wary; they had never had a dog in the hospital itself and were concerned with her manners. Week by week, she was increasingly greeted by more smiles and warm greetings, and even individuals I had never met spoke of her in high esteem. This facility is now enquiring about having Daisy visit multiple wards. They have noticed the difference she makes. She is the pebble in the pond.

Her positive effects on patients are not just physical, but mental. Bed-ridden hospital patients rise from their beds to greet her, while their frail arms that don't have the energy to put food into their own mouths ask to hold her leash. When we have regularly visited dementia wards, the patients remembered her, or recalled pertinent stories about their own family pets. Every week, it was usually the same story, but still as funny and quirky as the first time I heard it. These are powerful reminders of Daisy's positive influence when at times these patients can fail to remember or recognise their own children.

If you haven't figured it out by now, the other reason why Daisy is no ordinary dog is because of her 'breed' or really, because she has no pedigree. I think I have a pretty good idea of what she is. With my extensive experience as a veterinary nurse and dog trainer on two continents, we would call her a pit bull back home. Here in Australia, well, her DNA profile says something completely different, and that's okay. I just roll with it; to me she is simply a bully breed type. No different from my pedigreed, senior male American staffy, who is enjoying his nap in the Australian sun, and the same as the staffy patiently waiting to be placed into foster care from Renbury pound. No different from the weight-pull champion pit bull in Canada or the American pit bull terrier police dog in Oregon, USA.

When people ask me what breed Daisy is, I just shrug and say, 'I don't know; she was a rescue.' Most go on to categorise her as a bully type. Others will pull her in closer and give her an extra scratch under the chin – they used to have a dog like her, they tell me. To some politicians and council workers with a weekend education in Australia, a dog like her can't be a certified therapy dog. Canines who share the physical characteristics like hers in some states get an automatic death sentence, or are confined to a 3 metre by 3 metre concrete and steel pen. They are inherently dangerous – not because of their actions, but because of the way they look. So instead of gently crawling up onto a bed with a quadriplegic who somehow musters the strength and mental fortitude to set their hand on her back as she lays beside them and gives a gentle lick on the cheek, many must hide or are destroyed. Because this is what the vast majority of these types of dogs are wonderful at.

It's a bit frustrating, really. I can't get on a public platform with Daisy and say, 'This is what breed-specific legislation would destroy,' because to formally acknowledge her for what one individual may think of her appearance puts her under the gun in some states. That means the ever-constant sound of her footsteps on the tile of the hospital ward floor would fade to a memory. She would not be that pebble in the pond. So we keep our head down and just swim in our own little fishing hole.

If I'm asked to put into words what Daisy means to me, there are none. As I stated at the beginning of this story, every day I look at her and am in awe of how lucky I am. Through her, I have made friends and invaluable contacts throughout the world. I now see how the disadvantaged beginning of a rescue pet does not limit its potential. Daisy reminds me to use compassion and to reserve judgement. She has strengthened my personality with a desire for critical thinking, expanded my empathy infinitely, and instilled responsibility for myself, and for others and my community. She shows me to be an individual, as a happy personality will bust down more barriers. She emphasises how 'just a rescue dog' can be so much more. A dog can be more than a companion, more than an adventure buddy, but an inspiration for others.

Elisabeth, South Australia

Use PetRescue to Find Your New Best Friend!

Whether it's a dog, cat, guinea pig, or any kind of animal, really, we're here to help you find the perfect rescue pet for your family!

How it works

Rescue groups, pounds and shelters across Australia use the PetRescue website to list their pets for adoption. PetRescue.com.au makes it easy to search and find your perfect rescue pet!

Getting started

This is the fun part! Use the 'Find A Pet' buttons at PetRescue.com.au to search for the type of pet you are after.

Take some time to read their profiles and get to know their personalities – are they cuddly, or more the independent sort? Consider things like size, activity level, grooming requirements, need for training, and so on. You can then 'Favourite' any pets that capture your heart.

If you need more information about a particular pet, contact the rescue group that has the pet in their care. Their details are listed under 'Contact Information' on the pet's page.

First contact for the adoption

Generally, the adoption process is quite simple, although may differ slightly between organisations. The first contact is the initial email you send to the rescue group to register your interest in a particular pet and ask any questions you may have.

Application

The rescue group will then ask that you fill out an application form. While the form may seem quite long, with this information they're better able to find the pet that's right for you. In the event that the pet you were interested in has been adopted, the group might be able to suggest another based on the information you've provided.

Meet and greet

If your application seems like a good match, the rescue group will arrange a time for you and your family to meet the pet. Some rescue groups do a 'house check' on your property, too – they just want to make sure the fences are escape-proof and to watch out for any potential dangers your new pet may come across.

Adoption fees

For the most part, the adoption fee reflects the basic medical expenses the group has incurred for the pet. If the pet had any extra medical treatment, it's likely that the fee you are charged won't cover these costs and the rescue group will actually be out of pocket. The adoption fee for a rescue pet is usually somewhere between $150 and $500.

Interstate adoptions

Since PetRescue connects you with rescue groups from all over Australia, it's possible you may fall in love with a pet located interstate. Some rescue groups have networks of carers in various locations, and do allow interstate adoptions. If you decide to adopt a pet from interstate, bear in mind that the transport costs will most often be borne by you. It's usually not much, and certainly not if you think that a particular pet is perfect for your family, but it's still something to consider.

Well, what are you waiting for?

We wish you all the best in your search for your new best friend. Let us know how you go! Email us at info@PetRescue.org.au.

How Can You Help Rescue Pets?

1. Tell your friends

Share PetRescue.com.au with your friends and family, and let them know about the wonderful pets waiting for homes at rescue groups, shelters and pounds across Australia. Make sure their next pet is a rescue pet!

2. Foster

Foster carers provide a safe, nurturing environment for a rescue pet until a permanent home can be found. Become part of the community who give these dogs and cats a second chance by opening your heart and home to a foster pet. Visit PetFoster.com.au to find out more.

3. Spread the word

Every pet on PetRescue.com.au has a Facebook and Twitter icon. Use social media to reach out to animal lovers everywhere by sharing pet profiles and becoming a Facebook fan.

4. Donate

You can't take them all home but you can help them find homes. PetRescue relies on donations to continue to offer rehoming programs and tools to hundreds of rescue groups, shelters and pounds. Visit our website to make a tax-deductible donation.

5. Share your skills

Are you a knitter, designer, lawyer, photographer, accountant, writer? Can you sizzle a sausage, play with a puppy or cuddle a kitten? Make contact with your local rescue group to offer to lend your time as a volunteer.

6. Check your local pound

Pounds and shelters in Australia are implementing programs and services that allow them to save 90 per cent or more of the pets coming into their care. Some pounds have fallen dramatically behind. Find out more by Googling 'The No Kill Equation' and follow up with your local pound or shelter to find out what they are doing to save more lives.

7. Become an advocate

Write to your state and federal politicians and let them know that animal welfare issues matter to you. Tell them that the number of healthy pets killed in pounds and shelters each year is not acceptable to you and ask them to take action.

8. Desex!

There are huge advantages to desexing your pet. Desexing reduces territorial aggression in male dogs and cats, making them less likely to fight other animals. They are also less likely to mark their territories by spraying or cocking their leg in the house. For females, desexing eliminates the possibility of uterine cancer and greatly reduces the possibility of mammary gland (breast) cancer. Oh, and don't forget your council registration fees are considerably cheaper.

9. Make ethical choices

Don't support puppy factories. Only shop at pet stores that don't sell animals and let them know why you choose to support them.

10. Howl from the roof tops

Proudly tell everyone you meet that your pet is a rescue pet!

Contacts

PetRescue would like to thank all of our contributors to this book, and for the tireless work they do for the animals of Australia. We encourage you to support them.

Animal Aid
animalaid.org.au
enquiries@animalaid.org.au
PO Box 34, Coldstream VIC 3770

Animal Protection Society of WA
apswa.org
info@animalprotectionsociety.westnet.com.au
27 Talbot Road, Southern River WA 6110

Animal Welfare League Qld
awlqld.com.au
info@awlqld.com.au
PO Box 3253, Helensvale Town Centre QLD 4212

Animal Welfare League NSW
awlnsw.com.au
marketing@awlnsw.com.au
PO Box K1086, Haymarket NSW 1240

Australian Cavy Sanctuary
australiancavysanctuary.com
australiancavysanctuary@hotmail.com

Big Ears Animal Sanctuary Inc.
bigearsanimalsanctuary.com
bj2103@bigpond.com
PO Box 426, Prospect TAS 7250

Cat Haven
cathaven.com.au
admin@cathaven.com.au
23 Lemnos Street, Shenton Park WA 6008

CatRescue NSW
catrescue.com.au
info@catrescue.com.au
PO Box 847, Gladesville NSW 2111

Conservation Ecology Centre, Cape Otway
conservationecologycentre.org
lizzie@conservationecologycentre.org
635 Otway Lighthouse Road, Cape Otway VIC 3233

Diggers Herding & K9 Education
herding.webs.com
diggersherding@yahoo.com.au
Edwards Road, Diggers Rest VIC 3427

Dogs' Refuge Home, Shenton Park
dogshome.org.au
enquiries@dogshome.org.au
30 Lemnos Street, Shenton Park WA 6008

Edgar's Mission Farm Sanctuary
edgarsmission.org.au
info@edgarsmission.org.au
365 McHarg's Road, Willowmavin VIC 3764

Forever Friends Animal Rescue Inc.
foreverfriends.org.au
info@foreverfriends.org.au
PO Box 873, Pakenham VIC 3180

Friends of the Hound Inc., NSW
friendsofthehound.org.au
enquiries@friendsofthehound.org.au
PO Box 5065, Murwillumbah South NSW 2484

CONTACTS

Geelong Animal Welfare Society
gaws.org.au
admin@gaws.org.au
325 Portarlington Road, Moolap VIC 3221

German Shepherd Rescue NSW
petrescue.com.au/groups/10411

Gold Coast Guinea Pig Rescue
gcgpr.com.au
alex@gcgpr.com.au
PO Box 3480, Australia Fair QLD 4125

Good Samaritan Donkey Sanctuary Inc.
donkeyrescue.org.au
donkeysanctuary@bigpond.com

Greyhounds As Pets NSW
gapnsw.com.au
gap@grnsw.com.au
PO Box 170, Concord West NSW 2138

Greyhound Safety Net
greyhoundsafetynet.net
contactus@greyhoundsafetynet.org
PO Box 400, Doveton VIC 3177

Guy Fawkes Heritage Horse Association Inc.
guyfawkesheritagehorse.com
guyfawkesheritagehorse@hotmail.com
PO Box 442, Dorrigo NSW 2453

Harmony Reins Animal Haven
harmonyreins.com.au
catherine@harmonyreins.com.au
PO Box 486, Yarra Junction VIC 3797

Homeless and Abused Animal Rescue Team
haart.org.au
info@haart.org.au
PO Box 694, Northam WA 6401

Homeless Hounds Rescue Victoria
petrescue.com.au/groups/10249
homelesshoundsrrr@gmail.com

Horses Helping Humans
horseshelpinghumansaustralia.com
suespence@horseshelpinghumansaustralia.com

Humane Research Australia
humaneresearch.org.au
info@humaneresearch.org.au
Suite 704, 1 Princess Street, Kew VIC 3101

K9 Dog Rescue Inc.
www.k9dogrescue.com
k9rescue@southwest.com.au
PO Box 220, Mandurah WA 6210

Labrador Rescue Inc.
rescuealabrador.com
rescuealabrador@yahoo.com.au

Lort Smith Animal Hospital
lortsmith.com
info@lortsmith.com
24 Villiers Street, North Melbourne VIC 3051

Maremma Rescue Victoria Inc.
facebook.com/pages/Maremma-Rescue-Victoria/155734967813887
mjcawood@harboursat.com.au

Matt Aitken Animal Rescue
petrescue.com.au/groups/10171
mattaitken@optusnet.com.au

Melbourne Animal Rescue
melbourneanimalrescue.org
adoptions@melbourneanimalrescue.org.au

mindDog
minddog.org.au
info@minddog.org.au
PO Box 797, Surry Hills NSW 2010

Monika's Doggie Rescue, NSW
doggierescue.com
admin@doggierescue.com
2 McCowan Road corner Bloodwood Road, Ingleside NSW 2101

Native Animal Trust Fund Inc., Wildlife Rescue Service in the Hunter
hunterwildlife.org.au
secretary@hunterwildlife.org.au
PO Box 1052, Toronto NSW 2283

9 Lives Cat Rescue, WA
9livescatrescue.com.au
info@9livescatrescue.com.au

Peninsula Cat Rescue Inc.
peninsulacatrescue.com.au
enquiries@peninsulacatrescue.com.au
PO Box 3327, Mornington VIC 3931

Perth Rat Rescue & Rehab
prrr.org
contact@prrr.org

Pets Haven Animal Shelter
petshaven.com.au
shelter@petshaven.com.au
6/130 High Street, Woodend VIC 3442

Porsche's Rescue
porschesrescue.com
PO Box 66, Thornleigh NSW 2120

Pug Rescue & Adoption Victoria Inc.
pugrescue.org.au
info@pugrescue.org.au
PO Box 4802, Knox City Centre VIC 3152

Pussies Galore Rescue
pussiesgalore.com.au
contact@pussiesgalore.com.au
73 Upper Cairns Terrace, Red Hill QLD 4059

Rabbit Runaway Orphanage
rabbitrunaway.org.au
info@rabbitrunaway.org.au
19 Stanley Steet, Olinda VIC 3788

RSPCA Qld
rspcaqld.org.au
admin@rspcaqld.org.au
139 Wacol Station Road, Wacol QLD 4076

RSPCA South Australia
rspcasa.org.au
info@rspcasa.org.au
GPO Box 2122, Adelaide SA 5001

RSPCA Tasmania
rspcatas.org.au
rspca@rspcatas.org.au
PO Box 66, Mowbray TAS 7248

Save-A-Pet Inc., Victoria
maxine.atsap@gmail.com
PO Box 1237, Horsham VIC 3402

Saving Animals from Euthanasia
safe.asn.au
info@safeperth.com.au
PO Box 1297 Joondalup WA 6027

Seeing Eye Dogs Australia
seda.visionaustralia.org
info@seda.org.au
Locked Bag 3005, Burwood NSW 1805

Shar Pei Rescue Inc.
sharpeirescue.com.au
enquiries@sharpeirescue.org

Siberian Husky Club of NSW Inc.
shcnsw.org.au
rescue@shcnsw.org.au
Muscharry Road, Londonderry NSW 2753

Soi Dog Foundation, Thailand, the United States, Australia, the UK, France and Holland
soidog.org
nadege@soidog.org
PO Box 4156, Narre Warren South VIC 3805

South Australian Ferret Association
safa.advancedscripting.com.au/public

Staffy and Bully Breed Rescue Inc.
petrescue.com.au/groups/10305
sabbrwa@gmail.com

Sydney Dogs and Cats Home
sydneydogsandcatshome.org
sdch@sydneydogsandcatshome.org
77 Edward Street, Carlton NSW 2218

Sydney Pet Rescue & Adoption Inc., NSW
sydneypetrescue.com.au
PO Box 361, Jannali NSW 2226

Victorian Brumby Association
victorianbrumbyassociation.org
info@victorianbrumbyassociation.org
213 Lexton Road, Beaufort VIC 3373

Victorian Dog Rescue & Resource Group Inc.
victoriandogrescue.org.au
rescue@victoriandogrescue.org.au
PO Box 208, Elsternwick VIC 3185

Wildlife Help on Mornington Peninsula
helpforwildlife.org.au
helpforwildlife@bigpond.com
PO Box 181, Coldstream VIC 3770

Wrangler Jayne
wranglerjayne.com.au
mail@wranglerjayne.com.au
PO Box 112, Coldstream VIC 3770

Image credits

Page vii: Courtesy of the Ten Network

Page 29: Nathan Williams

Page 49: Nina Huynh

Page 55: Carrie Palmer

Page 60: Wendy Bright

Page 69: Newspix/Melvyn Knipe

Page 83: Lisa Davis

Page 109: Diana Leventhal, K9 Photography

Page 115 and 119: Alex Olguin, olguinphotography.com.au

Page 125: John Jore

Page 128: Claire Garrett, Petography

Page 144: Jeremy Jasinkski

Page 159: Natalie Brabham

Page 161 and 163: Mark Tyrrell

Page 180: Alvina Narayan

Pages 183 and 185: Tina-Louise Borg, Jet Photography

Page 191: Anita Fraser

Page 195: Shayne Neal

Page 229: Di Bennett OAM

Page 23: Lisa Winter

Page 235: Emma Turner, emmaturnerphotography.com.au

Page 249: Cindy Amey

Page 255: Stephan Miechel

Pages 233 and 260: Helen Stathy

Pages 205 and 224: Ruthless Photos

Acknowledgements

Saskia and PetRescue would love to thank the large and passionate editorial team who helped collect these stories from all over Australia and made this book possible. Anna, Chris, Lisa, Liz, Lynda, Miriam, Molly and Robin, you were fabulous! To the awe-inspiring rescue groups all over the country who save the lives of our deserving four-legged friends, please take a bow. You are changing the world – one life at a time. To the foster carers and adopters who sent their stories in – you are setting an example to everyone in your community about how rewarding it is to bring a rescue pet into your life. Keep up the great work!

But the biggest thanks, of course, goes to the animals who brighten our days, forgive us, keep vigil for us, transform us and, most of all, love us – unconditionally.

PetRescue's Amazing Dog Stories

EDITED BY SASKIA ADAMS AND VICKIE DAVY

Every dog has a tale . . .

This collection brings together stories of canine survival, loyalty and affection. These dogs have overcome troubled backgrounds to bring joy, companionship and adventure to the lives of their new families.

There's Fudge, who braved a house fire to save his owner; Barnaby, Australia's saddest dog, who conquered severe agoraphobia after being mistreated; the tale of a real-life Milo and Otis; Dusty's special bond with his eleven-year-old best mate; and Sasha, the three-legged assistant ambulance driver. There are also stories of doggie heroics, quirky skills and friendships that were just meant to be.